Visions of Sugarplums

Christmas 1992

Heritage House INC.®

THE SOUTHWESTERN COMPANY

Nashville, Tennessee

Visions of Sugarplums

Christmas 1992

Conceived, edited and published
under the direction of:

Ralph Mosley   Chairman of the Board
Thomas Milam   President and Publisher
Betty Ann Jones   Vice President of Marketing
Ron Hartman   Vice President of Operations
Debbie Seigenthaler   Executive Editor

Christmas 1992

Editor: Mary Jane Blount
Creative Director: Philip Sankey
Essayists: Ronald Kidd and Yvonne Martin Kidd
Art Director: Steve Newman
Project Leader: Mary Cummings
Crafts Editor: Kathleen English
Associate Editors: Georgia Brazil, Jane Hinshaw,
Linda Jones, Mary Wilson
Test Kitchen: Charlene Sproles
Illustrator: Barbara Ball
Contributing Editor: Laura Hill
Typographers: Pam Newsome, Sara Anglin
Production: John Moulton
Manufacturing Assistant: George McAllister

To my mom: Lucile K. Thomas
From: Barbara Elder
your daughter. 1992. (July)

Contents

Visions of
Sugarplums

A Season for Beginning
Introduction

*I*t just didn't feel like Christmas. The sun was shining, the poppies were in bloom, the temperature had risen into the nineties. I had just finished mowing the lawn, for crying out loud. This was nutty, even by California standards.

To make matters worse, Yvonne and I couldn't agree on how to celebrate the holiday. We had just recently married and moved into our Pasadena home, and Christmas hadn't yet been transformed from *his* and *hers* into *ours*. So we hadn't done anything. It was December 20, and we hadn't even bought a tree.

That was when Yvonne decided we needed a dog. She found a classified listing for twelve Airedale puppies in a place called Gorman and made an appointment for the following day.

When we woke up the next morning, it was pouring rain. We got into the car and splashed our way up into the mountains. At three thousand feet, an amazing thing happened.

It started to snow.

Yvonne and I looked at each other, afraid to speak for fear the sun would come out and surfers would appear by the roadside. Soon the flakes were falling thick and fast.

We located the address, and when we went inside we were attacked by twelve small bundles of fur. We played with them, wondering how we would ever be able to pick one.

As it turned out, the dog picked us. The one they called "Fuzz Face" kept nibbling Yvonne's hand. Twenty minutes later the puppy was ours, and Christmas had begun.

We named her Agatha, after Yvonne's favorite author Agatha Christie. Over the next few days we got ready for Christmas, with little Agatha stumbling along at our heels.

As Christmas Day approached, Yvonne said, "Do you think your parents would mind if we joined them for Christmas but stayed home on Christmas Eve? We have a house and a family. Maybe it's time we started a few traditions of our own." I knew she was right.

It was a magical Christmas Eve. Yvonne and I had a candlelight dinner by the tree, then opened presents. We laughed and sipped cider and snuggled by the fire. Agatha plopped down in Yvonne's lap, and I took their picture.

I love that photo. In it, Yvonne is wearing a floppy Santa Claus hat, and something that once resembled a doggie bone hangs limply from Agatha's mouth. When I look at that picture, I think of Agatha, long gone now, and of Yvonne, and of the holiday traditions she and I have kept alive over the years.

That was the year they started. That was the year we made Christmas ours.

A Season for Sharing
Food Gifts

The First Annual Christmas Cookie Exchange was a simple concept born of necessity.

My friend Carolyn and I were looking through holiday magazines one December evening, admiring the beautiful cookie baskets and bemoaning the fact that we'd never have enough time to prepare any of our own. After all, we were career women with full schedules during a very hectic season.

That's when the brilliant idea came to us. We would throw a pre-Christmas party and invite eight friends. Each friend would be asked to bring six dozen of her favorite homemade Christmas cookies. After a light dinner, we would divide up the goodies evenly among the group. Business done, all of us would go home with an ample assortment for gift-giving. Our party would be called the First Annual Christmas Cookie Exchange.

The event took place years ago. But, as with many precious memories in my life, the moments are preserved like photographs to be called upon and enjoyed as the years go by. I vividly recall Elvie taking "hat, coat, and umbrella duty" at the door. Elvie—a teddy bear of a woman—and JoAnne—a Disney princess look-alike—had never met before, but that night they mugged and hugged for my mental camera.

I distinctly remember Jill, cookie firmly inserted in mouth, announcing that her recipe had involved single-handedly cornering the market in both chocolate chips and butter.

I recall Robin's sheepish grin as she opened a shoebox filled with an enormous glop of chocolate and meringue. It seemed that in the damp weather, her Meringue Mushrooms had suffered a complete meltdown.

I chuckle as I remember ten grown women circling a table that was full of cookies. Like children, we were stuffing as many into our mouths as we put into our baskets. Our rationale: We needed the energy.

My final image summarizes the spirit of the evening. In this mental photo we are victors, each holding a cookie high in the air like a tiny Wimbledon trophy. Our expressions clearly announce the euphoria we felt. "Eureka! We have found the true meaning of life: good cookies and good friends."

Chocolate Almond Biscotti, Chocolate Chip Candy
Cookie Bars, Holiday Chocolate Shortbread Cookies,
Triple-Decker Fudge, pages 10, 12, 17 and 34

Cheery Christmas Cookies

APRICOT COOKIES

1 cup margarine, softened	1/3 cup margarine,
1/2 cup sugar	softened
2 cups all-purpose flour	1/4 cup sugar
Salt to taste	1/4 cup packed light
1 (21-ounce) can apricot	brown sugar
or peach pie filling	1/4 teaspoon salt
1 (4-ounce) jar apricot	3/4 cup all-purpose flour
preserves	

☐ Preheat oven to 350 degrees.
☐ Cream 1 cup margarine and 1/2 cup sugar in mixer bowl until light and fluffy. Add 2 cups flour and salt to taste; mix until crumbly. Press into greased 11-by-16-inch baking pan.
☐ Bake for 10 minutes. Cool slightly. Spread with mixture of pie filling and preserves.
☐ Combine 1/3 cup margarine, 1/4 cup sugar, brown sugar, 1/4 teaspoon salt and 3/4 cup flour in small bowl; mix well. Sprinkle over filling.
☐ Bake for 30 to 35 minutes. Cut into bars. May drizzle with glaze if desired.
☐ Yield: 3 dozen.

BUTTERCUP SQUARES

1 (2-pastry) package pie	1/2 cup fine cracker
crust mix	crumbs
1 cup sugar	1/2 cup coconut
1/4 cup light corn syrup	1 teaspoon almond extract
3 eggs	1/2 teaspoon salt
1/2 cup margarine,	2 tablespoons
softened	confectioners' sugar
10 to 12 cherries, chopped	

☐ Preheat oven to 375 degrees.
☐ Prepare pie crust mix using package directions. Line 8-by-10-inch baking pan with half the pastry.
☐ Combine sugar, corn syrup, eggs, margarine, cherries, cracker crumbs, coconut, almond extract and salt in bowl; mix well.
☐ Spoon mixture into prepared pan. Top with remaining pastry; seal edges and cut vents.
☐ Bake for 20 to 25 minutes or until golden brown. Sprinkle with confectioners' sugar. Cut into squares.
☐ Yield: 2 dozen.

CHOCOLATE ALMOND BISCOTTI

1/2 cup butter or	1/4 teaspoon salt
margarine, softened	1 cup sliced almonds
1 1/4 cups sugar	1 cup Hershey's
2 eggs	semisweet
1 teaspoon almond extract	chocolate chips
2 1/4 cups all-purpose flour	1 tablespoon shortening
1/4 cup Hershey's	1/4 cup Hershey's vanilla
premium European	milk chips
style cocoa	1 teaspoon shortening
1 teaspoon baking powder	Sliced almonds

☐ Preheat oven to 375 degrees.
☐ Cream butter and sugar in mixer bowl until light. Beat in eggs and almond extract.
☐ Mix flour, cocoa, baking powder and salt in bowl. Add to creamed mixture; mix well.
☐ Mix in 1 cup almonds with wooden spoon. Divide into 2 portions.
☐ Shape each portion into 11-inch log; place 2 inches or more apart on ungreased cookie sheet.
☐ Bake on middle oven rack for 30 minutes or until firm.
☐ Cool on cookie sheet for 15 minutes.
☐ Cut diagonally into 1/2-inch slices with serrated knife, discarding end pieces.
☐ Arrange slices cut side down close together on 2 cookie sheets.
☐ Bake for 26 minutes, turning cookies after 13 minutes. Cool on cookie sheets.
☐ Combine chocolate chips and 1 tablespoon shortening in glass bowl.
☐ Microwave on High for 1 to 1 1/2 minutes or until melted; stir until smooth.
☐ Dip ends of biscotti into chocolate glaze or drizzle with chocolate glaze.
☐ Combine vanilla chips and 1 teaspoon shortening in glass bowl.
☐ Microwave on High for 30 to 45 seconds or until melted; stir until smooth.
☐ Drizzle over chocolate glaze. Garnish with additional almonds.
☐ Store in airtight container.
☐ Serve with coffee or hot chocolate for dipping.
☐ Yield: 28 cookies.

CANDIED FRUIT BROWNIES

4 eggs	1 cup chopped candied
2 cups packed light	fruit
brown sugar	1 teaspoon cinnamon
1 tablespoon cold water	1/4 teaspoon salt
2 cups all-purpose flour	1 cup chopped pecans

□ Preheat oven to 375 degrees.
□ Beat eggs in mixer bowl until very light. Beat in brown sugar and water.
□ Mix flour, fruit, cinnamon and salt in bowl. Stir in pecans.
□ Add to egg mixture; mix well. Dough will be very stiff. Spoon into greased 9-by-13-inch baking pan.
□ Bake for 20 minutes. Cool on wire rack. Cut into bars.
□ Yield: 3 dozen.

PEANUT BUTTER CHOCOLATE BROWNIES

12/3 cups Reese's peanut	1 cup all-purpose flour
butter chips	1/2 teaspoon salt
1/2 cup butter or	13/4 cups Hershey's
margarine, softened	premium milk
1 cup sugar	chocolate chunks
3 eggs	1/4 cup chopped peanuts
1 teaspoon vanilla extract	

□ Preheat oven to 350 degrees.
□ Microwave peanut butter chips on High in glass bowl for 1 to 1 1/2 minutes or until melted; stir until smooth.
□ Cream butter and sugar in mixer bowl until light and fluffy. Beat in eggs, vanilla and melted peanut butter chips.
□ Add flour and salt; mix well. Stir in chocolate chunks and peanuts. Spread in greased 9-by-13-inch baking pan.
□ Bake for 25 to 30 minutes or until brownies begin to pull from sides of pan. Cool in pan. Cut into bars.
□ Yield: 3 dozen.

PRALINE BROWNIES

1 (22-ounce) package	2 tablespoons melted
brownie mix	margarine
1/2 cup packed light	1/2 cup chopped pecans
brown sugar	

□ Preheat oven to 350 degrees. Grease bottom of 9-by-13-inch baking pan.
□ Prepare brownie mix using package directions. Spread in prepared pan.
□ Combine brown sugar, margarine and pecans in bowl; mix well. Sprinkle over batter.

□ Bake for 30 minutes. Cool in pan on wire rack. Cut into squares. Frost with fudge frosting if desired.
□ Yield: 2 dozen.

TWO-WAY BROWNIES

1 cup butter or margarine,	1/2 teaspoon vanilla extract
softened	2 (1-ounce) squares
2 cups sugar	unsweetened chocolate,
4 eggs	melted
2 cups all-purpose flour	3/4 cup chopped pecans
1/2 teaspoon salt	3/4 cup chocolate chips

□ Preheat oven to 350 degrees.
□ Cream butter and sugar in mixer bowl until light. Beat in eggs.
□ Sift in flour and salt; mix well. Mix in vanilla. Divide into 2 portions.
□ Add chocolate and pecans to 1 portion; mix well. Spread in greased 9-by-13-inch baking dish.
□ Mix chocolate chips into second portion. Spread over first layer.
□ Bake for 30 to 33 minutes or until brownies pull from edge of pan. Cool in pan on wire rack. Cut into squares.
□ Yield: 2 dozen.

CHOCOLATE PEANUT BUTTER THUMBPRINTS

12/3 cups Reese's peanut	1 egg
butter chips	1 teaspoon vanilla extract
1/2 cup butter or	1 1/2 cups all-purpose flour
margarine, softened	1/2 cup Hershey's baking
1/2 cup packed light	cocoa
brown sugar	1/2 teaspoon baking soda
1/2 cup sugar	Sugar

□ Preheat oven to 375 degrees.
□ Microwave 1/2 cup peanut butter chips on High for 30 to 40 seconds or just until melted; stir until smooth.
□ Combine butter, brown sugar, 1/2 cup sugar, egg and vanilla in mixer bowl; beat until light and fluffy. Beat in melted peanut butter chips.
□ Mix flour, cocoa and baking soda in bowl. Add to batter; mix well.
□ Shape by tablespoonfuls into balls; roll in additional sugar. Place on ungreased cookie sheet. Flatten balls to 1/4-inch thickness with bottom of glass. Make indentation in center of each cookie with thumb.
□ Bake for 6 minutes or until set. Press indentation again with tip of spoon if necessary. Fill with remaining peanut butter chips. Let stand for 1 to 2 minutes; spread into swirl.
□ Remove to wire rack to cool completely.
□ Yield: 2 1/2 dozen.

CHOCOLATE CHIP CANDY COOKIE BARS

1²/3 cups all-purpose flour	1¹/2 cups Hershey's semi-sweet chocolate chips
2 tablespoons sugar	
³/4 teaspoon baking powder	1¹/2 cups sugar
¹/2 cup butter or margarine, chilled	¹/2 cup butter or margarine
	¹/2 cup evaporated milk
1 egg, slightly beaten	¹/2 cup corn syrup
2 tablespoons evaporated milk	1¹/2 cups sliced almonds
	¹/2 cup Hershey's semi-sweet chocolate chips

□ Preheat oven to 375 degrees.
□ Mix first 3 ingredients in medium bowl. Cut in ¹/2 cup butter until mixture resembles coarse crumbs.
□ Add egg and 2 tablespoons evaporated milk; mix to form ball. Press over bottom and ¹/4 inch up sides of 10-by-15-inch baking pan; prick with fork.
□ Bake for 12 minutes or until light brown. Sprinkle baked layer with 1¹/2 cups chocolate chips; do not spread.
□ Combine 1¹/2 cups sugar, ¹/2 cup butter, ¹/2 cup evaporated milk and corn syrup in 3-quart saucepan.
□ Bring to a boil over medium heat, stirring constantly. Stir in almonds. Cook to 240 degrees on candy thermometer, soft-ball stage. Spoon immediately over chips and crust; do not spread.
□ Bake for 10 to 15 minutes or just until golden brown. Cool for 5 minutes. Sprinkle with ¹/2 cup chocolate chips. Cool to room temperature. Cut into bars.
□ Yield: 4 dozen.

HOLIDAY CHOCOLATE CHIP SQUARES

1 cup butter or margarine, softened	¹/4 teaspoon salt
	2 cups chocolate chips
1¹/4 cups sugar	1 cup chopped pecans
1 egg	30 maraschino cherries
1 teaspoon vanilla extract	15 candy spearmint leaves, cut into halves lengthwise
1¹/4 teaspoons baking powder	
2¹/4 cups all-purpose flour	

□ Preheat oven to 350 degrees.
□ Cream butter and sugar in mixer bowl until light and fluffy. Beat in egg and vanilla.
□ Add mixture of baking powder, flour and salt; mix well. Stir in chocolate chips and pecans.
□ Spread in greased 9-by-13-inch baking dish. Press maraschino cherries into 5 rows of 6 cherries on top of batter. Place 1 candy at base of each cherry.
□ Bake for 25 to 30 minutes or until edges pull from sides of pan. Cool on wire rack. Cut into squares centered with cherries.
□ Yield: 2¹/2 dozen.

CHOCOLATE TOFFEE CRESCENT BARS

1 (8-count) can crescent rolls	1 cup margarine
	1¹/2 cups chopped pecans
1 cup packed light brown sugar	1 cup chocolate chips

□ Preheat oven to 375 degrees.
□ Separate roll dough into rectangles. Press over bottom of 10-by-15-inch baking pan; press perforations to seal.
□ Bring brown sugar and margarine to a boil in small saucepan, stirring constantly. Boil for 1 minute. Pour over dough. Sprinkle with pecans.
□ Bake for 14 to 18 minutes or until golden brown. Sprinkle with chocolate chips. Let stand for 2 minutes; swirl chocolate over top.
□ Let stand until cool. Cut into bars.
□ Yield: 4 dozen.

CREAM CHEESE PISTACHIO COOKIES

1 cup butter or margarine, softened	2¹/2 cups all-purpose flour
	1 tablespoon grated lemon rind
6 ounces cream cheese, softened	1 tablespoon lemon juice
²/3 cup sugar	¹/2 cup finely chopped pistachios
1 egg yolk	

□ Preheat oven to 350 degrees.
□ Cream butter, cream cheese and sugar in mixer bowl until light. Beat in egg yolk.
□ Add flour, lemon rind, lemon juice and pistachios. Mix to form stiff dough, kneading in last of ingredients on floured board.
□ Shape as desired. (See variations below.) Place on cookie sheets.
□ Bake using variation directions.
□ **Jamprints:** Shape dough by scant tablespoonfuls into balls. Roll half the balls in additional finely chopped pistachios. Place all balls on cookie sheet. Bake for 14 minutes. Press cookies with thumb; cool. Dust plain cookies with confectioners' sugar. Fill centers with jam. Yield: 5 dozen.
□ **Lemon Twists:** Roll dough by 2-tablespoon portions into 8-inch rolls on board sprinkled with sugar. Loop into twists; place on cookie sheet. Bake for 14 minutes. Yield: 29 twists.
□ **Swedish Bars:** Shape dough into three 1¹/2-by-13-inch ropes on cookie sheet. Make ¹/2-inch depressions down length of ropes with handle of wooden spoon. Fill depressions with jam; sprinkle with finely chopped pistachios. Bake for 22 minutes. Cool slightly; slice diagonally into bars. Yield: 3 dozen.

Cream Cheese Pistachio Cookies, page 12

COOKIE PRESS GINGERSNAPS

3/4 cup butter or
  margarine, softened
3/4 cup packed light
  brown sugar
3/4 cup molasses
1 egg
3 cups sifted all-purpose
  flour

1 1/2 teaspoons baking soda
1 teaspoon cinnamon
1 teaspoon ginger
1/4 teaspoon cloves
1/4 teaspoon salt
1/4 cup sugar sprinkles

□ Preheat oven to 375 degrees.
□ Cream butter and brown sugar in mixer bowl
until light and fluffy. Blend in molasses and egg.
□ Sift in flour, baking soda, cinnamon, ginger,
cloves and salt; mix well.
□ Spoon into cookie press. Press onto ungreased
cookie sheet.
Sprinkle with
sugar sprinkles.
□ Bake for 8
minutes or until
golden brown.
Remove to wire
rack to cool.
□ Yield: 4 dozen.

*Make our Chocolate-
Covered Speckled Apples
on page 32, coat with
favorite crunchies, and
wrap individually for
one-of-a-kind gifts.*

GINGER GIANTS

1 cup all-purpose flour
1/2 teaspoon baking
  powder
1/2 teaspoon baking soda
1/2 teaspoon cinnamon
1/2 teaspoon nutmeg
1/2 teaspoon ginger
1/2 teaspoon salt
1/3 cup sugar

1/2 cup butter or
  margarine, softened
1/2 cup packed light
  brown sugar
1 egg, beaten
1 teaspoon vanilla extract
1 cup oats
1 cup raisins

□ Preheat oven to 350 degrees.
□ Mix flour, baking powder, baking soda,
cinnamon, nutmeg, ginger and salt in bowl.
□ Combine sugar, butter, brown sugar, egg and
vanilla in mixer bowl; beat at high speed until
light and fluffy. Add dry ingredients gradually,
beating at low speed until blended.
□ Stir in oats and raisins. Drop by 1/4 cupfuls onto
ungreased cookie sheet.
□ Bake for 15 to 17 minutes or until golden brown.
Cool on wire rack.
□ Yield: 8 to 10 cookies.

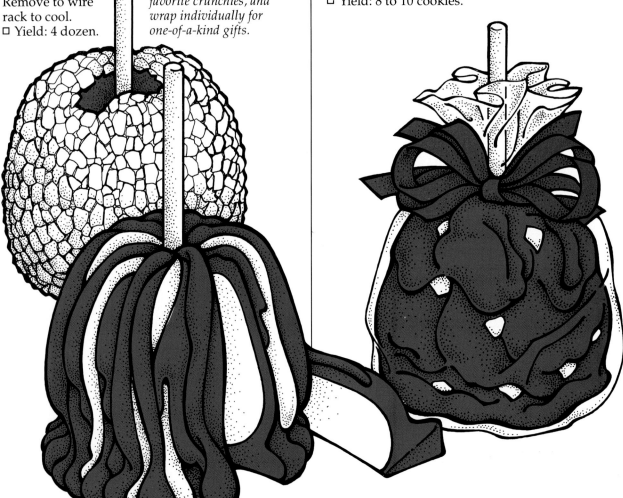

CHRISTMAS SURPRISE

1½ cups graham cracker
   crumbs
2 tablespoons sugar
½ cup melted margarine
2 cups miniature
   marshmallows
1½ cups coconut

1 cup chopped
   maraschino cherries
1 (14-ounce) can
   sweetened condensed
   milk
1 cup chopped pecans

□ Preheat oven to 350 degrees.
□ Mix cracker crumbs, sugar and margarine in bowl. Press into 9-by-13-inch baking dish.
□ Layer marshmallows, coconut and cherries in prepared dish. Drizzle with condensed milk. Press pecans into top.
□ Bake for 25 minutes. Cool. Cut into squares.
□ Yield: 2 dozen.

KITKAT BARS

1 cup butter or margarine
⅓ cup sugar
1 cup packed light brown
   sugar
2 cups finely crushed
   graham cracker crumbs
½ cup milk

2 (16-ounce) packages
   butter crackers
½ cup semisweet
   chocolate chips
½ cup butterscotch chips
⅔ cup creamy peanut
   butter

□ Combine first 5 ingredients in saucepan. Bring to a boil, stirring constantly. Cook for 5 minutes; cool.
□ Line 9-by-13-inch dish with 1 layer butter crackers. Pour half the sauce on top. Repeat layers. Top with crackers.
□ Melt chocolate chips, butterscotch chips and peanut butter in double boiler, stirring to mix well. Spread over crackers.
□ Chill until topping is firm. Cut into bars.
□ Yield: 2 dozen.

MOLASSES WAFERS

1 cup (scant) all-purpose
   flour
⅔ cup sugar
1 teaspoon ginger

½ cup molasses
½ cup butter
   or margarine

□ Preheat oven to 300 degrees.
□ Sift flour, sugar and ginger into bowl.
□ Heat molasses to the boiling point in saucepan; remove from heat.
□ Stir in butter. Add flour mixture; mix well.
□ Drop by teaspoonfuls 2 inches apart onto cookie sheet.
□ Bake for 15 minutes. Cool slightly.
□ Roll warm cookies around handle of wooden spoon. Let stand until cool. May fill with ice cream.
□ Yield: 5 dozen.

FILLED MERINGUES

3 eggs whites
¼ teaspoon cream of
   tartar
¼ teaspoon almond
   extract

1 cup sugar
8 ounces soft cream
   cheese with
   strawberries
1 cup strawberry preserves

□ Preheat oven to 300 degrees.
□ Beat first 3 ingredients at medium speed in mixer bowl until soft peaks form. Add sugar gradually, beating at high speed until stiff.
□ Drop by tablespoonfuls 3 inches apart onto baking sheet lined with baking parchment. Make well in center with spoon, building up sides.
□ Bake for 20 minutes. Turn off oven. Let meringues stand in closed oven for 30 minutes.
□ Fill with cream cheese and preserves.
□ Yield: 36 meringues.

MINT MELT-AWAY COOKIES

1 cup sugar
¾ cup butter or
   margarine, softened
1 cup vegetable oil
½ cup confectioners'
   sugar
1 cup crushed candy canes

2 eggs, beaten
2 teaspoons vanilla extract
4 cups all-purpose flour
1 teaspoon baking soda
½ teaspoon salt
1 cup crushed pecans

□ Preheat oven to 375 degrees.
□ Cream first 4 ingredients in mixer bowl until light. Add candy. Blend in eggs and vanilla. Stir in remaining ingredients. Drop by teaspoonfuls onto ungreased cookie sheet.
□ Bake for 8 to 9 minutes. Cool on cookie sheet for 2 minutes. Remove to wire rack to cool completely.
□ Yield: 8 dozen.

PIÑA COLADA COOKIES

1 cup margarine, softened
1 cup sugar
1 (4-ounce) package
   vanilla instant pudding
   mix
2 eggs

1 teaspoon vanilla extract
2¼ cups all-purpose flour
1 teaspoon baking soda
2 packets piña colada mix
1 cup shredded coconut

□ Preheat oven to 375 degrees.
□ Cream first 3 ingredients in mixer bowl until smooth. Blend in eggs and vanilla. Beat in mixture of flour and baking soda gradually. Stir in piña colada mix and coconut; batter will be stiff.
□ Drop by rounded teaspoonfuls 2 inches apart onto ungreased cookie sheet.
□ Bake for 8 to 10 minutes or until golden brown. Remove to wire rack to cool.
□ Yield: 5 dozen.

Creative Christmas Cookies, Cookie Pecan Critters, Mincemeat Peek-A-Boo Cookies, Stained Glass Cookies, Cinnamon Pinwheel Cookies, pages 16 and 17

CREATIVE CHRISTMAS COOKIES

1 (14-ounce) can Eagle®
  Brand sweetened
  condensed milk
3/4 cup margarine,
  softened
2 eggs
1 tablespoon vanilla
  extract or 2 teaspoons
  almond or lemon extract
3 1/2 cups all-purpose flour

1 tablespoon baking
  powder
1/2 teaspoon salt
1/4 cup margarine
1/4 cup water
1/2 cup baking cocoa
2 cups confectioners'
  sugar
1 teaspoon vanilla extract

□ Combine first 4 ingredients in mixer bowl; beat until smooth. Add mixture of flour, baking powder and salt; mix well. Chill for 2 hours.
□ Preheat oven to 350 degrees.
□ Knead dough on floured surface until smooth. Divide into 3 portions. Roll each portion 1/8 inch thick; cut as desired with cookie cutter. Place 1 inch apart on greased cookie sheet.
□ Bake for 7 to 9 minutes or just until edges are light brown; do not overbake. Remove to wire rack to cool.
□ Melt 1/4 cup margarine with water in small saucepan. Stir in cocoa; remove from heat.
□ Beat in remaining ingredients until smooth, adding additional water as needed for desired consistency. Spread frosting over cookies. May frost with decorator's frosting if desired.
□ Yield: 6 dozen.

- **Chocolate Cookies:** May decrease flour to 3 cups and add 1/2 cup baking cocoa to dough. Spread frosting on half the cookies and top with remaining cookies for chocolate sandwich cookies. Yield: 4 to 8 dozen.
- **Cookie Pecan Critters:** Arrange 3 pecan halves for each critter on ungreased baking sheet. Press 1-inch balls of dough over centers of arranged pecans. Bake for 8 minutes. Frost as on page 16. Yield: 6 dozen.
- **Mincemeat Peek-A-Boo Cookies:** Cut dough into 3-inch circles. Place 2 teaspoons mincemeat in centers of half the circles. Cut X in centers of remaining circles. Place over mincemeat; press edges lightly to seal. Bake on cookie sheet for 8 to 10 minutes or until light brown. Sprinkle with confectioners' sugar. Yield: 3 dozen.
- **Stained Glass Cookies:** Cut dough into desired 3-inch shapes; cut out holes in center. Place on foil-lined cookie sheet. Fill centers with crushed hard candies. Bake for 6 to 8 minutes or until candy melts. Cool in pan for 5 minutes. Yield: 8 dozen.
- **Cinnamon Pinwheel Cookies:** Decrease baking powder in recipe to 2 teaspoons. Roll into four 8-by-16-inch rectangles. Brush with melted margarine; sprinkle with mixture of 2 tablespoons sugar and 1/2 teaspoon cinnamon. Roll up tightly from 8-inch side. Freeze, tightly wrapped, for 20 minutes or until firm. Cut into 1/4-inch slices; place on cookie sheets. Bake for 12 to 14 minutes or until light brown. Yield: 6 dozen.

THREE-LAYER ALMOND BARS

2 cups graham cracker crumbs	1 (7-ounce) package coconut
2 tablespoons light brown sugar	1 cup semisweet chocolate chips
1/2 cup melted butter or margarine	1 cup butterscotch chips
1 (14-ounce) can sweetened condensed milk	1/4 cup butter or margarine
1 teaspoon vanilla extract	6 tablespoons chunky peanut butter
	1/3 cup chopped almonds

- Preheat oven to 325 degrees.
- Combine cracker crumbs, brown sugar and melted butter in small bowl; mix well. Press into greased 9-by-13-inch baking pan.
- Bake for 10 minutes. Cool to room temperature.
- Combine condensed milk, vanilla and coconut in bowl; mix well. Pour over prepared crust.
- Bake for 25 minutes. Cool to room temperature.
- Combine chocolate chips, butterscotch chips, 1/4 cup butter, peanut butter and chopped almonds in double boiler.

- Cook until melted, stirring constantly. Spread over cooled layer. Cool and cut into squares.
- Yield: 3 dozen.

ROLO COOKIES

1 cup margarine, softened	1/2 cup chopped pecans
1 cup sugar	48 Rolo caramel candies
1 cup packed light brown sugar	1 tablespoon sugar
2 eggs, beaten	1/2 cup chopped pecans
2 teaspoons vanilla extract	1 cup vanilla candy coating wafers or almond bark
2 1/2 cups all-purpose flour	1 tablespoon margarine
3/4 cup baking cocoa	
1 teaspoon baking soda	

- Cream 1 cup margarine, 1 cup sugar and brown sugar in mixer bowl until light and fluffy. Beat in eggs and vanilla.
- Stir in mixture of flour, cocoa and baking soda. Mix in 1/2 cup pecans.
- Chill dough for 1 hour.
- Preheat oven to 375 degrees.
- Divide dough into 4 portions; shape each portion into 12 balls. Press 1 unwrapped caramel into each ball, shaping to enclose completely.
- Mix 1 tablespoon sugar and 1/2 cup pecans in small bowl. Dip top of each cookie into mixture; arrange on greased cookie sheet.
- Bake for 10 minutes or until puffed and crackled. Remove to wire rack to cool.
- Melt vanilla candy wafers and 1 tablespoon margarine in saucepan. Drizzle over cookies.
- Yield: 4 dozen.

HOLIDAY CHOCOLATE SHORTBREAD COOKIES

1 cup butter or margarine, softened	1/2 cup Hershey's premium European style cocoa
1 1/4 cups confectioners' sugar	1 2/3 cups Hershey's vanilla milk chips
1 teaspoon vanilla extract	
1 3/4 cups all-purpose flour	

- Preheat oven to 300 degrees.
- Cream butter, confectioners' sugar and vanilla in large mixer bowl until light. Blend in flour and cocoa gradually.
- Roll or pat 1/4 inch thick between waxed paper. Cut into desired shapes with cookie cutters. Place on ungreased cookie sheet.
- Bake for 15 to 20 minutes or just until firm. Arrange vanilla chips flat side down in decorative pattern on warm cookies.
- Cool slightly on cookie sheet. Remove to wire rack to cool completely. Store in airtight container.
- Yield: 3 1/2 dozen.

SOUR CREAM SUGAR COOKIES

2 cups sugar
1 cup sour cream
3 1/2 cups all-purpose
    flour
1 cup butter or margarine,
    softened
1 teaspoon baking soda

□ Preheat oven to 400 degrees.
□ Combine all ingredients in bowl; mix well.
□ Drop by teaspoonfuls onto greased cookie sheet; press lightly with fork.
□ Bake for 8 minutes. Remove to wire rack to cool.
□ Yield: 5 dozen.

SUGAR COOKIE MACAROONS

1 package sugar cookie
    mix
1 egg white
1 teaspoon coconut or
    almond extract
1/2 cup coconut
1 egg white
1 1/4 cups coconut
15 candied cherries, cut
    into halves

□ Preheat oven to 325 degrees.
□ Combine cookie mix, 1 egg white and coconut extract in bowl; mix well. Stir in 1/2 cup coconut.
□ Shape into 1-inch balls. Dip into remaining egg white; coat with 1 1/4 cups coconut. Press 1 candied cherry half into center of each cookie. Place on ungreased cookie sheet.
□ Bake for 8 minutes or until coconut is light brown. Cool on cookie sheet for 1 minute. Remove to wire rack to cool completely.
□ Yield: 3 1/2 dozen.

COCONUT COOKIES

3 eggs, beaten
2 cups sugar
1 cup butter or margarine,
    softened
1 teaspoon baking soda
1/2 cup buttermilk
2 1/2 cups all-purpose flour
1 teaspoon cream of tartar
1 teaspoon salt
2 cups coconut
1 teaspoon vanilla extract

□ Preheat oven to 350 degrees.
□ Combine eggs, sugar and butter in mixer bowl; beat until smooth. Stir in mixture of baking soda and buttermilk.
□ Add mixture of flour, cream of tartar and salt; mix well. Stir in coconut and vanilla. Drop by tablespoonfuls onto greased cookie sheet.
□ Bake for 5 minutes or until edges are light brown. Remove to wire rack to cool.
□ Yield: 3 dozen.

Peanut Butter Chocolate Brownies, Chocolate Peanut Butter Thumbprints, Creamy Peanut Butter Chip Cheesecake, pages 11 and 171

TOFFEE COOKIES

1 cup butter or margarine,
    softened
1 cup packed light brown
    sugar
1 egg yolk
1 cup all-purpose flour
6 (1-ounce) milk
    chocolate candy bars
2/3 cup finely chopped
    pecans

□ Preheat oven to 350 degrees.
□ Cream first 3 ingredients in mixer bowl; beat until light. Add flour gradually, mixing well after each addition. Spread in greased 10-by-15-inch baking pan.
□ Bake for 15 to 20 minutes or until medium brown. Arrange chocolate candy bars over top.
□ Spread chocolate over top when melted. Sprinkle with pecans. Cool completely. Cut into diamonds.
□ Yield: 6 dozen.

TURTLE SQUARES

2 cups all-purpose flour
1/2 cup packed light
    brown sugar
1/2 cup butter or
    margarine, softened
1 1/2 cups pecan halves
1/2 cup packed light
    brown sugar
1 cup butter or margarine
1 cup chocolate chips

□ Preheat oven to 350 degrees.
□ Mix first 3 ingredients in bowl; mixture will be very dry. Press firmly into greased 9-by-13-inch baking pan. Sprinkle evenly with pecans.
□ Bring 1/2 cup brown sugar and 1 cup butter to a boil in saucepan. Cook for 50 seconds, stirring constantly. Pour over crust.
□ Bake for 20 minutes. Sprinkle with chocolate chips. Let stand until cool. Cut into squares.
□ Yield: 3 to 4 dozen.

WAFFLE COOKIES

3/4 cup butter or
    margarine, softened
3/4 cup shortening
1/4 cup sugar
1 1/2 cups packed light
    brown sugar
2 teaspoons vanilla extract
2 eggs
4 1/2 cups all-purpose flour
1/2 teaspoon salt
1 1/2 cups confectioners'
    sugar
1/4 cup milk
1/2 teaspoon maple extract

□ Preheat waffle iron.
□ Cream butter, shortening, sugar, brown sugar and vanilla in mixer bowl until light and fluffy.
□ Blend in eggs. Add flour and salt; mix well. Shape into 1-inch balls. Arrange 3 to 4 balls at a time in greased waffle iron.
□ Bake until golden brown. Cool on wire rack.
□ Beat confectioners' sugar, milk and maple extract in bowl until smooth. Drizzle over cookies.
□ Yield: 3 1/2 dozen.

Festive Christmas Breads

CRANBERRY AND APPLE BREAD

1/4 cup butter or
  margarine, softened
1 cup sugar
2 eggs, beaten
1 cup sour cream
2 teaspoons grated lemon
  rind
3 cups all-purpose flour
1/2 teaspoon baking soda

4 teaspoons baking
  powder
1/2 teaspoon salt
11/2 cups chopped
  cranberries
11/2 cups chopped peeled
  apples
1/2 cup chopped walnuts

□ Preheat oven to 350 degrees.
□ Beat butter and sugar in mixer bowl until
light and fluffy. Beat in eggs, sour cream and
lemon rind.
□ Sift flour, baking soda, baking powder and salt
together. Add to creamed mixture; mix well.
□ Fold in cranberries, apples and walnuts. Pour
into greased 5-by-9-inch loaf pan.
□ Bake for 60 to 70 minutes or until loaf tests done.
□ Cool in pan on wire rack for 15 minutes. Remove
to wire rack to cool completely. Let stand,
wrapped in foil, for 24 hours before slicing.
□ Yield: 1 loaf.

APRICOT PUMPKIN BREAD

11/2 cups canned
  pumpkin
1 cup sugar
1 cup oil
3 eggs
21/4 cups all-purpose flour
11/2 teaspoons baking
  soda
11/2 teaspoons baking
  powder

3/4 teaspoon cinnamon
3/4 teaspoon nutmeg
3/4 teaspoon salt
1 (4-ounce) package
  vanilla pudding and pie
  filling mix
11/2 cups chopped dried
  apricots
11/2 cups chopped walnuts

□ Preheat oven to 350 degrees.
□ Combine pumpkin, sugar and oil in bowl; blend
well. Beat in eggs.
□ Mix flour and next 6 dry ingredients in bowl.
Fold in pumpkin mixture. Mix in apricots and
walnuts. Pour into 2 greased and floured
5-by-9-inch loaf pans or 13-inch coffee cans.
□ Bake for 1 hour or until loaves test done.
□ Cool in pans for 10 minutes. Remove to wire rack
to cool completely.

□ Store, tightly wrapped, in freezer for up to 3
months. Do not use instant pudding mix.
□ Yield: 2 loaves.

CINNAMON PEAR BREAD

2 (16-ounce) cans pears,
  drained, chopped
3 eggs, beaten
1 cup vegetable oil
11/2 cups sugar
1/2 teaspoon grated lemon
  rind
1 teaspoon vanilla extract

3 cups all-purpose flour
1 teaspoon salt
1 teaspoon baking soda
1/4 teaspoon baking
  powder
11/2 teaspoons cinnamon
1 cup chopped pecans

□ Preheat oven to 325 degrees.
□ Combine pears, eggs, oil, sugar, lemon rind and
vanilla in mixer bowl; mix well.
□ Sift in flour, salt, baking soda, baking powder
and cinnamon; beat until well mixed. Fold in
pecans. Pour into 2 greased 5-by-9-inch loaf pans.
□ Bake for 11/4 hours or until loaves test done.
□ Yield: 2 loaves.

COCONUT AND PECAN LOAVES

2 cups butter or
  margarine, softened
4 cups sugar
1 (4-ounce) bottle of
  vanilla extract
2 eggs, beaten
1 (16-ounce) package
  flaked coconut

4 cups chopped pecans
1 (22-ounce) pound cake,
  crumbled
3/4 cup packed light
  brown sugar
3/4 cup butter or
  margarine
11/2 cups all-purpose flour

□ Preheat oven to 325 degrees.
□ Cream 2 cups butter and sugar in mixer bowl
until light and fluffy. Beat in vanilla and eggs. Add
coconut, pecans and pound cake crumbs; mix well.
□ Pour into 9 greased and floured 3-by-5-inch loaf
pans filling 2/3 full. Sprinkle with mixture of
remaining ingredients.
□ Bake for 45 minutes or until loaves test done.
□ Chill overnight. Loaves will sink in center.
□ Yield: 8 miniature loaves.

*Apricot Pumpkin Bread, Two-Way Apricot Topping,
pages 20 and 43*

BLUEBERRY BRUNCH BREAD

1 (2-layer) package lemon cake mix
1/4 cup butter or margarine, softened
3 ounces cream cheese, softened
1/3 cup water
2 eggs
1 (21-ounce) can blueberry pie filling

1/2 cup finely chopped almonds
1/2 cup confectioners' sugar
1 tablespoon butter or margarine, softened
2 to 3 teaspoons milk
1/4 teaspoon lemon extract

☐ Preheat oven to 350 degrees.
☐ Combine cake mix, 1/4 cup butter and cream cheese in mixer bowl. Beat at low speed until crumbly. Reserve 1 cup mixture for topping.
☐ Add water and eggs to remaining crumb mixture. Beat at high speed for 2 minutes.
☐ Pour into greased and floured 9-by-13-inch baking pan. Spread pie filling gently over batter. Sprinkle mixture of reserved mixture and almonds over top.
☐ Bake for 35 minutes or until bread tests done.
☐ Blend confectioners' sugar, 1 tablespoon butter, milk and lemon extract in small bowl. Drizzle over warm bread. Serve warm or cold.
☐ Yield: 12 servings.

CHEDDAR BUNDT BREAD

2 (8-ounce) loaves frozen bread dough, thawed
2 cups shredded Cheddar cheese
1/2 cup melted margarine
1/2 envelope onion soup mix

☐ Cut bread dough into 24 pieces. Make indentation in each. Fill with cheese; fold over and seal.
☐ Dip into mixture of margarine and soup mix. Arrange in bundt pan. Let rise, covered, until doubled in bulk.
☐ Preheat oven to 350 degrees.
☐ Bake for 30 to 35 minutes or until golden brown.
☐ Yield: 1 loaf.

Give the Earth a Christmas present by using recycled or reusable packaging. Some easy ideas include paper bags, dish towels, muslin, brown paper and even newspapers—including the comics! Trim with "biodegradables" such as candy canes and cinnamon sticks.

APRICOT TEA LOAF

1/2 cup packed light brown sugar	2 (16-ounce) cans apricots, drained, puréed
2 cups whole wheat flour	1/2 cup egg substitute
2 teaspoons baking soda	1/4 cup safflower oil
1/4 teaspoon cinnamon	2 teaspoons vanilla extract

☐ Preheat oven to 350 degrees.
☐ Combine brown sugar, whole wheat flour, baking soda and cinnamon in bowl.
☐ Mix apricot purée, egg substitute, oil and vanilla in bowl. Add to dry ingredients, mixing until just blended; do not over mix.
☐ Pour into greased and floured 5-by-9-inch loaf pan.
☐ Bake for 55 minutes or until loaf tests done.
☐ Cool in pan for several minutes. Remove to wire rack to cool completely.
☐ Yield: 1 loaf.

BANANA-APPLE BREAD

2 eggs	2 cups flour
2 very ripe bananas, mashed	2 teaspoons baking powder
1 teaspoon vanilla extract	1 teaspoon baking soda
1 teaspoon cinnamon	1/2 teaspoon salt
1 teaspoon allspice	1/3 cup raisins
1/4 cup honey	2 Granny Smith apples, peeled, chopped

☐ Preheat oven to 375 degrees.
☐ Combine eggs, bananas, vanilla, spices and honey in mixer bowl. Beat until blended.
☐ Add mixture of dry ingredients; mix well. Fold in raisins and apples.
☐ Spoon into greased and floured 5-by-9-inch loaf pan.
☐ Bake for 40 to 45 minutes or until loaf tests done.
☐ Remove to wire rack to cool completely.
☐ Yield: 1 loaf.

LEMON YOGURT BREAD

3 cups all-purpose flour	2 tablespoons lemon extract
1 teaspoon salt	1 tablespoon grated lemon rind
1 teaspoon baking soda	1 tablespoon grated lemon rind
1 teaspoon baking powder	2 cups lemon yogurt
13/4 cups sugar	1/2 to 1 cup chopped almonds
3 eggs	
1 cup vegetable oil	

☐ Preheat oven to 325 degrees.
☐ Combine first 5 ingredients in mixer bowl. Add eggs, oil, lemon extract, lemon rind and yogurt; beat until well mixed. Stir in almonds.
☐ Pour into 2 greased 5-by-9-inch loaf pans.

☐ Bake for 45 to 60 minutes or until loaves test done. Cool in pans for 10 minutes. Remove to wire rack to cool completely.
☐ Yield: 2 loaves.

CREAMY PECAN BREAD

8 ounces cream cheese, softened	1 teaspoon baking soda
1/3 cup sugar	1 teaspoon salt
1 egg	1/2 cup canola oil
21/4 cups flour	1/2 cup milk
1/3 cup sugar	2 eggs
1/3 cup packed light brown sugar	1 teaspoon grated lemon rind
	1 cup chopped pecans

☐ Preheat oven to 350 degrees.
☐ Combine cream cheese, 1/3 cup sugar and 1 egg in mixer bowl. Beat until blended.
☐ Combine flour, remaining 1/3 cup sugar, brown sugar, baking soda and salt in large bowl; mix well. Stir in mixture of oil, milk and remaining 2 eggs. Fold in lemon rind and pecans.
☐ Pour 1 cup batter into greased and floured 9-inch springform pan with ring insert. Spoon cream cheese mixture over batter. Top with remaining batter.
☐ Bake for 1 hour or until loaf tests done.
☐ Cool in pan for 10 minutes. Remove to wire rack to cool completely.
☐ Yield: 1 loaf.

PUMPKIN SWIRL BREAD

8 ounces cream cheese, softened	1 teaspoon cinnamon
1/4 cup sugar	1/2 teaspoon salt
1 egg, beaten	1/4 teaspoon nutmeg
13/4 cups all-purpose flour	1 cup canned pumpkin
11/2 cups sugar	1/2 cup melted margarine
1 teaspoon baking soda	1 egg, beaten
	1/3 cup water

☐ Preheat oven to 350 degrees.
☐ Blend cream cheese with 1/4 cup sugar and 1 egg in small bowl; set aside.
☐ Mix flour, 11/2 cups sugar, baking soda, cinnamon, salt and nutmeg in large bowl. Add pumpkin, margarine, 1 egg and water; mix just until moistened. Reserve 2 cups pumpkin batter.
☐ Pour remaining pumpkin batter into greased and floured 5-by-9-inch loaf pan. Add cream cheese mixture and reserved pumpkin batter. Cut through with knife to marbleize.
☐ Bake for 1 hour and 10 minutes or until loaf tests done. Cool in pan for 10 minutes. Remove to wire rack to cool completely.
☐ Yield: 1 loaf.

□ Drain spinach; squeeze dry. Combine with 2 eggs, feta cheese, oregano and garlic in bowl; mix well and set aside.
□ Combine 1 cup flour, dry yeast, sugar and salt in large mixer bowl.
□ Heat water and butter to 120 degrees in small saucepan.
□ Add to yeast mixture gradually. Beat at medium speed for 2 minutes.
□ Add 1/2 cup flour. Beat mixture at high speed for 2 minutes.
□ Stir in enough remaining flour to make soft dough. Knead on lightly floured surface for 4 to 6 minutes or until smooth and elastic.
□ Roll dough into 10-by-14-inch rectangle. Place on greased baking sheet.
□ Spread spinach filling down center third of rectangle.
□ Cut 1-inch strips from outer edge to filling on both sides. Fold strips alternately over filling to resemble braid.
□ Let rise, covered, in warm place for 15 minutes.
□ Brush with beaten egg white; sprinkle with sesame seed.
□ Preheat oven to 400 degrees.
□ Bake for 25 minutes or until golden brown. Let stand until cooled slightly before cutting.
□ Place on serving plate. Serve warm.
□ Yield: 1 loaf.

PEPPERY CHEESE BREAD

1 envelope dry yeast	1 egg
1/4 cup warm water	2 1/3 cups all-purpose flour
2 tablespoons sugar	1 cup shredded Cheddar
1 teaspoon salt	cheese
1/4 teaspoon baking soda	1/2 teaspoon freshly
1 cup sour cream	ground pepper

□ Dissolve yeast in warm water in mixer bowl.
□ Add sugar, salt, baking soda, sour cream, egg and 1 1/2 cups flour.
□ Beat at low speed for 30 seconds.
□ Beat at high speed for 2 minutes. Stir in remaining flour, cheese and pepper.
□ Spoon into 2 greased 1-pound coffee cans.
□ Let rise in warm place for 50 minutes; dough will rise only slightly.
□ Preheat oven to 350 degrees.
□ Bake for 40 minutes or until golden brown.
□ Remove loaves to wire rack to cool.
□ Yield: 2 loaves.

Spinach and Cheese Loaf

SPINACH AND CHEESE LOAF

1 (10-ounce) package frozen chopped spinach, thawed	1 envelope Fleischmann's RapidRise dry yeast
2 eggs, lightly beaten	1 tablespoon sugar
1 cup crumbled feta cheese	1 teaspoon salt
1 teaspoon Spice Islands oregano leaves	1 cup water
1 clove of garlic, minced	1 tablespoon butter or margarine
3 to 3 1/2 cups all-purpose flour	1 egg white, lightly beaten
	Sesame seed to taste

NO-KNEAD BUNDT BREAD

1 envelope dry yeast	1/2 cup sugar
1/4 cup warm water	1 teaspoon salt
11/4 cups milk, scalded	4 cups all-purpose flour
3/4 cup margarine	1 egg
1 egg	

□ Dissolve yeast in warm water. Stir hot milk with margarine in mixer bowl until margarine melts. Let stand until cool.
□ Add 1 egg, sugar, salt, dissolved yeast and 1 cup flour; mix well. Mix in remaining 3 cups flour and 1 egg gradually; dough will be sticky.
□ Let rise, covered, in warm place for 11/2 hours or until doubled in bulk.
□ Punch dough down. Place in greased bundt pan. Let rise until doubled in bulk.
□ Preheat oven to 350 degrees.
□ Bake for 45 minutes or until golden brown.
□ Yield: 1 loaf.

LEMON POPPY SEED MUFFINS

2 cups all-purpose flour	3/4 teaspoon salt
11/2 cups quick-cooking oats	11/2 cups reconstituted frozen lemonade concentrate
1/3 cup sugar	
1 tablespoon light brown sugar	2 eggs, beaten
1 teaspoon poppy seed	1/3 cup oil
1 teaspoon baking powder	1 tablespoon grated lemon rind
1/2 teaspoon baking soda	

□ Preheat oven to 400 degrees.
□ Combine first 8 ingredients in bowl; mix well.
□ Add mixture of lemonade, eggs, oil and lemon rind; mix just until moistened.
□ Fill greased or paper-lined muffin cups 2/3 full.
□ Bake for 20 to 25 minutes or until golden brown.
□ Yield: 11/2 dozen.

PIÑA COLADA MUFFINS

1 (2-layer) package yellow cake mix	1 cup flaked coconut
1/3 cup vegetable oil	1/2 cup chopped walnuts
3 eggs	1 cup drained crushed pineapple
1 teaspoon coconut extract	Confectioners' sugar glaze
1 teaspoon rum extract	

□ Preheat oven to 350 degrees.
□ Prepare cake mix using oil and eggs according to package directions.
□ Add extracts, coconut, walnuts and pineapple. Mix for 1 minute; do not over mix.
□ Fill paper-lined muffin cups 3/4 full.
□ Bake for 15 to 20 minutes or until golden brown.

□ Drizzle with confectioners' sugar glaze.
□ Yield: 21/2 dozen.

MACADAMIA NUT MUFFINS

2 cups baking mix	1 cup chopped macadamia nuts
3/4 teaspoon baking soda	
1/2 cup packed light brown sugar	1 egg, beaten
	1 cup crushed pineapple

□ Preheat oven to 400 degrees.
□ Combine first 4 ingredients in bowl. Beat egg with undrained pineapple. Stir into dry ingredients.
□ Fill greased or paper-lined muffin cups 3/4 full.
□ Bake for 12 to 15 minutes or until golden brown.
□ Yield: 14 muffins.

ORANGE SUNSHINE MUFFINS

1 (2-layer) package orange supreme cake mix	1 (11-ounce) can mandarin oranges, drained, chopped
1/3 cup corn oil	1/2 cup orange juice
1 cup orange juice	2 cups confectioners' sugar
3 eggs	

□ Preheat oven to 350 degrees.
□ Combine first 4 ingredients in mixer bowl. Beat for 3 minutes. Fold in chopped oranges.
□ Pour into greased and floured or paper-lined miniature muffin cups.
□ Bake for 10 minutes. Let stand for several minutes; remove muffins. Place on wire rack.
□ Combine remaining 1/2 cup orange juice and confectioners' sugar in bowl; mix well. Spoon over muffins. Let stand to cool completely.
□ Yield: 4 dozen.

CRANBERRY AND YOGURT COFFEE CAKE

1 (2-layer) package yellow cake mix	1 cup plain yogurt
	1/4 cup vegetable oil
1 (4-ounce) package vanilla instant pudding mix	1 (16-ounce) can whole cranberry sauce
4 eggs	1/2 cup chopped walnuts

□ Preheat oven to 350 degrees.
□ Mix dry cake mix and pudding mix in large mixer bowl. Add eggs, yogurt and oil. Beat at high speed for 3 minutes.
□ Pour 2/3 of the batter into greased 9-by-13-inch baking pan.
□ Spoon cranberry sauce over batter. Top with remaining batter. Sprinkle with walnuts.
□ Bake for 45 to 50 minutes or until coffee cake tests done.
□ Yield: 1 coffee cake.

CINNAMON BUBBLE RING

1 (12-ounce) package hot
  roll mix
2 tablespoons butter or
  margarine, softened
1 egg
2 tablespoons sugar

1 cup hot water
1/4 cup melted butter or
  margarine
2 cups sugar
2 tablespoons cinnamon

□ Combine flour mix and yeast from roll mix in bowl; mix well.
□ Add softened butter, egg, 2 tablespoons sugar and hot water; mix well.
□ Knead on floured surface until smooth. Let rest, covered, for 5 minutes.
□ Shape into small balls. Dip in melted butter; coat with mixture of 2 cups sugar and cinnamon. Place in greased bundt pan.
□ Let rise, covered with towel, in warm place for 30 minutes or until doubled in bulk.
□ Preheat oven to 375 degrees.
□ Bake for 15 to 20 minutes or until golden brown. Invert onto tray or wire rack.
□ Yield: 1 bubble ring.

CREAM CHEESE COFFEE CAKE

1 (2-layer) package lemon
  supreme cake mix
2 eggs
1 cup all-purpose flour
1 envelope dry yeast
2/3 cup warm water
16 ounces cream cheese,
  softened
2 eggs
1/4 cup sugar

1 tablespoon all-purpose
  flour
1 tablespoon milk
6 tablespoons butter or
  margarine, softened
1 cup confectioners' sugar
1 tablespoon light corn
  syrup
1 tablespoon water

□ Preheat oven to 350 degrees.
□ Combine 1 1/2 cups cake mix, eggs, 1 cup flour, dry yeast and 2/3 cup warm water in mixer bowl.
□ Beat at medium speed for 2 minutes. Spread in greased 9-by-13-inch baking pan.
□ Combine cream cheese, eggs, sugar, 1 tablespoon flour and milk in mixer bowl. Beat until well blended. Spoon over batter in baking pan.
□ Cut butter into remaining cake mix in small bowl. Sprinkle over cream cheese layer.
□ Bake for 40 to 45 minutes or until golden brown.
□ Blend confectioners' sugar with corn syrup and 1 tablespoon water in small bowl. Drizzle over hot coffee cake.
□ Yield: 1 coffee cake.

YULETIDE COFFEE CAKE

1 cup packed light brown
  sugar
1/2 cup flaked coconut
1/2 cup chopped pecans
1 teaspoon cinnamon
2 cups all-purpose flour
1 cup sugar
2 teaspoons baking
  powder

1 teaspoon salt
2 (4-ounce) packages
  vanilla instant
  pudding mix
1 cup water
3/4 cup vegetable oil
1 teaspoon vanilla extract
4 eggs

□ Mix brown sugar, coconut, pecans and cinnamon in bowl; set aside.
□ Combine flour, sugar, baking powder, salt and pudding mix in mixer bowl.
□ Add water, oil, vanilla and eggs.
□ Beat at low speed for 30 seconds. Beat at medium speed for 2 minutes.
□ Layer batter and coconut mixture 1/2 at a time in greased and floured 9-by-13-inch baking pan.
□ Chill overnight.
□ Preheat oven to 325 degrees.
□ Bake for 40 to 60 minutes or until coffee cake tests done.
□ Yield: 1 coffee cake.

BLENDER CROISSANTS

1 cup warm water
2 envelopes dry yeast
1 (5-ounce) can evaporated
  milk
1 egg
1/4 cup melted butter
  or margarine

1/3 cup sugar
5 cups all-purpose flour
1 cup chilled butter or
  margarine, coarsely
  chopped
1 egg, beaten
1 tablespoon water

□ Combine warm water, yeast, evaporated milk, 1 egg, melted butter and sugar in blender or food processor container; process until smooth. Add 1 cup flour gradually, processing until smooth.
□ Place remaining 4 cups flour in large bowl. Add 1 cup chopped butter and yeast mixture; mix gently until moistened.
□ Chill, covered, for 4 hours or longer.
□ Divide dough into 4 portions. Remove 1 portion at a time from refrigerator. Roll into 16-inch circle on floured surface. Cut into 8 wedges.
□ Roll up from wide ends; shape into crescents. Place point side down 2 inches apart on nonstick baking pan. Let rise, covered, for 3 to 4 hours or until doubled in bulk.
□ Brush with mixture of 1 egg and water.
□ Preheat oven to 400 degrees.
□ Bake for 12 to 15 minutes or until golden brown. Serve warm.
□ Yield: 32 croissants.

Merry Christmas Cakes

SPICED CHOCO-APPLE CAKE ROLL

1 (21-ounce) can apple pie filling, chopped
1 1/2 cups whipped topping
4 egg whites, at room temperature
1/2 cup sugar
4 egg yolks, at room temperature
1/3 cup sugar
1 teaspoon vanilla extract
1/2 cup all-purpose flour
1/4 cup Hershey's baking cocoa
1/2 teaspoon baking powder
1/4 teaspoon baking soda
1/2 teaspoon cinnamon
1/4 teaspoon cloves
1/8 teaspoon salt
1/3 cup water
Confectioners' sugar
Cocoa Glaze

□ Preheat oven to 375 degrees. Line 10-by-15-inch cake pan with foil; grease foil.
□ Combine pie filling and whipped topping in bowl; mix well. Chill until time to fill cake.
□ Beat egg whites in mixer bowl until foamy. Add 1/2 cup sugar gradually, beating until stiff.
□ Beat egg yolks at high speed in mixer bowl until thick and lemon-colored. Add 1/3 cup sugar and vanilla gradually; beat for 2 minutes longer.
□ Mix next 7 dry ingredients in bowl. Fold into egg yolk mixture alternately with water. Fold into egg whites. Spread in prepared pan.
□ Bake for 9 minutes or until top springs back when lightly touched in center.
□ Loosen cake from sides of pan. Invert onto towel sprinkled with confectioners' sugar; discard foil. Roll cake in towel, starting at narrow end. Cool on wire rack.
□ Unroll cake. Spread with apple mixture. Reroll cake to enclose filling. Place on serving plate. Spread with Cocoa Glaze.
□ Yield: 8 to 10 servings.

COCOA GLAZE

2 tablespoons butter or margarine
2 tablespoons Hershey's baking cocoa
2 tablespoons water
1 cup confectioners' sugar
1/2 teaspoon vanilla extract

□ Melt butter in small saucepan over low heat. Stir in cocoa and 2 tablespoons water.
□ Cook until thickened, stirring constantly; do not boil. Remove from heat.

□ Add confectioners' sugar and vanilla; whisk until smooth. Whisk in additional water 1/2 teaspoon at a time if needed for desired consistency.
□ Yield: 3/4 cup.

HOT APPLESAUCE CHRISTMAS CAKES

3 cups hot applesauce
2 cups sugar
1 cup melted shortening
1 teaspoon salt
4 1/2 cups sifted all-purpose flour
4 teaspoons baking soda
1 teaspoon nutmeg
1 teaspoon cinnamon
1 teaspoon allspice
1/2 teaspoon cloves
1 (15-ounce) package golden raisins
1 (15-ounce) package raisins
1 pound candied mixed fruit
3 cups chopped pecans
1/2 (16-ounce) package red and green fruit-flavored gumdrops

□ Combine first 4 ingredients in bowl; mix well. Let stand overnight.
□ Preheat oven to 275 degrees.
□ Sift flour, baking soda and spices into bowl. Add to applesauce mixture; mix well.
□ Stir in raisins, candied fruit, pecans and gumdrops. Spoon into 3 greased loaf pans.
□ Bake for 1 3/4 hours. Cool in pans for 10 minutes. Remove to wire rack to cool completely.
□ Yield: 36 servings.

SHERRY EGGNOG CAKE

1 (2-layer) package yellow cake mix
1 (4-ounce) French vanilla instant pudding mix
1 teaspoon nutmeg
4 eggs
3/4 cup vegetable oil
3/4 cup cream sherry
2 teaspoons vanilla extract
Confectioners' sugar

□ Preheat oven to 350 degrees. Grease and flour bundt pan.
□ Combine first 7 ingredients in bowl. Beat at medium speed for 5 minutes. Spoon into prepared pan.
□ Bake for 40 to 45 minutes or until cake tests done. Cool in pan.
□ Invert onto serving plate. Sift confectioners' sugar over top. Serve with fresh fruit.
□ Yield: 24 servings.

CHOCOLATE ALMOND TORTE

4 egg yolks
1/2 cup sugar
3/4 cup ground blanched almonds
1/3 cup all-purpose flour
1/3 cup Hershey's baking cocoa
1/2 teaspoon baking soda
1/4 teaspoon salt
1/4 cup water

1 teaspoon vanilla extract
1/4 teaspoon almond extract
4 egg whites
1/4 cup sugar
Cherry Filling
Chocolate Glaze
Sliced almonds and maraschino or candied cherry halves

□ Preheat oven to 375 degrees. Grease bottoms of three 8-inch cake pans. Line bottoms with waxed paper and grease again; do not grease sides of pans.
□ Beat egg yolks at medium speed in small mixer bowl for 3 minutes. Add 1/2 cup sugar. Beat for 2 minutes longer.
□ Mix ground almonds, flour, cocoa, baking soda and salt in bowl. Add to egg yolk mixture alternately with water, beating at low speed just until blended. Stir in vanilla and almond extract.
□ Beat egg whites in large mixer bowl until foamy. Add 1/4 cup sugar gradually, beating constantly until stiff peaks form.
□ Fold a small amount of stiffly beaten egg whites into chocolate mixture; fold chocolate mixture into stiffly beaten egg whites. Spread evenly in prepared cake pans.
□ Bake for 14 minutes or until tops spring back when lightly touched. Cool in pans for 10 minutes. Remove to wire rack to cool completely.
□ Spread Cherry Filling between cake layers. Spread top with Chocolate Glaze, allowing glaze to run down side.
□ Garnish with sliced almonds and cherry halves.
□ Yield: 10 to 12 servings.

CHERRY FILLING

1 cup whipping cream
1 1/2 teaspoons kirsch or 1/4 teaspoon almond extract

1/4 cup confectioners' sugar
1/3 cup chopped red candied cherries

□ Combine cream with kirsch and confectioners' sugar in small mixer bowl.
□ Beat until soft peaks form. Fold in cherries.
□ Yield: 2 1/2 cups.

CHOCOLATE GLAZE

1 tablespoon butter or margarine
2 tablespoons Hershey's baking cocoa

2 tablespoons water
1 cup confectioners' sugar
1/4 teaspoon vanilla extract

□ Melt butter in small saucepan over low heat. Stir in cocoa and water. Cook until thickened, stirring constantly; remove from heat.
□ Add confectioners' sugar and vanilla; beat until mixture is smooth and of spreading consistency. Beat in additional water 1/2 teaspoon at a time if needed for desired consistency.
□ Yield: 1 1/4 cups.

MACADAMIA NUT FUDGE CAKE

1 cup all-purpose flour
3/4 cup sugar
1/4 cup Hershey's baking cocoa
1 1/2 teaspoons instant coffee granules
3/4 teaspoon baking soda
1/4 teaspoon salt

1/2 cup butter or margarine, softened
3/4 cup sour cream
1 egg
1/2 teaspoon vanilla extract
Fudge Nut Glaze
Macadamia nuts

□ Preheat oven to 350 degrees. Grease 9-inch cake pan. Line bottom with waxed paper; grease and flour pan.
□ Combine first 6 ingredients in large mixer bowl.
□ Add butter, sour cream, egg and vanilla; blend at low speed. Beat at medium speed for 3 minutes. Spoon into prepared pan.
□ Bake for 30 to 35 minutes or until toothpick inserted in center comes out clean. Cool in pan for 10 minutes. Remove to wire rack to cool completely, discarding waxed paper.
□ Place cake on serving plate. Pour Fudge Nut Glaze evenly over cake, allowing glaze to run down side. Garnish with macadamia nuts. Chill for 1 hour or until glaze is firm. May substitute hazelnuts or pecans for Macadamia nuts.
□ Yield: 8 to 10 servings.

FUDGE NUT GLAZE

1/2 cup whipping cream
1/4 cup sugar
1 tablespoon butter or margarine
1 1/2 teaspoons light corn syrup

1/3 cup Hershey's semisweet chocolate chips
1/2 teaspoon vanilla extract
3/4 cup macadamia nuts, hazelnuts or pecans

□ Combine first 5 ingredients in small saucepan.
□ Bring to a boil over medium heat, stirring constantly. Cook for 5 minutes, stirring constantly; remove from heat.
□ Cool for 10 minutes. Stir in vanilla and macadamia nuts.
□ Yield: 1 1/2 cups.

Chocolate Almond Torte, Macadamia Nut Fudge Cake, page 28

EVER-SO-EASY FRUITCAKE

1 (28-ounce) jar None
  Such® ready-to-use
  mincemeat
1 (14-ounce) can Eagle®
  Brand sweetened
  condensed milk
1 pound mixed candied
  fruit

2 eggs, slightly beaten
1 cup coarsely chopped
  pecans
2 1/2 cups all-purpose flour
1 teaspoon baking soda
2 cups confectioners' sugar
2 to 3 tablespoons milk

□ Preheat oven to 300 degrees. Grease and flour
10-inch bundt pan.
□ Combine mincemeat, condensed milk, candied
fruit, eggs and pecans in bowl; mix well.
□ Add mixture of flour and baking soda; mix well.
Spoon into prepared pan.
□ Bake for 45 to 50 minutes or until wooden pick
inserted in cake comes out clean.
□ Cool in pan for 15 minutes. Invert onto serving
plate to cool completely.
□ Beat confectioners' sugar with enough milk in
mixer bowl to make of glaze consistency.
□ Spoon glaze over fruitcake.
□ Yield: 24 servings.
□ **Fruitcake-in-a-Can:** Spoon batter into 2 greased
1-pound coffee cans and bake for 1 hour and 20
minutes to 1 hour and 25 minutes. May spoon 1
cup batter into each of eight 10-ounce soup cans
and bake for 50 to 55 minutes. Yield: 2 loaves.
□ **Fruitcake Bars:** Spread batter into greased
2-by-10-by-15-inch baking pan and bake for 40 to
45 minutes or until firm. Cool and glaze as desired.
Yield: 4 dozen.

QUICK AND EASY JAM CAKE

1 (2-layer) package spice
  cake mix
4 eggs
1 cup seedless blackberry
  jam

1/3 cup vegetable oil
2/3 cup raisins
2/3 cup chopped pecans
Brown Sugar Frosting

□ Preheat oven to 350 degrees. Grease and flour
three 9-inch cake pans.
□ Combine cake mix, eggs, jam and oil in mixer
bowl; beat until smooth. Stir in raisins and pecans.
Spoon into prepared pans.
□ Bake for 18 minutes or until wooden pick
inserted in center comes out clean. Remove to
wire rack to cool.
□ Spread Brown Sugar Frosting between layers and
over top and side of cake.
□ Yield: 16 servings.

BROWN SUGAR FROSTING

1/2 cup margarine
1 cup packed light brown
  sugar
1/4 cup milk

2 ounces cream cheese,
  softened
1 (1-pound) package
  confectioners' sugar

□ Heat margarine and brown sugar in saucepan
until brown sugar dissolves, stirring to mix well.
□ Add to milk, cream cheese and confectioners'
sugar in mixer bowl, beating until smooth.
□ Yield: 4 cups.

BUTTER PECAN CAKE

1 (2-layer) package butter
  pecan cake mix
1 can coconut and pecan
  frosting
1 cup coconut
1/3 cup vegetable oil

1 cup water
4 eggs, at room
  temperature
Salt to taste
1 cup chopped pecans

□ Preheat oven to 300 degrees. Grease and flour
10-inch tube pan.
□ Combine cake mix, canned frosting and coconut
in mixer bowl. Add oil, water, eggs and salt.
□ Beat at medium speed for 2 to 3 minutes,
scraping bowl frequently.
□ Fold in pecans. Spoon into prepared pan.
□ Bake for 1 hour and 20 minutes or until cake tests
done. Cool in pan for 10 minutes. Remove to
serving plate to cool completely. Chill in
refrigerator before slicing.
□ Yield: 16 servings.

NUTTY RICH RUM CAKE

1/2 cup chopped pecans
1 (2-layer) package butter
  pecan cake mix
4 eggs, beaten
1/2 cup vegetable oil
1 (4-ounce) package
  vanilla instant
  pudding mix

1/2 cup water
1/2 cup light rum
1/2 cup butter or
  margarine
1 cup sugar
1/4 cup water
1/4 cup rum

□ Preheat oven to 325 degrees. Grease and flour
10-inch bundt pan; sprinkle with pecans.
□ Combine cake mix, eggs, oil, pudding mix, 1/2
cup water and 1/2 cup rum in large bowl; beat until
smooth. Pour into prepared pan.
□ Bake for 40 minutes.
□ Combine butter, sugar, 1/4 cup water and 1/4 cup
rum in saucepan. Bring to a boil. Cook for 10
minutes, stirring constantly.
□ Pour over warm cake in pan. Let stand in pan for
1 or 2 days. Invert onto serving plate.
□ Yield: 16 servings.

FUDGE RIBBON CAKE

1 (2-layer) package
  chocolate cake mix
8 ounces cream cheese,
  softened
2 tablespoons margarine,
  softened
1 tablespoon cornstarch
1 (14-ounce) can Eagle®
  Brand sweetened
  condensed milk

1 egg
1 teaspoon vanilla extract
1 1-ounce square
  semisweet chocolate
1 tablespoon margarine
2 tablespoons water
3/4 cup confectioners'
  sugar
1/2 teaspoon vanilla extract
Confectioners' sugar

☐ Preheat oven to 350 degrees.
☐ Prepare cake mix using package directions.
Spoon into greased and floured 10-inch bundt pan
or 3 round cake pans.
☐ Beat next 3 ingredients in mixer bowl until fluffy.
Beat in condensed milk gradually. Add egg and 1
teaspoon vanilla; mix well. Spoon over cake batter.
☐ Bake for 50 to 55 minutes or until cake tests done.
☐ Cool in pan for 15 minutes. Remove to serving
plate to cool completely.

Fudge Ribbon Cake, Fudge Ribbon Cupcakes,
Grasshopper Ribbon Cake

☐ Melt chocolate with 1 tablespoon margarine and
water in small saucepan; remove from heat.
☐ Stir in confectioners' sugar and 1/2 teaspoon
vanilla; mix until smooth. Frost cake or garnish
with confectioners' sugar.
☐ Yield: 16 servings.
☐ **Fudge Ribbon Cupcakes:** Spoon cake batter into
30 paper-lined muffin cups. Top each with 2
tablespoons cream cheese mixture. Bake for 20
minutes or until cupcakes test done. Frost with
ready-to-spread frosting. Yield: 30 cupcakes.
☐ **Grasshopper Ribbon Cake:** Substitute 1
teaspoon peppermint flavoring and several drops
of green food coloring for vanilla in cream cheese
mixture and bake in 9-by-13-inch cake pan until
cake tests done.
☐ Yield: 16 servings.

Heavenly Christmas Candy

CHOCOLATE-COVERED SPECKLED APPLES

8 large Granny Smith
  apples, stems removed
8 wooden popsicle sticks
  or skewers
1¹/3 cups confectioners'
  sugar
¹/2 cup Hershey's baking
  cocoa

¹/2 cup vegetable oil
1 cup Hershey's
  semisweet or milk
  chocolate chips
2 cups chopped Hershey's
  vanilla milk chips

□ Wash and dry apples. Insert popsicle stick into
stem end of each apple. Place on waxed paper-
lined tray.
□ Combine confectioners' sugar, cocoa and oil in
glass bowl; mix well. Add chocolate chips.
□ Microwave on High for 1 minute; mix well.
Microwave for 15 to 30 seconds longer if necessary
to melt any remaining chips.
□ Twirl apples in chocolate mixture or spoon
mixture over apples; tap popsicle sticks on edge of
pan to remove excess coating. Return to tray. Let
stand for 5 minutes.
□ Coat with vanilla milk chips. Chill for 1 to 2
hours or until firm. Store wrapped in plastic wrap.
□ May drizzle coated apples with melted caramel
or milk chocolate or white chocolate and coat with
chopped pecans or candy.
□ Yield: 8 servings.

CHEWY APPLE SQUARES

2 envelopes unflavored
  gelatin
¹/2 cup cold water
1¹/4 cups grated apple
2 cups sugar
1 teaspoon lemon juice

1 cup finely chopped
  pecans
1 teaspoon vanilla extract
¹/2 cup confectioners'
  sugar
1 tablespoon cornstarch

□ Soften gelatin in cold water in bowl. Add ¹/2 cup
apple. Let stand for 10 minutes.
□ Combine ³/4 cup apple, sugar and lemon juice in
saucepan. Add gelatin mixture. Bring to a simmer,
stirring constantly. Simmer for 15 minutes.
□ Let stand for 30 minutes or until cooled to
lukewarm. Mix in pecans and vanilla.
□ Pour into greased 8-inch square pan. Let stand
for 24 hours.

□ Cut into squares; coat with mixture of
confectioners' sugar and cornstarch. Place in
paper bonbon cups.
□ Yield: 2 dozen.

MICROWAVE CARAMELS

1 cup butter or margarine,
  melted
1 (14-ounce) can
  sweetened condensed
  milk
1 cup light corn syrup

1 (1-pound) package light
  brown sugar
1 teaspoon vanilla extract
2 cups semisweet
  chocolate chips, melted

□ Blend first 4 ingredients in large microwave-safe
bowl. Microwave on High for 17 minutes, stirring
every 3 minutes. Mix in vanilla.
□ Pour into buttered 9-by-13-inch pan. Chill in
refrigerator overnight.
□ Pour melted chocolate over caramels. Cut into
1-inch squares.
□ May substitute almond bark for chocolate chips
or increase amount of chocolate and dip caramel
squares into chocolate to coat on all sides.
□ Yield: 10 dozen.

CHERRY CANDY

1 (14-ounce) package
  chocolate fudge
  frosting mix
1 (1-pound) package
  confectioners' sugar
¹/2 (14-ounce) can
  sweetened condensed
  milk
1 (4-ounce) jar
  maraschino cherries,
  drained, chopped

1¹/2 teaspoons vanilla
  extract
¹/4 cup butter or
  margarine, softened
2 cups white chocolate
  chips
1 to 2 tablespoons melted
  paraffin
1 (8-ounce) package
  chopped peanuts

□ Combine first 6 ingredients in bowl; mix well.
□ Shape into balls. Chill until firm if necessary.
□ Melt white chocolate chips with paraffin in
double boiler over hot water; blend well.
□ Dip balls into melted white chocolate; roll in
peanuts to coat. Place in paper bonbon cups. Let
stand until firm. Store in refrigerator.
□ Yield: 2 to 3 dozen.

Easy Nut Brittle

1 cup sugar
1/2 cup light corn syrup
1/8 teaspoon salt
11/2 cups mixed nuts,
   roasted peanuts
   or cashews

1 teaspoon corn oil
   margarine
1 teaspoon vanilla extract
1 teaspoon baking soda

□ Spray baking sheet and metal spatula with nonstick cooking spray. Combine sugar, corn syrup and salt in 2-quart microwave-safe bowl; blend well with wooden spoon.
□ Microwave on High for 7 to 8 minutes or until syrup is pale yellow. Stir in mixed nuts.
□ Microwave for 1 to 2 minutes or until nuts are lightly browned. Add margarine, vanilla and baking soda; stir until foamy.

Easy Nut Brittle

□ Pour onto prepared baking sheet; spread evenly with spatula. Cool. Break into pieces and store in tightly covered container.
□ Yield: 11/4 pounds.

Nut Clusters

12 ounces semisweet
   chocolate chips

12 ounces almond bark
2 cups mixed nuts

□ Melt chocolate chips and almond bark in double boiler. Stir in mixed nuts.
□ Drop by teaspoonfuls onto waxed paper-lined surface. Let stand until firm.
□ Yield: 3 dozen.

COCONUT PEAKS

1/4 cup butter or margarine	3 cups flaked coconut
2 cups confectioners' sugar	1 teaspoon vanilla extract
1/4 cup light cream or evaporated milk	1/2 cup semisweet chocolate chips
	2 tablespoons butter or margarine

□ Melt 1/4 cup butter in saucepan over medium heat. Cook until golden brown, stirring constantly; remove from heat.
□ Add confectioners' sugar, cream, coconut and vanilla; mix well. Drop by spoonfuls onto plate.
□ Chill until firm enough to shape into cones with flattened bottoms; place in paper bonbon cups.
□ Melt chocolate chips with 2 tablespoons butter in saucepan over low heat, stirring constantly.
□ Drizzle melted chocolate mixture over tops of cones and allow to run down sides of cones to resemble mountains.
□ Yield: 1 to 2 dozen.

TRIPLE-DECKER FUDGE

1 (10-ounce) package Hershey's vanilla milk chips	1 (10-ounce) package Hershey's milk chocolate chunks
1 (10-ounce) package Hershey's semisweet chocolate chunks	2 (14-ounce) cans sweetened condensed milk

□ Place vanilla milk chips, semisweet chocolate, and milk chocolate in separate microwave-safe bowls. Add 3/4 cup condensed milk to each of the chocolate bowls. Pour remaining condensed milk into vanilla milk bowl.
□ Microwave each bowl on High for 50 seconds or until melted; blend well. Melt each as needed.
□ Layer milk chocolate, vanilla milk and semisweet chocolate in foil-lined 9-by-13-inch pan.
□ Chill until firm.
□ Remove from pan, peel off foil and cut into 1-inch squares. Place in paper bonbon cups. Store in refrigerator.
□ Yield: 8 dozen.

PEPPERMINT PECANS

1 cup sugar	1 teaspoon peppermint extract
1/4 cup water	4 cups pecan halves
1 tablespoon light corn syrup	
1 tablespoon (heaping) marshmallow creme	

□ Bring sugar, water and corn syrup to a boil in saucepan. Boil for 1 minute; remove from heat.

□ Add marshmallow creme and peppermint extract; blend well. Add pecans; stir until coated.
□ Drop onto waxed paper; separate into clusters. Cool. Store in tightly covered container.
□ Yield: 4 cups.

SUGARPLUM DELIGHTS

1 cup margarine, softened	2 cups graham cracker crumbs
8 ounces cream cheese, softened	1 cup chopped pecans
1 tablespoon vanilla extract	31/2 cups semisweet chocolate chips
1 cup shredded coconut	3 tablespoons melted paraffin
1 (1-pound) package confectioners' sugar	

□ Cream margarine and cream cheese in mixer bowl until light and fluffy. Add next 5 ingredients; mix well.
□ Shape into 1-inch balls; place on waxed paper. Chill for 1 hour or longer.
□ Melt chocolate chips with paraffin in double boiler over hot water; blend well. Remove and dip 6 balls at a time into chocolate to coat; place in paper bonbon cups. Let stand until firm.
□ Yield: 5 dozen.

TIGER BUTTER

1 cup white chocolate candy coating wafers	1 cup chocolate candy coating wafers, melted
1/2 cup chunky peanut butter	

□ Melt white chocolate wafers in double boiler over hot water, stirring constantly. Blend in peanut butter.
□ Alternate strips of peanut butter and chocolate mixtures on waxed paper-lined tray; swirl with knife. Let stand until firm. Break into pieces.
□ Yield: 11/4 pounds.

TOFFEE CLUSTERS

1 pound white almond bark	1 (10-ounce) package almond brickle chips
2 cups semisweet chocolate chips	

□ Microwave almond bark in glass bowl on High for 5 minutes or until melted, stirring frequently.
□ Add chocolate chips. Microwave for 1 minute or until melted. Stir in almond brickle chips.
□ Drop by spoonfuls into paper bonbon cups. Let stand until firm.
□ Yield: 3 dozen.

Wrap our Cappucino Mix or Coffee Vienna Mix (page 43) in pretty mugs and tie on pepperment stick stirrers.

TRUFFLE MICE

4 ounces semisweet
  chocolate, chopped
1/3 cup sour cream
1 cup finely crushed
  chocolate wafers

1/3 cup confectioners'
  sugar
Gold or silver shot
Sliced almonds
Black licorice whips

□ Melt chocolate in double boiler over hot water, stirring constantly; remove from heat. Blend in sour cream.
□ Add wafer crumbs; mix well. Chill for 1 hour or until firm.
□ Roll by teaspoonfuls in confectioners' sugar; shape into oval for body of mouse.
□ Place 2 gold or silver shot for eyes, 2 almond slices for ears and desired length of licorice whip for tail.

□ Store in refrigerator.
□ Yield: 20 candies.

WALNUT BONBONS

8 ounces cream cheese,
  softened
7 cups confectioners'
  sugar

1 teaspoon walnut extract
1 1/2 cups walnut halves
2 cups flaked coconut

□ Combine first 3 ingredients in bowl; mix well.
□ Shape a small amount of cream cheese mixture around each walnut half; roll in coconut to coat. Place in paper bonbon cups.
□ Chill until set. Serve at room temperature.
□ Yield: 5 dozen.

Favorite Christmas Treats

BOSTON CREAM CHEESECAKE

1 (1-layer) package yellow cake mix	2 tablespoons water
16 ounces cream cheese, softened	2 (1-ounce) squares unsweetened chocolate
1/2 cup sugar	3 tablespoons margarine
1 teaspoon vanilla extract	1 cup confectioners' sugar
2 eggs	1 teaspoon vanilla extract
1/3 cup sour cream	

□ Preheat oven to 350 degrees.
□ Prepare cake mix using package directions. Pour into 9-inch springform pan greased on bottom only.
□ Bake for 20 minutes.
□ Beat cream cheese with sugar and 1 teaspoon vanilla extract until light and fluffy.
□ Beat in eggs 1 at a time. Mix in sour cream. Spread over baked layer.
□ Bake for 35 minutes longer.
□ Cool in pan for several minutes. Loosen from edge of pan. Let stand until cooled completely. Remove side of pan.
□ Heat water, chocolate and margarine in saucepan until melted, stirring constantly; remove from heat.
□ Beat in confectioners' sugar and vanilla. Spread over cheesecake.
□ Chill until serving time.
□ Yield: 10 to 12 servings.

FUDGE TRUFFLE CHEESECAKE

1 1/2 cups vanilla wafer crumbs	24 ounces cream cheese, softened
1/2 cup confectioners' sugar	1 (14-ounce) can sweetened condensed milk
1/3 cup baking cocoa	
1/3 cup melted butter or margarine	4 eggs
2 cups semisweet chocolate chips	2 teaspoons vanilla extract

□ Preheat oven to 300 degrees.
□ Combine crumbs, confectioners' sugar, cocoa and butter in bowl; mix well. Press over bottom of 9-inch springform pan.

□ Melt chocolate chips in heavy saucepan over very low heat, stirring frequently.
□ Beat cream cheese in mixer bowl until smooth. Add melted chocolate, condensed milk, eggs and vanilla; beat until smooth and creamy. Pour into prepared pan.
□ Bake for 1 hour or until set in center. Let stand until cooled to room temperature.
□ Place on serving plate; remove side of pan. Chill until serving time.
□ Yield: 10 to 12 servings.

CHOCOLATE APPLE TART

2 cups all-purpose flour	1/2 teaspoon cinnamon
2 tablespoons sugar	1/8 teaspoon nutmeg
1/2 teaspoon baking powder	1 cup whipping cream
1/2 teaspoon salt	1 egg yolk, beaten
1/2 cup butter or margarine, softened	1/4 cup Hershey's baking cocoa
3 tablespoons water	1/2 cup sugar
1/2 cup sugar	3 cups peeled sliced apples

□ Preheat oven to 350 degrees.
□ Combine first 4 ingredients in bowl. Cut in butter until crumbly. Add water; mix until mixture forms ball. Press pastry over bottom and up side of 11-inch round tart pan with removable bottom.
□ Mix 1/2 cup sugar with spices in bowl; set aside. Whisk whipping cream with egg yolk in bowl until blended. Stir in cocoa and 1/2 cup sugar.
□ Sprinkle 2 tablespoons spice-sugar mixture over pastry. Pour cocoa mixture into prepared tart pan.
□ Bake for 20 minutes.
□ Toss apple slices with remaining spice-sugar mixture. Arrange apple slices in overlapping spoke pattern on top of tart.
□ Bake for 50 to 55 minutes longer or until chocolate mixture is set and apples are tender. Cut into wedges.
□ Serve warm with ice cream.
□ Yield: 12 servings.

Spiced Choco-Apple Cake Roll, Chocolate-Covered Speckled Apples, Chocolate Apple Tart, pages 27, 32 and 36

Ever-So-Easy Fruitcake, Fruitcake-in-a-Can, Fruitcake Bars, Cranberry Mince Streusel Pie, pages 30 and 38

CRANBERRY MINCE STREUSEL PIE

1¹/₃ cups None Such® ready-to-use mincemeat
1 (9-inch) unbaked pie shell
1 (16-ounce) can whole cranberry sauce
2 tablespoons sugar
1¹/₂ teaspoons grated orange rind

¹/₂ cup all-purpose flour
¹/₂ cup packed light brown sugar
¹/₂ cup quick-cooking oats
¹/₄ cup melted margarine
¹/₃ cup chopped pecans
1 teaspoon allspice or cinnamon

□ Preheat oven to 425 degrees.
□ Spread mincemeat over bottom of pie shell. Combine cranberry sauce, sugar and orange rind in bowl; mix well. Spread over mincemeat.
□ Mix flour, brown sugar, oats and margarine in small bowl until crumbly. Stir in pecans and allspice. Sprinkle over top.
□ Bake for 15 minutes. Reduce oven temperature to 350 degrees. Bake for 35 minutes longer or until golden brown. Cover edge of pie with foil if necessary. Serve warm or cool.
□ Yield: 6 to 8 servings.

BUTTERED RUM POPCORN

9 cups popped popcorn
2 cups mixed nuts
¹/₂ cup butter or margarine
¹/₂ cup light corn syrup

1 cup packed light brown sugar
1¹/₂ teaspoons rum extract
1 teaspoon baking soda

□ Preheat oven to 250 degrees.
□ Combine popcorn and mixed nuts in lightly greased shallow baking pan.
□ Bring butter, corn syrup and brown sugar to a boil in saucepan over medium heat. Cook for 5 minutes; remove from heat.
□ Stir in rum extract and baking soda.
□ Pour over popcorn mixture; toss to coat.
□ Bake for 1 hour, stirring every 15 minutes.
□ Spread mixture on waxed paper to cool, stirring gently to separate.
□ Store in airtight container.
□ Yield: 10 cups.

Fruity Party Mix

4 cups bite-sized
   shredded wheat cereal
1/2 cup mixed nuts
1/2 cup shredded coconut
1/3 cup butter or
   margarine

1/4 cup frozen orange or
   pineapple juice
   concentrate, thawed
2 tablespoons honey
3/4 teaspoon ginger
1 cup raisins

□ Preheat oven to 275 degrees.
□ Combine cereal, mixed nuts and coconut in large
bowl; toss lightly to mix.
□ Combine butter, orange juice concentrate, honey
and ginger in saucepan. Cook until butter melts,
stirring frequently. Add raisins. Cook for 2
minutes or until raisins are plumped, stirring
frequently. Pour over cereal mixture; toss lightly.
□ Spread on baking sheet. Bake for 45 minutes,
stirring every 15 minutes. Bake for 15 minutes
longer or until light brown; watch carefully to
prevent over browning. Cool to room temperature.
□ Store in airtight container.
□ Yield: 6 cups.

Sugar and Spice Snack

1 (6-ounce) package
   bugle-shaped corn
   snacks
2 cups mixed nuts
2 tablespoons orange juice
2 egg whites

1 1/3 cups sugar
1 tablespoon grated
   orange rind
1 teaspoon cinnamon
1 teaspoon allspice
1 teaspoon ginger

□ Preheat oven to 275 degrees.
□ Mix corn snacks and nuts in large bowl. Beat
orange juice and egg whites with wire whisk in
bowl until foamy. Whisk in sugar, orange rind
and spices.
□ Pour over nut mixture, tossing to coat. Spread in
greased 10-by-15-inch baking pan.
□ Bake for 45 minutes, stirring every 15 minutes.
Spread mixture on waxed paper to cool, stirring
gently to separate.
□ Store in airtight container.
□ Yield: 10 cups.

BING CHERRY JAM

4 cups chopped pitted Bing cherries	1/2 teaspoon cloves
1 envelope pectin	1/4 cup almond liqueur or 1 teaspoon almond extract
1/4 cup lemon juice	
1/4 teaspoon salt	4 1/2 cups sugar
1/2 teaspoon cinnamon	

□ Combine cherries, pectin, lemon juice, salt, cinnamon, cloves and almond liqueur in large saucepan. Bring to a full rolling boil.
□ Stir in sugar. Boil for 2 minutes; remove from heat and skim.
□ Ladle into hot sterilized 1-pint jelly jars, leaving 1/4-inch headspace; seal with 2-piece lids. Process in boiling water bath for 10 minutes.
□ Yield: 7 1/2-pints.

FESTIVE FRUIT JAM

2 cups chopped peeled peaches	1 unpeeled orange, thinly sliced
1 cup chopped peeled plums	2 cups green grape halves Sugar
1 (14-ounce) can pineapple chunks	1 cup chopped pecans

□ Combine peaches, plums, undrained pineapple, orange slices and grapes in bowl; mix well. Measure fruit mixture. Mix with equal measure of sugar in saucepan.
□ Bring to a simmer, stirring frequently. Simmer, uncovered, for 40 minutes, stirring occasionally.
□ Stir in pecans. Bring to a full rolling boil.
□ Cook for 1 to 2 minutes, stirring constantly.
□ Ladle into hot sterilized 1-pint jelly jars, leaving 1/4-inch headspace; seal with 2-piece lids.
□ Yield: 6 to 8 pints.

GRAPE FREEZER JELLY

2 (6-ounce) cans frozen grape juice concentrate, thawed	1 3/4 cups lemon-lime soda
	3/4 cup water
	1 envelope pectin
5 cups sugar	

□ Combine grape juice concentrate and sugar in bowl; mix well. Stir in lemon-lime soda.
□ Bring water and pectin to a boil in saucepan, stirring constantly.
□ Stir hot mixture into grape juice mixture. Stir for 3 minutes.
□ Ladle into small 1-pint freezer containers; seal. Let stand at room temperature for 24 hours.
□ Store in freezer.
□ Yield: 5 2/3 pints.

PICKLED PEACHES

2 cups sugar	1 tablespoon whole allspice
2 cups water	
3 cups vinegar	24 firm ripe peaches, peeled or 48 canned peach halves
1 (2-inch) piece of fresh peeled gingerroot	
2 cinnamon sticks	4 cups sugar
1 teaspoon whole cloves	

□ Combine first 7 ingredients in large saucepan. Bring to a boil, stirring until sugar is dissolved.
□ Add peaches several at a time. Cook until heated through but not soft; remove with slotted spoon. Return all peaches to hot syrup.
□ Let stand until cooled to room temperature. Drain, reserving syrup.
□ Heat reserved syrup and 2 cups sugar in saucepan until sugar dissolves, stirring frequently. Add peaches to hot syrup.
□ Let stand overnight. Remove peaches with slotted spoon; pack into hot sterilized 1-quart jars.
□ Add remaining 2 cups sugar to syrup. Heat until sugar dissolves, stirring frequently. Cook until of desired consistency.
□ Ladle over peaches in jars, leaving 1/2-inch headspace; seal with 2-piece lids. Process in boiling water bath for 10 minutes.
□ Yield: 3 quarts.

SQUASH PICKLES

8 cups sliced yellow squash	2 tablespoons salt
	3 cups sugar
2 cups sliced onions	2 cups vinegar
3 green bell peppers, cut into strips	2 teaspoons mustard seed
	2 teaspoons celery seed

□ Combine first 3 ingredients in large bowl. Sprinkle with salt. Let stand for 1 hour; drain.
□ Combine sugar, vinegar, mustard seed and celery seed in large saucepan. Bring to a boil, stirring until sugar dissolves; remove from heat.
□ Add vegetables; mix gently. Ladle into hot sterilized 1-pint jars, leaving 1/4-inch headspace; seal with 2-piece lids. Process in boiling water bath for 10 minutes.
□ Yield: 5 pints.

Pickled Peaches, Eight Herb Vinegar, Pickled Sweet Peppers, pages 40 and 42

SWEET GARLIC PICKLES

1 (1-quart) jar kosher dill pickles	3 cloves of garlic, sliced
1 cup sugar	2 dried hot red peppers
1 cup apple cider vinegar	3 cinnamon sticks, broken

☐ Drain pickles; slice into rounds. Combine with remaining ingredients in large bowl; mix gently.
☐ Let stand, covered, at room temperature for 3 days, stirring 2 or 3 times each day.
☐ Drain, reserving liquid. Pack pickle slices into 1-pint jars. Add reserved liquid; seal with 2-piece lids.
☐ Store in refrigerator for 3 days or longer before serving.
☐ Yield: 2 or 3 pints.

EIGHT HERB VINEGAR

Opal basil	Rosemary
Marjoram	Celery Seed
Thyme	Chervil
Winter savory	1 gallon white wine
Sage	vinegar

☐ Wash herbs; shake dry. Pack into sterilized 1-gallon jar.
☐ Heat vinegar in saucepan until very hot; do not boil. Pour over herbs; seal.
☐ Let stand for 4 to 6 weeks. Strain twice. Decant into hot sterilized 1-quart jars. Place sprigs of herbs in jar; seal.
☐ May use only 1 type of herb if desired. May use vinegar for salad dressing, pickled peppers or antipasto mix.
☐ Yield: 3 1/2 quarts.

PICKLED SWEET PEPPERS

2 large red bell peppers	1/4 cup honey
2 large yellow bell peppers	1 teaspoon black peppercorns
2 cups water	4 large cloves of garlic, thinly sliced
1/2 cup Eight Herb Vinegar	1 cup sliced onion

☐ Cut bell peppers into halves lengthwise; discard seed and membranes. Cut lengthwise into 1-inch wide strips; set aside.
☐ Combine water, Eight Herb Vinegar, honey, peppercorns and garlic in saucepan. Bring to a boil. Add peppers and onion.
☐ Bring to a boil; cover. Reduce heat. Simmer for 20 minutes or until peppers are very tender. Let stand until cool.
☐ Store in airtight containers in refrigerator.
☐ Yield: 5 cups.

APPLE RELISH

12 large apples, cored	2 cups apple cider vinegar
6 red bell peppers, seeded	1 cup packed light brown sugar
6 green bell peppers, seeded	5 cups sugar
4 large onions, peeled	1 cup prepared mustard
3 hot peppers	

☐ Force unpeeled apples, red and green peppers, onions and hot peppers through food grinder.
☐ Mix remaining ingredients in large saucepan. Bring to a boil, stirring frequently. Simmer for 5 minutes, stirring frequently.
☐ Ladle into hot sterilized 1-pint jars, leaving 1/2-inch headspace. Seal with 2-piece lids.
☐ Serve with cream cheese and crackers or as an accompaniment with meat or beans.
☐ Yield: 13 pints.

RHUBARB AND ONION RELISH

8 cups sliced rhubarb	1 teaspoon ginger
4 cups sliced onions	1 cup vinegar
4 cups sliced light brown sugar	1 clove of garlic, minced
2 teaspoons salt	1 tablespoon mixed pickling spices
1 teaspoon cinnamon	

☐ Combine first 7 ingredients in heavy saucepan; mix well. Tie garlic and pickling spices in cheesecloth bag. Add to rhubarb mixture.
☐ Bring mixture to a simmer, stirring frequently. Simmer for 2 minutes or until rhubarb is tender-crisp, stirring frequently; do not overcook. Discard spice bag.
☐ Ladle into hot sterilized 1-pint jars, leaving 1/2-inch headspace; seal with 2-piece lids. Process in boiling water bath for 5 minutes.
☐ Yield: 5 pints.

FRUIT SALSA

1 green bell pepper, chopped	1 papaya or mango, chopped
1 yellow bell pepper, chopped	1 pineapple, peeled, chopped
1 red bell pepper, chopped	1/2 cup finely chopped cilantro
Minced jalapeño pepper to taste	1 purple onion, chopped

☐ Combine all ingredients in bowl; mix well.
☐ Ladle into hot sterilized 1-pint jars. Store in refrigerator.
☐ Serve as dip with corn chips or as an accompaniment with grilled fish or chicken.
☐ Yield: 3 to 4 pints.

TWO-WAY APRICOT TOPPING

3¼ cups water
2 (8-ounce) packages
dried apricots
½ cup sugar

Cinnamon to taste
2 tablespoons lemon juice
1 tablespoon apricot
brandy or nectar

□ Combine water, apricots and sugar in 2-quart saucepan. Bring to a boil; reduce heat.
□ Simmer for 10 to 15 minutes or until liquid is reduced to 1 cup; remove from heat.
□ Stir in cinnamon, lemon juice and brandy.
□ Purée in blender container.
□ Pour into sterilized 1-pint jars; seal.
□ Store in refrigerator.
□ May use puréed topping as fruit topping or spread for toast or muffins.
□ Yield: 2 pints.
□ **Microwave Topping:** Reduce water by 1¼ cups. Combine water, apricots and sugar in glass bowl. Microwave, covered, on High for 10 to 12 minutes or until apricots are almost tender. Let stand for 5 minutes. Proceed as instructed above.

CARAMEL CRACKERS

½ cup sugar
½ cup light corn syrup
¼ cup margarine
1 teaspoon baking soda

1 teaspoon vanilla extract
1 (16-ounce) package
oyster crackers
1 cup peanuts

□ Preheat oven to 225 degrees.
□ Combine sugar, corn syrup and margarine in saucepan. Bring to a simmer over low heat.
□ Cook for 5 minutes; remove from heat. Stir in baking soda and vanilla.
□ Pour over crackers and peanuts in lightly greased 9-by-13-inch baking pan; toss to coat.
□ Bake for 45 minutes or until golden brown, stirring every 15 minutes.
□ Pour onto waxed paper to cool, stirring gently to separate.
□ Store in airtight container.
□ Yield: 5 to 6 cups.

SCRAMBLE

1 pound cashews
1 pound mixed nuts
1 pound pecan halves
1 (15-ounce) package
wheat Chex
1 (15-ounce) package
round oat cereal

2 (8-ounce) packages
pretzel sticks
2 cups vegetable oil
1 teaspoon garlic salt
1 tablespoon seasoned
salt

□ Preheat oven to 250 degrees.
□ Combine cashews, mixed nuts, pecans, cereals and pretzels in large roasting pan.

□ Mix vegetable oil, garlic salt and seasoned salt in bowl. Pour over nut mixture; mix gently with wooden spoon.
□ Bake for 2 hours, stirring every 15 minutes.
□ Let stand until cooled to room temperature.
□ Store in airtight container.
□ Yield: 35 cups.

SALT SUBSTITUTE

1 teaspoon chili powder
2 teaspoons oregano
2 teaspoons pepper
1 tablespoon garlic
powder
2 tablespoons dry mustard

6 tablespoons onion
powder
3 tablespoons paprika
3 tablespoons poultry
seasoning

□ Combine chili powder, oregano, pepper, garlic powder, dry mustard, onion powder, paprika and poultry seasoning in bowl; mix well.
□ Divide among pretty jars with shaker tops or salt shakers.
□ Use on meat, poultry, seafood or vegetables.
□ Yield: 3½ cups.

CAPPUCINO MIX

1 (8-quart) package
nonfat dry milk powder
1 (16-ounce) jar powdered
nondairy creamer
1 (20-ounce) package
instant cocoa mix

1 (8-ounce) jar instant
coffee powder
1 (1-pound) package
confectioners' sugar

□ Combine all ingredients in large container; mix well.
□ Divide into smaller containers; seal tightly.
□ Attach instructions to mix ¼ cup dry mix with 1 cup boiling water for each serving.
□ Yield: 20 cups mix.

COFFEE VIENNA MIX

2 cups instant cocoa mix
2 cups powdered
nondairy creamer
1½ cups instant coffee
powder

1½ cups confectioners'
sugar
1 teaspoon cinnamon
1 teaspoon nutmeg

□ Combine all ingredients in large container; mix well.
□ Divide into smaller containers; seal tightly.
□ Attach instructions to mix 3 to 4 teaspoons dry mix with 1 cup boiling water for each serving.
□ Yield: 7 cups mix.

Visions of Sugarplums

A Season for Giving

Homemade Gifts

It was supposed to be the year of the bicycle.

I was seven years old, and more than anything in the world I wanted a Schwinn bike for Christmas. I imagined myself astride it like a knight on his horse, battling the forces of evil and little David Lovelace down the street. The bike was all I could think about as the holidays drew near, and by Christmas Eve the image was so real I could almost hop on and ride it.

Carol, my four-year-old sister, had other things on her mind. "You'll never guess what I'm giving you," she said.

"A bicycle pump?" I asked.

"No, a paper angel!"

The moment she said it, her face turned pale. In her excitement she had told me something I wasn't supposed to know.

Carol ran to her room. She stayed there until the next morning, when we gathered beneath the Christmas tree. Sure enough, there was my bicycle. I was itching to take it outside for a test ride, but first we had to finish unwrapping presents. I plowed through my other gifts, until there was just one left: a lumpy package wrapped in wrinkled green paper. *To Ronald*, said the tag, *Love, Carol*. I glanced at my sister. Her eyes were downcast.

"I wonder what this is," I said.

Carol looked up.

"Maybe it's a bicycle pump," I said.

Carol stared at me, amazed. "Don't you remember?" she said.

"Remember what?" I asked. I unwrapped the package and found a rough figure made of construction paper and covered with glitter.

"It's an angel!" I exclaimed. "This is great!"

"He didn't remember!" Carol said. She gave me a big hug. I hugged her back, and as I did, I saw my mother smiling at me.

"Let's put it on the tree," I suggested. My father lifted Carol up, and she placed the angel at the very top.

It was supposed to be the year of the bicycle, and in fact I rode that bike until the paint faded and the seat wore out. But these days it's the angel I remember most often, and the excitement on my little sister's face, and the lesson I learned that year about receiving: that if it's done right, it's more like giving than getting.

Looking back, that may have been the best gift of all.

Kitten Barrette and Necklace, Flop-Eared Bunny Barrette,
Gold Lamé Picture Frame, pages 78 and 79

Paper Reindeer Garland

Here's a project that your child will enjoy doing and you will enjoy displaying—a paper-doll style reindeer garland. Not only can your little herd encircle a tree, you can tape them to the shelves of a hutch, swag a mantel, or put them out to pasture on your child's headboard.

MATERIALS

1 (4-by-5-inch) piece cardboard
Scissors
White butcher paper or freezer wrap paper
Transparent tape
See Patterns

DIRECTIONS

- □ Transfer pattern to cardboard and cut out.
- □ Cut butcher paper into 5-inch-by-desired length strips.
- □ Fold butcher paper accordion-style into 4-inch segments.
- □ Lay cardboard pattern on paper with fold edges aligned and trace design.
- □ Cut out, cutting through all thicknesses at once.
- □ Tape strips of garland together to create longer segments.

Cross-Stitch Grandbaby Stockings

We call these grandbaby stockings because they're perfect little stockings for a grand-mother to make and fill with goodies. They could spawn a whole new tradition—Grandmother could tuck a special gift in them every year.

MATERIALS

1 (6-by-8-inch) 11-count Aida cloth white fabric piece
Embroidery floss in desired colors to match fabric
1 (#24) embroidery needle
1/4 yard (45-inch wide) plaid fabric
1 (5-by-9-inch) white cotton fabric piece
1 yard (1/2-inch wide) white binding
1 yard (1-inch wide) pregathered white lace for girl's stocking
See Patterns

DIRECTIONS

- □ Transfer pattern piece A for small stocking to Aida cloth.
- □ Mark center of cross-stitch fabric both ways with long running stitch using needle and thread.
- □ Work name for ornament on graph paper before stitching to check placement. Adjust solid ornament area as necessary.
- □ Work cross-stitch according to chart and color key, beginning at intersection of arrows on chart to ensure proper placement of design on fabric.
- □ Use 2 strands of floss for cross-stitch and 1 strand for back-stitch.
- □ Press finished work.
- □ Cut 1 of pattern piece B from plaid fabric.
- □ Cut 1 of pattern piece C from plaid fabric and white cotton backing. Cut one 1-by-7-inch strip for hanger. Make a 24-inch-long (1/2-inch wide) binding strip from remaining fabric.
- □ Position stocking top on cross-stitched stocking with right sides facing, and stitch together. Turn up and press.
- □ Use this as pattern to cut white cotton backing.
- □ Position stocking top on backing and finish edges with plaid binding.
- □ Position large stocking on backing and finish edges of large stocking with white binding.
- □ Center small stocking on center front of large stocking piece and slipstitch in place leaving top open as for a pocket.
- □ Fold long sides of plaid strip to inside so raw edges meet. Press.
- □ Fold in half lengthwise and press. Stitch along folded edges.
- □ Turn ends under 1/2-inch and tack to front and back of stocking for hanger.
- □ Slipstitch lace along white binding and hanger for girl's stocking.

Bashful Reindeer Shirt

This shy little reindeer will delight your youngster both in the making and in the wearing. Its antlers are made with a child's hand prints! And if you're allergic to needle and thread, this is a safe project to take on. Fusible web fabric, safety pins, and paint work the magic.

Paper Reindeer Garland, Cross-Stitch Grandbaby Stockings, Bashful Reindeer Shirt, Reindeer Baby Bib, pages 46 and 48

MATERIALS FOR BASHFUL REINDEER SHIRT

1 (6-by-7-inch) piece brown fabric
Fusible web fabric
Turtleneck shirt in desired color
Red Tulip™ Slick Paint
Newspaper
Silver glitter pen
2 safety pins
1 (1¾-inch diameter) red pom-pom
Ribbon bow
See Patterns

DIRECTIONS

□ Transfer pattern to fabric and fusible web and cut out.
□ Determine placement of triangle reindeer head. Following manufacturer's directions, fuse triangle to shirt.
□ Coat child's hands with red paint and have child blot them on newspaper to test paint consistency. Make hand print antlers on reindeer, referring to photograph for placement.
□ Transfer eye details to face and paint with glitter pen. Outline head with glitter pen.
□ Attach pom-pom nose to reindeer face with safety pin.
□ Pin bow to a corner below antler.

Reindeer Baby Bib

D ress baby in a bib that carries a bonus—stuffed reindeer that can't get thrown on the floor. Ribbon holders keep them in reach of little hands, and Velcro attachments allow you to tuck them out of the way when feeding begins. If you add jingle bells make sure you remove them before baby begins to play with the reindeer.

MATERIALS

1 (½-inch diameter) plastic ring
1 purchased white terry cloth bib with inset fabric
   border
⅓ yard (¾-inch wide) green grosgrain ribbon
1 (9-inch) square of green felt
Scraps of red and white dotted fabric
White embroidery floss
1 (#24) embroidery needle
2 (½-inch) Velcro dots
⅔ yard (¼-inch wide) green satin ribbon
Jingle bells if desired
See Patterns

DIRECTIONS

□ Sew plastic ring to center front of bib just below ribbed neck.
□ Sew green grosgrain ribbon across bib centered in fabric border area and with raw edges folded around sides and stitched to back of bib.
□ Transfer reindeer pattern to felt 4 times and to fabric 1 time. Reverse pattern and transfer to fabric 1 time. Cut out 6 reindeer.
□ Layer 2 felt reindeer below each fabric reindeer. Pin together.
□ Sew around edges with buttonhole stitch using 3 strands of white floss.
□ Sew half of Velcro dot to reindeer and half to bib for each reindeer, referring to photograph for placement.
□ Fold satin ribbon in half, and knot fold through plastic ring. Sew ends to back of reindeer. Trim excess ribbon.
□ Tie jingle bells on with a length of floss threaded through reindeer's neck, and remove before baby begins to play with reindeer, if desired.

Heart and Bow Glitter Shirt

W ant to add a touch of glamour to your wardrobe for the holidays? Here's an idea that won't break the bank. Raid your reserves for bits of lace and some baubles, pick up gold and glitter paint pens, and transform a plain white T-shirt into a glitter shirt! Here, it's shown layered over other shirts, but you can totally change the look by topping it with everything from a dressy cardigan to a jeans jacket. And by using different colors or sweatshirts, you can customize gifts for friends and family.

MATERIALS

1 white T-shirt
Scraps of lace
DMC® gold machine embroidery thread
Gold Tulip™ paint pen
Tulip™ gold iridescent paint writer
Tulip™ brush-on gold liquid glitter
Medium flat paintbrush
Acrylic gemstones, pearls, or other embellishments
Adhesive sealant (E-6000)
See Patterns

DIRECTIONS FOR HEART AND BOW GLITTER SHIRT

◻ Transfer heart pattern to shirt just under collar band 3 times: 1 in center, and 1 to each side between center heart and shoulder seam.

◻ Cut a piece of lace larger than heart, and pin over heart design.

◻ Sew a tight zig-zag stitch with gold machine embroidery thread along heart outline. Cut extra lace close to stitching line in front. Cut T-shirt heart out at stitching line in back.

◻ Transfer bow pattern and details to shirt underneath center heart.

◻ Draw over lines with gold paint writer. Let dry.

◻ Draw along some of lines with gold paint writer to accent.

◻ Fill in bow with brush-on glitter paint.

◻ Add a light wash of paint around bow and hearts with brush-on glitter paint.

◻ Glue baubles at random around hearts and bow using adhesive sealant. Draw a line with glitter pen around each bauble.

Noah's Ark Pillow

What better way to share the story of the flood with little ones than with a stenciled Noah's Ark Pillow? Its ark pocket on front is filled with little stuffed pairs of animals, and on back there's another pocket just right for holding a Noah's Ark storybook.

MATERIALS

1/2 yard (45-inch wide) blue pindot fabric
1 (5-by-9 3/4-inch) thin quilt batting piece
3/4 yard (45-inch wide) muslin
Stencil-Ease® Design: K-20 Noah's Ark
Masking tape
Stencil-Ease® Fab-Tex Paint: Country Blue, Olde Rose, Colonial Golde
Stenciling brushes: 3/4 inch to 1 inch in diameter, 1 brush for each color
Paper plate or saucer
Paper towels
Polyester stuffing
1/8 yard (45-inch wide) coordinating print
1 3/4 yards (1/4-inch) cording
1 (14-inch) pillow form
Noah's Ark storybook
See Patterns

DIRECTIONS

◻ Cut two 12-by-15-inch pieces from pindot and set aside.

◻ Transfer ark pattern to pindot 2 times and batting 1 time and cut out.

◻ Stack pindot pieces, with right sides facing, and batting piece on top. Stitch with a 1/4-inch seam, leaving an opening for turning.

◻ Trim excess batting from seam, clip curves, and turn. Slipstitch opening closed.

◻ Machine topstitch 3 rows of decorative stitching 1/4-inch apart across top of ark.

◻ Cut a 14-inch square from muslin. Locate center of square and measure 1 inch above center for placement of ark house.

◻ Position ark hull below house placement and lightly mark outline.

◻ Review the manufacturer's directions for paint, and follow directions for stenciling on page 54.

◻ Stencil house, roof, giraffe, doves, and waves on pillow front.

◻ Stencil 2 each of the animals on remaining muslin, leaving 2 inches between each animal.

◻ Reverse stencils and repeat.

◻ Cut out muslin about 3/4 inch from painted edges, loosely following contour of designs.

◻ Place animal front and back together, right sides facing, matching painted designs.

◻ Stitch, leaving an opening for turning.

◻ Turn, stuff firmly with polyester stuffing, and slipstitch closed.

◻ Position ark hull on front of pillow. Machine topstitch along sides and bottom to form hull pocket.

◻ Cut four 1 3/4-by-14-inch strips from coordinating print. Stitch to sides of pillow front.

◻ Make a 1-inch hem along a 15-inch side of both pindot backing pieces.

◻ Lay pieces together with wrong sides up and with hemmed sides to middle to form a 15-inch square. Pin together.

◻ Sew cording to right sides of pillow front matching raw edges.

◻ Place pillow backing on pillow front with right sides facing so that back pocket formed by overlapped pieces will open to top of pillow.

◻ Stitch with a 1/4-inch seam, unpin back overlap, and turn.

◻ Insert pillow form.

◻ Place animals in hull pocket and storybook in back pocket.

Quilted Angel Ornaments

*J*ust like cousins, these little angels have many things in common. The main differences are with their clothes and hairstyles. Our city angel's pretty pink skirt is edged in lace and her blond tresses are made with bullion knots. Her country cousin has crocheted lace wings and a jute halo, and their elegant Victorian cousin has a crazy quilt skirt and a sparkling gold halo. Depending on your style, you can make a twin or add new members to the family tree.

MATERIALS

Scraps of fabric, lace, and ribbon
Polyester batting
3¹/2 inches gold cord, gold trim, or jute
Embroidery floss or perle cotton in desired colors
See Patterns

DIRECTIONS FOR CITY ANGEL

□ Cut 1 of pattern piece A from background fabric.
□ Cut 2 of pattern piece B from background fabric.
□ Cut 2 of pattern piece C from wing fabric.
□ Cut 1 of pattern piece D from background fabric.
□ Cut 1 of pattern piece E from skirt fabric.
□ Cut 1 of pattern piece F from face fabric.
□ Cut 1 of pattern piece G from backing fabric.
□ Cut 1 of pattern piece G from batting.
□ Sew pieces together as indicated (Figure 1), using a ¹/8-inch seam.
□ Gather a 4-inch piece of ³/8-inch lace and tack to skirt hem.
□ Cut a 3¹/2-inch piece of gold cord for halo. Tack ends to ornament as indicated (Figure 2).
□ Turn raw edges of angel face under ¹/8 inch, and appliqué as indicated (Figure 3).
□ Embellish face and stitch hair as desired.
□ Stack pieces as follows: angel right side up, backing right side down, and batting. Stitch through all layers with a ¹/4-inch seam leaving an opening for turning.
□ Clip batting from seam, turn, and slipstitch opening closed.
□ Quilt as desired.
□ Cut 6¹/2 inches of ¹/8-inch wide satin ribbon. Fold in half and tack ends to top of ornament for hanger. Make bows from ¹/8-inch wide and ¹/16-inch wide ribbon and tack to top corner.

DIRECTIONS FOR COUNTRY ANGEL

□ Cut 3 of pattern piece A from background fabric.
□ Cut 1 of pattern piece D from background fabric.
□ Cut 1 of pattern piece E from skirt fabric.
□ Cut 1 of pattern piece F from face fabric.
□ Cut 1 of pattern piece G from backing fabric.
□ Cut 1 of pattern piece G from batting.
□ Sew pieces together as indicated (Figure 1).
□ Cut two 2-inch long pieces of 1-inch wide crocheted lace for wings. Turn under side edges, and tack in place. Gather bottom edge of each and tack to center of ornament.
□ Cut a 3¹/2-inch piece of jute for halo, and tack ends to ornament as indicated (Figure 2).
□ Make face and hair as for city angel.
□ Make hanger as for city angel, using ¹/4-inch wide grosgrain ribbon.

DIRECTIONS FOR VICTORIAN ANGEL

□ Cut 1 pattern piece E from muslin. Assemble small bits of fabric, lace, and various embroidery stitches using muslin piece as backing to make a crazy quilt piece for skirt.
□ Follow assembly as for Country Angel, using white lace for wings and gold trim for halo.
□ Make hanger as for other angels, using ³/8-inch wide white damask ribbon.

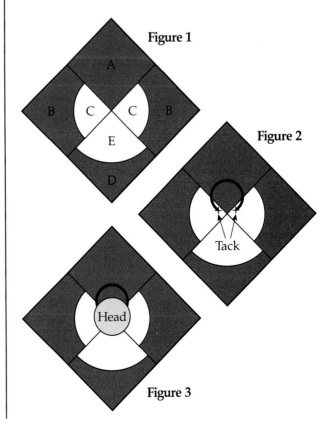

Figure 1

Figure 2

Tack

Head

Figure 3

Civil War Doll

Harking back to a time when baby dolls were harder to come by but were needed more than ever, this little Civil War doll demonstrates that sweetness comes mostly from inspiration. A man's handkerchief, a bit of stuffing, and scraps of ribbon and lace are all you need. Just gather the center of one end of a handkerchief into a ball, and stuff it firmly with polyester stuffing. Tie the stuffed area off with a string for the head, and tack a length of lace around it to define the face. Knot her hands, tie a pretty ribbon around her neck, and trim the bottom of her dress with lace. Then tack the edges of her hem together to keep baby's skirt tidy.

Molly Mop Doll

Despite Molly's humble beginnings, she is a doll sure to win the heart of any little girl. A fluffy string mop, available at craft stores, makes a cuddly friend just by tying a couple of bows and dressing her in a lacy bonnet.

MATERIALS

1 (10-inch) mop
14 inches string to match
1³/₄ yards (¹/₈-inch wide) blue satin ribbon
¹/₄ yard print fabric
16¹/₂ inches (1¹/₄-inch wide) ecru lace

DIRECTIONS

□ Define head by cinching end of mop with matching string.
□ Gather 2 equal bunches of mop string for arms and bring to front of body.
□ Tie arm sections tightly halfway between neck and bottom of doll with 18 inches of satin ribbon.
□ Cut mop string 1¹/₂ inches below bow to make hands.
□ Cut a 6-by-16¹/₂-inch piece of fabric. Align raw edges. Sew lace to 1 long side of fabric. Press open.
□ Fold long sides of fabric together with wrong sides facing. Sew along lace edge with a ¹/₈-inch seam. Sew another seam ¹/₄ inch from first for ribbon casing.
□ Sew a seam ¹/₄ inch from fold for another casing.

□ Insert a 30-inch piece of ribbon in casing on lace edge and a 12-inch piece of ribbon in casing on fold edge. Slip bonnet over head, and tighten gathers to fit.
□ Tie ends of ribbon in casing on lace edge in a bow under doll's chin. Tie ribbon in back casing in bow at back of neck.

Heirloom Holiday Bookmark

Mark this season's place in the string of holidays past and present with a lacy cross-stitched bookmark. Whether you want to personalize a special volume you're giving or have noticed that Grandma's favorite bookmark has gotten a little tattered, this handmade gift will recall your thoughtfulness page after page.

MATERIALS

1 (1³/₄-by-7-inch) piece 18-count Aida cloth white fabric
1 (#24) embroidery needle
DMC® Embroidery Floss = 8m skeins (1 skein each):
  #666 Red, #700 Green
1 (1³/₄-by-7-inch) fusible webbing piece
1 (1³/₄-by-7-inch) white backing fabric
¹/₂ yard (¹/₂-inch wide) white lace
Fabric glue
See Patterns

DIRECTIONS

□ Mark center of cross-stitch fabric both ways with long running stitch using needle and thread.
□ Work cross-stitch according to chart and color key, beginning at intersection of arrows on chart to ensure proper placement of design on fabric.
□ Each square on chart represents 1 fabric thread. Use 1 strand of floss for cross-stitch and back-stitch.
□ Press finished work.
□ Use manufacturer's instructions to fuse back of fabric to wrong side of fusible webbing.
□ Cut lace to fit around edges. Overlap lace to front of bookmark by ¹/₈ inch; glue lace in place.

Noah's Ark Pillow, Quilted Angel Ornaments, Civil War Doll, Molly Mop Doll, pages 50, 51 and 52

Embossed Greeting Cards

*I*f you do much stenciling, you probably have a collection of favorite designs stored away for future use. This season, give those old standards new life by making stunning embossed greeting cards. Whether you want to make up a batch of special cards for family and your closest friends, or create a surefire bestseller for the church bazaar, these cards will fill the bill.

MATERIALS

Precut stencils
Blank note cards
Masking tape
Engraving tool or 1/2-inch sharpened dowel, sanded smooth

DIRECTIONS

□ Position stencil on front of blank card and tape in place. Hold paper and stencil up to sunny window with stencil to glass. Press paper carefully into stencil cuts with engraving tool or sharpened dowel. Continue to emboss rest of design.
□ Raised areas can be tinted with watercolor washes or lightly applied inks or dyes.

Ivy Basket Cards and Tags

A basket brimming with vines of ivy adorns these delicate note cards and gift tags. The design is so simple, and so easy to shorten and extend, that you can use it any number of ways: stencil with sprigs on ribbon ends before tying bows around packages, add a strand below the return address on your Christmas card envelopes, place a basket on the same page as your inscription in a gift book. And for the person on your list who still maintains the gentle art of correspondence, make a gift of a bunch of note cards bound with ribbon and bearing your unwritten message of good tidings.

MATERIALS

Blank note cards or artist's watercolor or charcoal paper
Stencils by Zula: MD21 Basket and Border
Masking tape
Stenciling paint: Christmas Red, Christmas Green, Gold
Paper plate or saucer
Stenciling brushes: 3/8 inch to 1/2 inch in diameter, 1 brush for each color
Paper towels
Hole punch

DIRECTIONS

□ Cut artist's paper into 1 1/4-inch pieces for small tags and 3 1/2-by-5-inch pieces folded into 2 1/2-by-3 1/2-inch cards for larger tags.
□ Follow directions for stenciling below.
□ Punch hole in finished tags to thread through ribbons tied around packages, if desired.

DIRECTIONS FOR STENCILING

□ Place stencil in position and tape in place with masking tape.
□ Review paint manufacturer's instructions. Place a small amount of paint on a paper plate or saucer.
□ Dip tip of brush into paint. Wipe off excess on a paper towel until brush is "dry" and paint is light and smooth in appearance.
□ Hold brush perpendicular to surface. Start at outside edge of cut-out area and work in clockwise motion from edge across design area.
□ Reverse to counter-clockwise motion and continue building up color to desired shade.
□ Align Print 2, if using more than 1 print, using register marks as a guide. Stencil Print 2. Continue until the design is complete.
□ Clean stencils and brushes gently following paint manufacturer's directions and allow to air dry before using again.

Create Popcorn and Gumdrop Ornaments by cutting 12-inches thin wire. Thread 4 pieces popped popcorn and 1 gumdrop at a time onto wire until wire is covered. Twist ends together. Glue bow made from a 12-inch length of 7/8-inch wide ribbon over twisted wire.

Heirloom Holiday Bookmark, Embossed Greeting Cards, Ivy Basket Cards and Tags, pages 52 and 54

Etched-Glass Vanity Mirror

Create a stunning focal point for a vanity with this romantic mirror. It looks like an expensive designer piece, but it's actually a recycled old picture frame fitted with a new mirror and covered with beautiful floral fabric. Etching cream and stencils embellish the mirror itself, and a wide fabric bow "hanger" completes the effect. For added impact, use the same floral fabric to make a ruffled skirt for a vanity table.

MATERIALS

Mirror and corrugated cardboard cut to fit frame
Clear contact paper
1 (12-by-15-inch) frame
Fine point permanent marker
Stencils by Zula: Periwinkle #9105
Single edge razor blade
Glass etching cream, available at craft stores
1 (1-inch) paintbrush
Acrylic paint in coordinating color
2 yards (45-inch wide) floral fabric
Adhesive sealant (E-6000)
Wire brads
Staple gun
Sawtooth picture hanger
1 (1/2-inch diameter) plastic ring

DIRECTIONS

□ Cover mirror with 3 layers of contact paper.
□ Place mirror in frame and mark borders with permanent marker.
□ Remove mirror and measure 1/2 inch inside marked border. Draw off this smaller rectangle for placement of stencils.
□ Position stencils on line and trace designs with permanent marker.
□ Reverse stencil for opposite sides and add designs as desired around edges of mirror.
□ Cut and remove contact paper within design areas with single edge razor blade. Make sure contact paper edges around designs are pressed flat on glass.
□ Apply glass etching cream following manufacturer's directions.
□ Rinse and remove contact paper.
□ Paint the inside edge of the frame with coordinating acrylic paint. Apply several coats until smooth. Let dry.

□ Cut eight 6-by-45-inch fabric strips. Join strips end-to-end using a 1/2-inch seam allowance.
□ Fold long sides under 1/2 inch and sew 1/4 inch from folded edge.
□ Run a gathering stitch along seam lines. Gather fabric to fit around frame.
□ Apply adhesive sealant on front edge of frame. Place ruffle on this edge. Nail in place with wire brads, concealing brads in folds of fabric.
□ Ungather 1 inch of fabric at end, fold to inside, and overlap opposite raw end.
□ Wrap fabric to back of frame and staple in place.
□ Secure mirror and backing in frame and attach hanger to top back.
□ Cut one 8-by-45-inch fabric strip for bow. Determine streamer length by measuring distance from top back of frame to desired point on streamer. Cut 2 pieces of fabric 8 inches wide by desired length.
□ Sew 3 strips end-to-end with 45-inch long piece in middle, using a 1/2-inch seam allowance.
□ Fold in half lengthwise, right sides facing, and sew raw edges together with a 1/2-inch seam. Turn and position this seam in center back. Press.
□ Cut ends at an angle. Turn 1/2-inch to inside, press, and slipstitch closed.
□ Tie a bow in center of strip. Sew plastic ring to center back of bow.
□ Center bow above mirror and staple streamers to back of frame.

Cosmetic Travel Bag

Banish any worries about spills in the suitcase with this pretty and practical travel bag. Zip-top bags are the secret. Just secure them under grosgrain ribbon, make a few quick passes with the sewing machine, and you have a bag that will safely transport shampoo and make-up to any port of call.

MATERIALS

1 (12-by-17-inch) piece reversible quilted fabric
6 sandwich-sized zip-top bags
1 yard (1-inch wide) coordinated grosgrain ribbon
24 inches (3/8-inch wide) coordinated satin ribbon

□ Round corners on fabric piece.
□ Bind raw edges of fabric with machine set on tight zig-zag stitch.
□ Mark center line on fabric running parallel to 12-inch sides.
□ Position 3 bags on 1 half of fabric as follows: Place 1 even with each side and center remaining 1 on top so that all 3 bottoms line up on center mark. Repeat for other side with remaining bags.
□ Cut a 12½-inch piece of grosgrain ribbon. Turn ends under ¼ inch and pin along center line over bottoms of bags. Stitch along both sides and ends of ribbon securing bags in seams.
□ Cut remaining grosgrain ribbon in half for handles. Position 1 piece on inside of bag with both ends ⅛ inch from end of bag and loop to inside. Stitch ends to bag, and turn up handle. Repeat for other handle.
□ Cut satin ribbon in half for ties.
□ Fold end of 1 satin ribbon piece under ½ inch, and stitch folded end to outside of bag centered between sides of handle. Repeat for other side.

Poinsettia Garland Shawl

Summon the romance of times past with a silken shawl ornamented with a garland of cross-stitch poinsettias. Rose, crimson, and flaxen blooms ring the edges, linked by swirling green satin ribbon. You can stitch as many or as few flowers as your time permits, and use the ribbon to fill in the spaces. Then drape the shawl around your shoulders for holiday parties, or use it to dress up a table for the season.

MATERIALS

Charles Craft Keepsake Shawl
1 (#24) embroidery needle
DMC® Embroidery Floss = 8m skeins (1 skein each):
  #307 Lemon, #310 Black, #321 Christmas Red,
  #444 Dk. Lemon, #471 Lt. Avocado Green,
  #522 Fern Green, #602 Med. Cranberry,
  #605 Very Lt. Cranberry, #666 Red,
  #700 Bright Christmas Green, #703 Chartreuse,
  #725 Topaz, #729 Med. Old Gold, #743 Med. Yellow,
  #745 Lt. Yellow, #776 Med. Pink,
  #815 Med. Garnet, #962 Med. Wild Rose,
  #973 Bright Canary, #3078 Very Lt. Golden Yellow,
  #3346 Hunter Green, #3687 Mauve
4 yards (³⁄8-inch wide) green satin ribbon
See Patterns

DIRECTIONS

□ Machine stitch a row 4 threads outside the basket-weave border of shawl. Remove threads up to stitched row to form fringe. Knot fringe if desired.
□ Mark center of corner squares both ways with long running stitch using needle and thread. Mark center of cross-stitch fabric border parallel to edge.
□ Determine placement of flowers along border and mark crossing centers for each design.
□ Work cross-stitch according to chart and color key, beginning at intersection of arrows on chart to ensure proper placement of design on fabric.
□ Each square on chart represents 2 fabric threads. Use 2 strands of floss for cross-stitch and 6 strands for back-stitch.
□ Press finished work.
□ Cut ribbon into desired lengths to link flowers. Fold raw ends under and tack ribbon in place along both long sides.

Painted Canvas Place Mats

The durability of canvas floor cloth comes to the table with these colorfully stenciled place mats. They offer the perfect combination for young diners—wipe-clean convenience and charming, personalized designs. Every busy Mom will appreciate the thoughtfulness behind this gift.

MATERIALS

1 (12½-by-16½-inch) floor cloth canvas piece
Stencils by Zula: 9175 Bunnies or 9177 Royal Guard
Masking tape
Stencil paint: Lt. Blue, Pink, and Mint Green for
  Bunnies; Navy and Cranberry for Royal Guard
Stenciling brushes: ³⁄4 inch to 1 inch in diameter,
  1 brush for each color
Paper plate or saucer
1 (1-inch) sponge brush
Paper towels
Polyurethane

DIRECTIONS FOR PLACE MATS

□ Mark lines for designs lightly with a pencil on canvas mat to aid in placement.
□ Review manufacturer's directions for paint, and follow directions for stenciling on page 54.
□ Allow paint to dry thoroughly.
□ Apply a coat of polyurethane with sponge brush. Work sponge brush first from side to side with overlapping strokes. Repeat brush strokes from top to bottom using overlapping strokes. Work out any puddles.
□ Repeat to apply a total of 5 to 6 coats.

Child-Art Tea Cozy

*M*ake a present Grandma will treasure more than all the jewels in the world. Let your child draw a picture of a teapot, either one you're giving her as a gift or one you "borrow" from her, and then stitch up a tea cozy. Every time she sits down for an afternoon cup, she'll feel warm, even before she takes the first sip.

MATERIALS

Tracing paper
Embroidery transfer pencil
1/3 yard (36-inch wide) white cotton fabric
1/3 yard (36-inch wide) prequilted white fabric
Paint pens in colors to match teapot artwork
2 1/4 yards (5/8-inch wide) rickrack in coordinating color
1 1/2 yards (1 1/4-inch wide) pregathered white eyelet lace
See Patterns

DIRECTIONS

□ Have child draw a picture of teapot.
□ Photocopy artwork as needed to make it fit within tea cozy pattern.
□ Lay tracing paper over photocopy of artwork. Trace design. Turn tracing paper over. Draw over traced lines using embroidery transfer pencil.
□ Transfer tea cozy pattern to white fabric and prequilted fabric, as indicated on pattern. Cut out 1 fabric piece and 2 prequilted fabric pieces.
□ Position artwork over white fabric piece with transfer pencil lines against fabric. Transfer artwork to fabric following manufacturer's instructions.

□ Draw over transferred lines with paint pens, referring to artwork and teapot for details.
□ Pin front fabric piece to 1 prequilted piece with wrong sides facing. Baste around edges.
□ Cut a 25-inch long piece of rickrack. Position rickrack around curved side of cozy front with edge of rickrack even with raw edges of fabric.
□ Cut a 25-inch long piece of eyelet lace, and position over rickrack so that bottom edge of lace is even with raw edge of fabric.
□ Cut another 25-inch long piece of rickrack, and position over lace even with first rickrack piece.
□ Baste through all layers of trim at fabric edge to secure.
□ Pin quilted back to front with right sides facing.
□ Sew through all layers along curved edge using a 1/4-inch seam allowance. Cut trims even with edge, clip curves, and turn. Press.
□ Cut a 30-inch long piece of eyelet lace. Align bottom edge of lace with raw edge of tea cozy's bottom beginning in center of back of cozy. Stitch together with a 1/4-inch seam. Turn lace down and press flat.
□ Cut a 30-inch long piece of rickrack. Topstitch to cozy along bottom edge beginning in center back.

Stenciled Jar Covers and Recipe Cards

*E*veryone appreciates a gift from the kitchen, especially when the recipe is included. Spice up your culinary presents this year with decorative jar covers and matching recipe cards. You'll be the talk of the coffee klatch.

MATERIALS

Muslin, osnaburg, burlap, or other light-colored fabric scraps
Pinking shears
Stencils by Zula: MD45 Flower Borders
Masking tape
Desired colors of stencil paint
Paper plate or saucer
Stenciling brushes: 3/8 inch to 1/2 inch in diameter, 1 brush for each color
Paper towels
Assorted ribbons and trims
Index cards

Painted Canvas Place Mats, Child-Art Tea Cozy, pages 58 and 61

DIRECTIONS FOR STENCILED JAR COVERS AND RECIPE CARDS

☐ Cut circles to desired size to fit jar tops from fabric scraps using pinking shears.
☐ Follow directions for stenciling on page 54.
☐ Decorate with ribbon and trim as desired.
☐ Stencil matching recipe cards.

Cinnamon Dinosaur Ornaments

What child can resist playing with dough and making dinosaurs? What Mom can resist the delicious scent of cinnamon streaming from these ornaments? It's a perfect combination. Set aside time to make a herd of these ornaments with your little one this year. You'll have all the ingredients for an afternoon of fun, and you'll have something more—memories to linger like the fragrance of cinnamon filling the air.

MATERIALS

1 cup (about 3.2 ounces) ground cinnamon
2 tablespoons ground allspice
1 cup applesauce
1/4 cup craft glue
Cookie cutters
Drinking straw
Whole cloves

DIRECTIONS

☐ Combine cinnamon and allspice in glass bowl.
☐ Add applesauce and glue; mix well. Mixture will be stiff.
☐ Add water or additional cinnamon, if needed, to achieve a clay-like consistency.
☐ Roll out dough between sheets of waxed paper to 1/2-inch thickness.
☐ Remove top sheet of waxed paper. Cut with cookie cutters. Remove excess dough.
☐ Make holes for hanging with straw. Insert cloves for eyes.
☐ Air dry on flat surface for a few days.

Shadow-Quilted Wreath Ornament

Shadow-quilting adds lovely softness to a handcrafted ornament. A sheer film of voile makes this little wreath seem as though it's being seen through soft winter light or lightly falling snow. Stitch up a sprinkling for your tree this year.

MATERIALS

Tracing paper
Scraps of red and green cotton
Fusible web fabric
Scrap of off-white voile or organza
Scrap of thin quilt batting
Scrap of muslin
Embroidery floss: Green, Red
7 inches (1/8-inch wide) red satin ribbon piece
See Patterns

DIRECTIONS

☐ Transfer patterns using tracing paper to cotton and fusible web and cut out.
☐ Cut four 4³/4-by-5³/4-inch rectangles: 1 from voile, 1 from batting, and 2 from muslin.
☐ Fuse web wreath and bow to wrong sides of fabric wreath and bow following manufacturer's directions.
☐ Position wreath and bow on 1 piece of muslin, referring to photograph for placement.
☐ Place voile over wreath, aligning edges with muslin.
☐ Outline-quilt around wreath and bow as indicated on pattern using green floss for wreath and red floss for bow.
☐ Make French knots randomly using red floss on wreath.
☐ Stack wreath piece right side up, remaining piece of muslin, and batting. Stitch, leaving an opening for turning.
☐ Clip corners and turn. Slipstitch opening closed.
☐ Fold ribbon in half. Tack ends to back for hanger.

Stenciled Jar Covers and Recipe Cards, Cinnamon Dinosaur Ornaments, Shadow-Quilted Wreath Ornament, Cinnamon Stick Dowel Tree, pages 61, 62, and 64

Cinnamon Stick Dowel Tree

*T*ry a fragrant twist on the traditional dowel tree. Use cinnamon sticks, instead! For extra aroma, dry strips of orange rind around pencils and glue on hangers and bows. The bright little pendants complement the soft brown tree, and make use of kitchen scraps!

MATERIALS

Craft foam block
Small container
Hot glue gun
10-inch long cinnamon sticks
Gold cord
Excelsior

DIRECTIONS

☐ Cut foam block to fit into container.
☐ Cover bottom of block with hot glue and position in container.
☐ Insert 1 cinnamon stick all the way through foam block. Glue another stick to top of first.
☐ Repeat to make tree desired height, snapping sticks as needed to vary the length.
☐ Glue cinnamon stick "limbs" onto tree, and lash in place with gold cord.
☐ Cover foam block with excelsior.
☐ Add ornaments.

Expandable Quilted Carryall

*O*ne of the problems when you travel is bringing back all the loot. This expandable carryall solves the problem beautifully. It grows from a roomy tote to a large duffle to a giant duffle in the flash of an eye—all thanks to a series of straps along the sides. The top is simply folded inside to make it tote-size, and pulled out to reveal the handles for each larger size. If you know someone who is always on the go, this is the gift to give.

MATERIALS

1¼ yards (45-inch wide) quilted fabric
¼ yard (36-inch wide) coordinating solid fabric
5¾ yards (1-inch wide) elastic strapping
23 inches (½-inch wide) double fold bias tape

DIRECTIONS

☐ Cut a 34-by-44-inch rectangle from quilted fabric. Cut two 8½-by-11-inch rectangles from quilted fabric. Cut two 8½-by-11-inch rectangles from solid fabric.
☐ Note: All seams are ½ inch and sewn with zig-zag stitch.
☐ Fold large quilted rectangle in half with right sides facing and 34-inch (side) edges together. Sew side seam. Turn.
☐ Fold edge of one end ½ inch to inside and hem.
☐ Sew 1 small quilted rectangle to 1 solid rectangle along both 11-inch sides with right sides facing. Turn. Repeat for 2 remaining rectangles.
☐ Cut strapping into 6 pieces: 2 to measure 81 inches and 4 to measure 11 inches.
☐ Pin a pocket, solid side out, centered 5 inches from unsewn bottom of 1 side of bag.
☐ Sew bottom edge of pocket to bag with tight zig-zag stitch.
☐ Fold 81-inch strapping piece in half and position on front of bag so that raw ends are even with bottom of bag and strapping covers ½ inch of pockets (Figure 4). Pin in place.

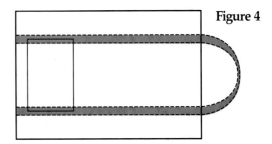

Figure 4

☐ Pin an 11-inch piece of strapping 3½ inches above pocket and parallel to it, tucking ends under side pieces of strapping.
☐ Pin another 11-inch piece of strapping 8 inches above first, tucking ends under side strapping.
☐ Stitch along both edges of side pieces of strapping, catching pocket and handles in seams, and stopping 5 inches from top of bag.
☐ Repeat to attach pocket and handles to other side.
☐ Turn bag. Place bottom edge together; cover with bias tape. Stitch together to strengthen seam. Fold corners into points with seam in middle to square bottom of bag, and sew 3 inches from tip. Turn.

Poinsettia-Snowflake Egg Ornaments

*H*atch a batch of ornaments made from painted wooden eggs. Bright red and green poinsettias and little white snowflakes on a clear blue field will brighten the tree. And if you're building an ornament collection to pass on, you can paint a child's name or the date opposite the design to recall your gift in years to come.

MATERIALS

Sandpaper
2¼-inch diameter wooden eggs
Tack cloth
Paintbrushes: small flat brush, liner
Water base varnish
Delta Ceramcoat® Acrylic Paints: Lt. Ivory, Ocean Reef, Tompte Red, Jubilee Green, Crimson, Bright Yellow
Toothpicks
Very fine tip black permanent marker
Shiny paints in squeezable bottles: Red, Green, White
1¼ yards (³/16-inch wide) satin picot ribbon for each ornament, white for snowflake and ecru for poinsettia
Acrylic sealant (E-6000)

GENERAL DIRECTIONS

□ Sand eggs, and wipe with tack cloth. Seal with 1 coat of varnish.
□ Apply several coats of base color paint (ivory for poinsettia, ocean reef for snowflake) until smooth. Paint designs as directed below.
□ Cut one 13-inch length of ribbon and knot ends for bow and hanger. Glue knot to top of ornament using acrylic sealant. Tie a bow around knot with remainder of ribbon.

DIRECTIONS FOR POINSETTIA ORNAMENT

□ Paint ends of eggs either red or green, referring to photograph for placement.
□ Centered between painted ends, paint 6 small poinsettia petals in crimson. Paint 6 more petals between first 6, using half crimson and half tompte red.
□ Fill center of flower with dots using a toothpick dipped in yellow paint.
□ Paint small leaves with green, referring to photograph for placement.

□ Outline petals and leaves with black marker.
□ Apply 1 coat of varnish.
□ Use shiny paints to add a row of dots along edges of painted ends, referring to photograph.
□ Write name on opposite side with shiny paints.

DIRECTIONS FOR SNOWFLAKE ORNAMENT

□ Write name or desired word in center of Christmas ornament.
□ Squeeze 4 drops of shiny paint in a diamond shape to make snowflake. Use toothpick to draw lines from dots to center.
□ Dip toothpick in white paint and draw small lines between first 4 lines radiating from center. Scatter snowflakes randomly over ornament.

Cross-Stitch Decorating Accents

*L*ovely holiday designs, cross-stitched into framable decorating accents, add elegance to mantels, tabletops, or the entryway. Their holiday sentiments will echo your hospitality throughout the season.

MATERIALS FOR TREE

1 (8½-by-8½-inch) piece 11-count Aida cloth ecru fabric
1 (#24) embroidery needle
DMC® Embroidery Floss = 8m skeins (1 skein each):
   #700 Bright Green, #904 Dk. Parrot Green, #729 Md. Old Gold, #783 Christmas Gold, #780 Dk. Topaz, #326 Dark Rose, #498 Dark Red, #910 Dk. Emerald Green, #797 Royal Blue, #208 Dk. Lavender
See Patterns

DIRECTIONS

□ Mark center of cross-stitch fabric both ways with long running stitch using needle and thread.
□ Work cross-stitch according to chart and color key, beginning at intersection of arrows on chart to ensure proper placement of design on fabric.
□ Each square on chart represents 1 fabric thread. Use 2 strands of floss for cross-stitch and 1 strand for back-stitch.
□ Press finished work.
□ Frame as desired.

MATERIALS FOR CROSS-STITCH ORNAMENT

1 (7-by-9-inch) piece 11-count Aida cloth ecru fabric
1 (#24) embroidery needle
DMC® Embroidery Floss = 8m skeins (1 skein each):
   #700 Bright Green, #783 Christmas Gold, #666 Red
See Patterns

DIRECTIONS

☐ Mark center of cross-stitch fabric both ways with long running stitch using needle and thread.
☐ Work cross-stitch according to chart and color key, beginning at intersection of arrows on chart to ensure proper placement of design on fabric.
☐ Each square on chart represents 1 fabric thread. Use 2 strands of floss for cross-stitch and 1 strand for back-stitch.
☐ Press finished work.
☐ Frame as desired.

Ribbon Tree Shirt

A plain black long sleeve T-shirt is transformed into stylish and distinctive holiday attire with the addition of ribbons, glittering gold trim, and jingle bells. If you're looking for sparkle and drama, this is the shirt for you.

MATERIALS

51 inches (1¹/₄-inch wide) plaid satin ribbon
Fusible web
Black long sleeved T-shirt
Gold glitter pen
2 yards gold trim
Hot glue gun
3¹/₃ yards (³/₈-inch wide) red satin ribbon
3¹/₃ yards (³/₈-inch wide) green satin ribbon
8 (¹/₂-inch) jingle bells

DIRECTIONS

☐ Cut plaid ribbon into 8 pieces measuring as follows: 1 inch, 3 inches, 5 inches, 7 inches, 9 inches, 11 inches, 13 inches, and 2 inches.
☐ Cut fusible web into 8 pieces 1¹/₄ inches wide and the same lengths as ribbon pieces.
☐ Arrange first 7 ribbon strips on shirt in rows from smallest to largest, each row ¹/₂ inch apart to make tree. Refer to photograph for placement.
☐ Turn 2-inch piece sideways and center below tree for trunk. Refer to photograph for placement.

☐ Follow manufacturer's directions to fuse ribbon to shirt. Outline ribbon with gold glitter pen.
☐ Swirl gold trim from top along side of each ribbon strip to bottom for tree garland. Glue to ribbon at sides and random points between to hold in place.
☐ Cut red and green satin ribbon into eight 12-inch long pieces, and tie in bows.
☐ Glue a bow and jingle bell at top, at alternating sides of middle ribbon strips, and at both sides of bottom ribbon strip.

Holly and Tree Accessories

E very Christmas outfit benefits from festive accessories like these holly and tree hair barrettes and earrings. They're made from torn watercolor paper brightened with paints and trims. Let the barrettes do double duty sprucing up a belt—just tie a length of gold fabric in an overhand knot and clip a barrette over the knot.

MATERIALS

140# or 300# watercolor paper
Small paintbrush
Watercolors: Green, Red, and Brown
Small acrylic rhinestones, confetti, and metallic ribbon
Waxed paper
Mod Podge® sealer
Jewelry glaze
Hot glue gun
Barrette backs
Earring posts or clips

DIRECTIONS

☐ Sketch a rough tree or holly shape onto paper, and tear along lines.
☐ Use a dime to sketch berries, and cut out.
☐ Paint desired shades with even coating of watercolor. Let dry.
☐ Arrange leaves and berries, and cover with Mod Podge®. Let dry.
☐ Position metallic ribbon garland to tree.
☐ Cover tree with Mod Podge® and while sealer is still wet, arrange rhinestones and confetti. Let dry.
☐ Follow manufacturer's directions for jewelry glaze and coat ornaments. Let dry.
☐ Trim with scissors if there is excess glaze.
☐ Hot glue backs onto accessories.

Candlelit Heart Ornament

A flickering candle lighting a rosy heart is a lovely symbol of the spirit of the season. Cast the glow for all to see with this sweet cross-stitched ornament.

MATERIALS

1 (3-by-3-inch) piece 18-count Aida cloth white fabric
1 (#24) embroidery needle
DMC® Embroidery Floss = 8m skeins (1 skein each):
    #600 Cranberry, #503 Blue Green, #729 Gold
Gold heart-shaped ornament frame
See Patterns

DIRECTIONS

□ Mark center of cross-stitch fabric both ways with long running stitch using needle and thread.
□ Work cross-stitch according to chart and color key, beginning at intersection of arrows on chart to ensure proper placement of design on fabric.
□ Each square on chart represents 1 fabric thread. Use 1 strand of floss for cross-stitch.
□ Press finished work.
□ Position ornament backing over stitched design and mark outline.
□ Cut out heart shape, and assemble ornament.

Santa's Helper Ornament

D on't Santa's reindeer deserve star status? Cast your "yes" vote by stitching this cute Santa's helper ornament. Then spread the message by tying them onto packages, taking them to bazaars, and spangling your tree with the dear little deer.

MATERIALS

1 (4-by-4-inch) 18-count Aida cloth white fabric piece
1 (#24) embroidery needle
DMC® Embroidery Floss = 8m skeins (1 skein each):
    #938 Brown, #700 Green
Gold star-shaped ornament frame
See Patterns

DIRECTIONS

□ Mark center of cross-stitch fabric both ways with long running stitch using needle and thread.
□ Work cross-stitch according to chart and color key, beginning at intersection of arrows on chart to ensure proper placement of design on fabric.
□ Each square on chart represents 1 fabric thread. Use 1 strand of floss for cross-stitch and back-stitch.
□ Press finished work.
□ Position ornament backing over stitched design and mark outline.
□ Cut out star shape, and assemble ornament.

Holiday Handle Cover

T he next time you're invited to a potluck dinner, take along a friend from the barnyard. This button-eyed rooster will make that warm skillet easier to carry and dress up your contribution to the holiday table.

MATERIALS

1 (2¹/2-by-10¹/2-inch) piece green pindot quilted fabric
Scraps of Christmas print fabric
2 (¹/2-inch) red buttons
¹/2 yard (¹/4-inch wide) red satin ribbon
See Patterns

DIRECTIONS

□ Transfer pattern to quilted fabric folded in half lengthwise. Cut out.
□ Fold a small square of Christmas print fabric in half twice to form triangle for beak. Pin in place, point to inside, as indicated on pattern.
□ Finger-fold a piece of Christmas fabric to form comb. Pin in place, raw edges to outside and folds to inside, as indicated on pattern.
□ Sew buttons on each side for eyes as indicated on pattern.
□ Turn under bottom edge ¹/2 inch and machine stitch hem.
□ Fold holder with right sides facing, and stitch remaining raw edges with a ¹/4-inch seam.
□ Turn and tie ribbon in bow around neck.

Candlelit Heart Ornament, Santa's Helper Ornament, Holiday Handle Cover, Holiday Potholder, Santa Gift Bag, Holiday Casserole Carrier, pages 70 and 72

Holiday Potholder

*C*ooking and Christmas go together like turkey and dressing. And it seems as if every time you turn around, you're looking for a potholder. This year, make up a big batch of these easy and festive potholders. Not only will you enjoy the colorful touch in your own kitchen, you can include them in gifts to fellow cooks and take them along as a crowning touch when food is the price of party admittance.

MATERIALS

2 (7¹/2-inch) squares of green pindot quilted fabric
33¹/2 inches (¹/2-inch wide) coordinating double fold
   bias tape
Thread to match

DIRECTIONS

□ Pin fabric together with wrong sides facing.
□ Pin bias tape around all edges, leaving a 3¹/2-inch length at 1 corner. Turn raw edges at end of extending tape ¹/4 inch to inside. Press flat.
□ Zig-zag stitch tape to fabric, and continue stitching along edge of extending strip.
□ Fold strip in half to form hanger. Tack hanger to potholder.

Santa Gift Bag

*T*ake a cue from St. Nick, and pack up your goodies in bright little Santa bags. Not only will you delight all the lucky people on your list, you can get decorating mileage out of them by filling them early and arranging them on a bed of greenery. (And if you make a few extras, you won't be caught empty handed if a surprise guest drops by with a gift.)

MATERIALS

Scraps of white velour
1 (1¹/2-by-5¹/2-inch) piece beige fabric
1 (7¹/2-by-24-inch) Christmas print piece
White thread
Black and red embroidery floss
20 inches (¹/4-inch wide) green satin ribbon
See Patterns

DIRECTIONS

□ Transfer beard pattern to velour and cut out. Transfer mustache appliqué lines to beard piece.
□ Cut a ³/4-by-7¹/2-inch strip from velour.

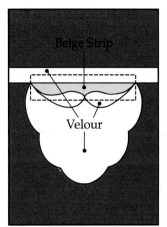

Figure 5

Figure 6

□ Position velour appliqués over beige strip on bag as indicated (Figure 5).
□ Set sewing machine for appliqué. Appliqué velour pieces to bag using satin stitch and white thread. Satin stitch along mustache lines.
□ Satin stitch eyes with black floss and mouth with red floss, referring to photograph.
□ Fold Christmas print piece in half, short ends together and right sides facing, to form bag. Stitch sides with a ¹/4-inch seam.
□ Fold corners into points with seam in middle, and sew 1 inch from tip to square bag's bottom (Figure 6).
□ Turn right side out. Fold top edge under ³/4 inch, and sew with a ¹/2-inch seam.
□ Snip an opening in center back of top hem, and insert ribbon drawstring. Tie ribbon ends together in a knot.

Holiday Casserole Carrier

*T*aking your famous casserole to the office luncheon this year? Tuck it into this festive carrier for the trip. The thick quilted fabric will keep your dish warm, and two strong handles make transporting the dish a snap.

MATERIALS

¹/2 yard (45-inch wide) green pindot quilted fabric
¹/2 yard (45-inch wide) Christmas print fabric
4 yards (¹/2-inch wide) coordinating double fold
   bias tape
1¹/2 yards (¹/4-inch wide) red satin ribbon

DIRECTIONS FOR CASSEROLE CARRIER

☐ Cut two 16-inch diameter circles from quilted fabric. Cut two 16-inch diameter circles from print fabric.
☐ Draw a 5-inch diameter circle in center of 1 quilted circle and cut out (Figure 7).
☐ Cut a straight line from center circle to edge (Figure 8).

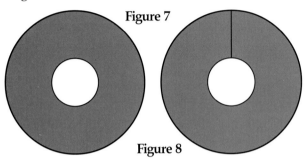

Figure 7

Figure 8

☐ Repeat to cut inner circle and straight line on 1 print circle.
☐ Place circles together, wrong sides facing, and bind straight edges with bias tape to make carrier top. Bind inner circle, attaching tape to allow opening for ribbon drawstring.
☐ Cut two 2-inch-by-15-inch strips from quilted fabric and two 2-inch-by-15-inch strips from print fabric for straps. Put 1 print and 1 quilted piece together, wrong sides facing. Bind long edges with bias tape. Repeat to make other strap.
☐ Position straps on quilted side of carrier top, with quilted side up parallel with straight cut and 3 inches apart (Figure 9). Trim ends of straps to match curve of carrier top.
☐ Put remaining 2 circle pieces together, wrong sides facing and print side up, for carrier bottom. Pin carrier top to bottom and bind with bias tape.
☐ Insert ribbon in center circle for drawstring.

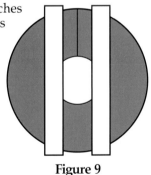

Figure 9

Kiddie Basket Desk

*T*his sturdy and practical basket desk offers a work surface and stowaway center in one. Since it's portable, you can fill it with toys for car trips. And, stocked with school supplies, it might even make doing homework more fun!

MATERIALS

Small plastic storage basket
1 piece 1/4-inch plywood or paneling
Scroll saw or bandsaw
3/4-by-3/4-inch pine trim strip
Router with rabbet bit
Wood glue
C-clamps
Desired paint, stain and embellishments
Polyurethane

DIRECTIONS

☐ Add 1 inch to basket's top dimensions for desk top's measurements.
☐ Cut out top with scroll saw, rounding corners.
☐ Cut 2 pieces from trim strip the same length as basket's long side.
☐ Measure basket lip to determine bit width, and rout groove.
☐ Position strips under top so that basket is centered (Figure 10).
☐ Glue strips in place and secure with C-clamps.
☐ Let dry. Paint strips and bottom of desk top a bright, coordinating color.
☐ Stain or paint top, and embellish with a painted design, stencils, or stickers, if desired.
☐ Seal with coat of polyurethane.

Figure 10

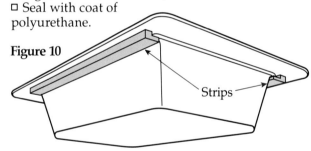

Strips

Handy Auto Safety Bucket

*W*hat do you give the man who has everything? If he spends much time in his car, you can give him some peace of mind this year. Cover a bucket with a "work apron," fill it with emergency items, and you have a handy safety kit. You can put kitty litter for traction inside the bucket, and include a flare, a scraper, cleaning cloths, a flashlight, and other aids in the apron's pockets. Or, for the gardener on your list, substitute garden tools, seeds, and fertilizer.

MATERIALS FOR HANDY AUTO SAFETY BUCKET

Plastic bucket with snap-on lid
Tracing paper
Red ticking or fabric
Denim fabric
1/2-inch wide navy grosgrain ribbon
Miscellaneous car items

DIRECTIONS

☐ Make pattern by measuring height, top circumference, and bottom circumference of bucket. Divide 2 circumference numbers into fourths, and add 2 inches to both numbers. Add 3 inches to height, and draw this shape onto tracing paper.
☐ Transfer pattern to ticking and cut 4 pieces. Determine denim pockets measurements by adding 2 inches to ticking's side measurements and reducing its height measurement by half.
☐ Make pattern, transfer to denim, and cut 4.
☐ Set sewing machine for appliqué, and bind all raw edges with satin stitch.
☐ Center 1 denim piece over 1 ticking piece with right sides up and bottom edges even.
☐ Sew a vertical seam through center of both pieces from bottom to top of denim piece. This divides denim into 2 pockets.
☐ Take a 1-inch tuck in center bottom of each pocket and pin in place.
☐ Sew denim and ticking together along bottom edge catching tucks in seam.
☐ Repeat for 3 remaining pieces.
☐ Sew 2 quarter panels together along one side with right sides facing. Repeat for 2 remaining quarter panels.
☐ Determine position for drawstring casing, and sew a 1½-inch strip of denim on the inside of both ticking pieces for casing.
☐ Sew remaining 2 sides together with right sides facing, stopping just under casing openings.
☐ Thread 2 pieces of grosgrain ribbon through both sides of casing for drawstring. Turn, slip apron over bucket, and cinch ribbon on each side to fit.
☐ Fill bucket and pockets with desired items.

Use washing detergent buckets for the Handy Auto Safety Bucket. You'll be doing a good deed for recycling.

Lollipop Backpack

Send the little one back to school in 1993 with a brightly stenciled lollipop backpack. Your creative touch will make it easy for your child to keep track of it. And the acrylic paint will hold up through mud puddle cleanups galore.

MATERIALS

Stencils by Zula: 9178 Alphabet, 9179 Lollipops
Acrylic Paint in desired colors
Masking tape
Purchased backpack
Paper plate or saucer
Stenciling brushes: 3/4 inch to 1 inch in diameter, 1 brush for each color
Paper towels

DIRECTIONS

☐ Stencil name onto newspaper or scrap paper to plan placement.
☐ Place a strip of masking tape on backpack to guide stenciling.
☐ Place a thick magazine inside backpack for firm stenciling surface.
☐ Follow directions for stenciling below.

DIRECTIONS FOR STENCILING

☐ Place stencil in position and tape in place with masking tape.
☐ Review paint manufacturer's instructions. Place a small amount of paint on a paper plate or saucer.
☐ Dip tip of brush into paint. Wipe off excess on a paper towel until brush is "dry" and paint is light and smooth in appearance.
☐ Hold brush perpendicular to surface. Start at outside edge of cut-out area and work in a clockwise motion from edge across design area.
☐ Reverse to a counter-clockwise motion and continue building up color to desired shade.
☐ Align Print 2 if using more than 1 print, using register marks as a guide. Stencil Print 2. Continue until the design is complete.
☐ Clean stencils and brushes gently following manufacturer's directions and allow to air dry before using again.

Kiddie Basket Desk, Handy Auto Safety Bucket, Lollipop Backpack, pages 73 and 74

Pop-Up Cards and Tags

*E*veryone enjoys opening a card and finding a hidden pop-up surprise. Use these cards to teach your children how much fun it is to send messages of love by mail. You know Grandma will keep hers forever.

MATERIALS FOR STAR GIFT TAG

Glue stick
Silver gift wrap
2 (8¹/2-by-11-inch) sheets red cardstock
Scissors
Silver paint markers: medium and fine tip
Silver gummed stars
See Patterns

DIRECTIONS

☐ Glue a 3-inch square of silver wrapping paper to corner of 1 cardstock piece.
☐ Transfer star pattern to silver paper and cut out.
☐ Fold star in half, as indicated on pattern, with silver side to outside.
☐ Cut remaining cardstock into two 5¹/2-by-8¹/2-inch pieces. Fold into two 4¹/4-by-5¹/2-inch cards. Crease folds well.
☐ Mark lightly a point ¹/2 inch from top of 1 card on folded edge.
☐ Mark another point 4 inches from top on folded edge.
☐ Mark a point 1¹/4 inch from back fold on top edge of card. Draw a line from this point to ¹/2-inch point on fold line, and cut out.
☐ Draw a line from same top point to 4-inch point. Fold along this line, creasing well and folding it to both sides of the card.
☐ Fold this triangle to inside of card to make pop-up triangle.
☐ Position folded star on this fold so that star's edges are concealed when card is closed. Glue star to pop-up triangle.
☐ Lay a line of glue on outside edges of card, avoiding pop-up triangle. Slip other card over inner card, and press together along glue lines.

☐ Mark a silver border on outside of card with wide silver marker. Write sentiment and glue gummed stars randomly around words.
☐ Write desired message on inside of card and glue on more gummed stars.

MATERIALS FOR TREE CARD AND GIFT TAG

1 (8-by-10¹/2-inch) matching blue paper piece, for large card
Glue stick
1 (9-by-12-inch) piece silver wrapping paper
1 (5-by-7-inch) piece silver wrapping paper
1 (8¹/2-by-11-inch) sheet green cardstock
Scissors
1 (8¹/2-by-11-inch) piece blue cardstock for large card
Silver snowflake sequins
Adhesive sealant (E-6000)
Silver paint markers: medium and fine tip
1 (8¹/2-by-11-inch) piece yellow cardstock, for gift tag

DIRECTIONS FOR LARGE CARD

☐ Fold blue paper into 5¹/4-by-8-inch card. Unfold and cover inside of card with glue stick. Center on large silver paper piece, and refold to crease silver paper.
☐ Glue small silver paper piece to corner of green cardstock. Transfer tree patterns to silver paper and cardstock. Cut out 2 small trees and 1 large tree from silver paper. Cut out 2 small trees and 1 large tree from green cardstock. Center green trees on silver trees as indicated on pattern, and glue in place.
☐ Fold blue cardstock into an 5¹/2-by-8¹/2-inch card. Mark lines inside card along fold as indicated (Figure 11). Cut lines and push 3 sections to inside of card to make pop-up tabs. Crease well.
☐ Lay a line of glue along outside edges of card and center blue and silver card over it. Press together firmly. Trim away excess silver paper.
☐ Glue 3 trees to tabs with largest tree in middle.
☐ Glue snowflakes to inside and to front card with adhesive sealant.
☐ Write sentiments with silver markers.

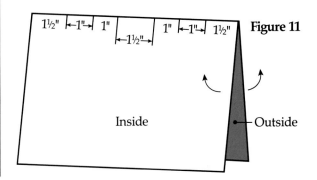

Figure 11

Pop-Up Cards and Tags, Gift Bag Handles, pages 77 and 78

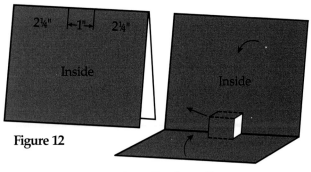

Figure 12

DIRECTIONS FOR POP-UP GIFT TAG

□ Cut yellow cardstock into two 5½-by-8½-inch pieces. Fold both into 4¼-by-5½-inch cards. Crease well.

□ Mark lines inside card along fold as indicated (Figure 12). Cut lines and push section to inside of card to make pop-up tab. Crease well.

□ Lay a line of glue along outside edges of this card and center other card over it. Press cards together firmly.

□ Transfer tree pattern to green cardstock and cut out.

□ Outline tree with medium paint marker and make scattered silver dots over tree. Glue tree to tab.

□ Draw borders along sides of card front with medium paint marker.

□ Write sentiments with silver markers.

Gift Bag Handles

Dress up your gift bags with festive handle covers. A bright red bow, a deep blue star and a rich green tree change even a plain sack to a Christmas goodie bag. Since the handle covers are just cut from heavy paper and glued in place, it's a great way to involve the kids in the fun.

MATERIALS

Heavy-weight paper: Red, Green, and Blue
Craft glue
See Patterns

DIRECTIONS

□ Transfer patterns to paper. Cut out 2 handle covers for each bag.

□ Position handle covers outside bag handles and just inside top edge of bag for tree and star bags. Glue in place.

□ Glue 1 bow to each bag handle for bow, leaving bag handle free at top for carrying.

Kitten Barrette and Necklace

Delight the little kitten in your house with a gift of kitty cat jewelry. Purchased wooden hearts turned upside down become puffy cheeks and a pointed wisp of fur. Then, folded ribbon ears and your paintbrush make pretty kitties for a necklace and barrette.

MATERIALS

1 (2-inch wide) ⅛-inch thick wooden heart
3 (1-inch wide) ⅛-inch thick wooden hearts
Acrylic paint: White, Gray, Peach, Black, Gold, Blue
Paintbrushes: Medium flat, liner
Tracing paper
Graphite or carbon paper
Clear spray sealer
Scraps of ½-inch wide peach, gray, and white ribbon
Adhesive sealant (E-6000)
Dark peach embroidery floss
¾ yard (1½-inch wide) peach satin ribbon
Barrette back
¾ yard (⅛-inch wide) peach satin ribbon
2 (¼-inch diameter) gold beads
See Patterns

DIRECTIONS

□ Paint large heart white and small hearts gray, white, and peach.

□ Transfer patterns onto tracing paper. Place graphite or carbon paper between patterns and hearts.

□ Trace over pattern to transfer image onto hearts.

□ Paint as indicated. Let dry.

□ Spray with sealer. Let dry.

□ Make ears with ½-inch wide ribbon in coordinating colors. Glue to back of face.

□ Make embroidery floss bows and glue to fronts of ears, referring to photograph for placement.

□ Make a large bow from 1½-inch wide ribbon. Glue large kitty face to front of bow and back of barrette to back of bow.

□ Glue a kitten face onto ⅛-inch wide ribbon and string a gold bead next to it for necklace.

□ Repeat to attach remaining heart faces and bead.

Flop-Eared Bunny Barrette

Make a pretty ponytail even prettier by topping it with this flop-eared bunny. If you're a seamstress, you can even coordinate it with a pretty dress or pinafore by using the scraps from the dress for bunny's ears.

MATERIALS

Scraps of muslin and print fabrics
Polyester stuffing
Acrylic paints: Pink, Dark Brown, Ivory
Paintbrushes: small round, liner
Pink makeup blush
1 yard (1/4-inch wide) blue satin ribbon
Hot glue gun
7 inches (2-inch wide) ecru lace
Barrette back
See Patterns

DIRECTIONS

◻ Transfer patterns to fabric and cut out.
◻ Sew 2 head pieces together, leaving an opening for turning.
◻ Turn, stuff firmly with polyester stuffing, and slipstitch closed.
◻ Transfer face details to fabric front.
◻ Paint nose pink.
◻ Paint eyes, eyelashes, mouth, and whiskers dark brown.
◻ Paint ivory dots in eyes, and use blush to tint cheeks.
◻ Sew ear piece together with right sides facing, leaving an opening for turning. Turn and slipstitch opening closed.
◻ Cut two 12-inch long pieces of ribbon.
◻ Tie tightly around ear piece where indicated on pattern. Tie ribbon in bows.
◻ Position ears on top of head with ears slightly overlapping sides of face, referring to photograph.
◻ Glue ears in place on top of head and on sides of face.
◻ Run a gathering stitch 1/2 inch from edge along 1 long side of lace.
◻ Gather to fit along bottom of face, and glue in place.
◻ Make a bow from remaining satin ribbon, and glue in center of lace on gathering line. Glue back of barrette to back of bunny head.

Gold Lamé Picture Frame

Set off your favorite photo in a frame of glittering gold lamé. Your artistry adds the finishing touch with delicately painted flowers accenting the frame's corners. Short on wall space? Use a plate stand or easel to display it on a tabletop.

MATERIALS

1 (8-by-10-inch) ready-cut mat
1 (8-by-10-inch) sheet of white paper
1 (11-by-13-inch) quilted gold lamé fabric piece
Craft glue
1 (8-by-10-inch) heavy cardboard backing
Gold wrapping paper
Scribbles® Paint: Shiny Bright Green, Shiny Lipstick Pink, Iridescent Champagne Ice, Crystal Gel Clover Green, Crystal Gel Pink Lemonade
Paintbrushes: small round, liner
Very fine tip black permanent marker
See Patterns

DIRECTIONS

◻ Place mat on paper and trace outline and center opening. Cut out to make backing. Set aside.
◻ Position lamé on right side of mat to extend 1 1/2 inches on all sides. Glue to mat.
◻ Clip corners, fold excess to wrong side of mat and glue in place.
◻ Cut center opening in lamé leaving 1 1/2 inches to turn to wrong side. Clip corners, fold over, and glue in place.
◻ Glue paper backing over raw edges of lamé.
◻ Cover both sides of back piece with gold wrapping paper. Glue back to lamé-covered front along side and top edges with wrong sides facing.
◻ Transfer patterns to frame front.
◻ Paint flower petals and leaves with shiny colors. Let dry.
◻ Brush thin coat of crystal gel over painted areas, matching gel colors to regular colors.
◻ Outline pink flowers with Pink Lemonade gel and leaves with Clover Green gel.
◻ Outline all flowers, flower details, leaves, and stems with black marker.

Visions of
Sugarplums

A Season for Reminiscing
Memories

*E*very year during the Christmas season, no matter what we plan, sooner or later we end up at the Starbirds'. We're drawn there like kids to cookies, like reindeer to rooftops, like shepherds to a star.

I went to school with Mike, the younger son, and the two of us have stayed in touch over the years. Since our family and Mike's always return to Southern California for the holidays, it's convenient to meet at the Pasadena home of Mike's parents, Bill and Mary Ellen Starbird. Those are the facts. But facts aren't the issue, as any child on Christmas morning can tell you.

The Starbirds' home is full of fun and full of memories.

There's Mary Ellen greeting you at the door, wearing a big smile, a Christmas dress, an apron, and tennis shoes shaped like frogs.

There's the little chuckle Bill gives as he watches his grandkids chase each other around the tree.

There are the dolls spread out on the kitchen floor, and the giggles of children from around the corner.

There are the goodies in the refrigerator, always including chocolate cake and ice cream.

There are the milk mustaches.

There are the riddles Santa Claus leaves, telling where he's hidden the gifts.

There's the annual Rose Parade Run on New Year's Eve, beginning at the Starbirds' front porch. The idea is to run/walk/stagger the length of the parade route, checking out the crowd and practicing the mechanical wave made famous by the Rose Queen and her court.

There's the way Bill pushes back his chair after dinner and tosses out light-hearted questions such as "What's your philosophy of education?" and "How do you define energy?" Sometimes people actually answer.

There's the jigsaw puzzle in the den. At some point each Christmas, all of us cluster around the puzzle and, fortified by brownies, work late into the night putting in the pieces.

There's Starbird Charades, where instead of book titles and quotations, you're asked to act out the meaning of individual words, such as *quibble* and *procrastination*.

And there's *The Messiah*, performed every year in its entirety by the Starbirds and a group of thirty to forty friends, with Bill at the piano. The notes aren't perfect, but the spirit is.

What are your plans for the holidays? If you'll be spending it with friends and family, talking and laughing and making memories, then, whether you know it or not, you're going to the same place where we always go.

We'll see you at the Starbirds'.

1992 Holiday Calendar

Tuesday December **1**	Wednesday December **2**	Thursday December **3**	Friday December **4**
Wednesday December **9**	Thursday December **10**	Friday December **11**	Saturday December **12**
Thursday December **17**	Friday December **18**	Saturday December **19**	Sunday December **20**
Friday December **25**	Saturday December **26**	Sunday December **27**	Monday December **28**

December   1992
S M T W T F S
          1 2 3 4 5
6 7 8 9 10 11 12
13 14 15 16 17 18 19
20 21 22 23 24 25 26
27 28 29 30 31

January   1993
S M T W T F S
                1 2
3 4 5 6 7 8 9
10 11 12 13 14 15 16
17 18 19 20 21 22 23
24 25 26 27 28 29 30
31

Saturday December **5**	Sunday December **6**	Monday December **7**	Tuesday December **8**
Sunday December **13**	Monday December **14**	Tuesday December **15**	Wednesday December **16**
Monday December **21**	Tuesday December **22**	Wednesday December **23**	Thursday December **24**
Tuesday December **29**	Wednesday December **30**	Thursday December **31**	Friday January **1**

Family Favorites

Somehow not only for Christmas but all the long year through,
The joy that you give to others is the joy that comes back to you,
And the more you spend in blessing the poor and lonely and sad,
The more of your heart's possessing returns to make you glad.
attributed to John Greenleaf Whittier

*H*ave everyone on your gift list fill in the chart below to help you decide what to give them.

Names					
Favorite Charity					
Favorite Color					
Favorite Flower					
Favorite Food					
Favorite Gift Certificate					
Favorite Music					
Favorite "Night Out"					
Favorite Scent					
Favorite Sport					
Favorite Toy or Gadget					
Favorite Type Book					
What I'd Love To Have					

Christmas Gift Size Chart

To give a gift that's wrapped with your love
And tied with your heart strings
Is to give a most precious gift—
One that'll last a lifetime.

Have friends and family fill out the size chart below to be sure your gift is "fitting."

Names						
Bathrobe						
Belt						
Blouse						
Coat						
Dress						
Gloves						
Hat						
Pajamas						
Ring						
Shirt						
Shoes						
Skirt						
Slacks						
Suit						
Sweater						

Christmas Gift Ideas

INFANTS AND TODDLERS

Activity quilt
Children's dinnerware set
Christmas ornament
Clothes
Clutch ball
Crib toys
Mesh net for holding stuffed
   animals
Mint or Proof coin set from
   birth year

Mobile
Multi-colored quilt
Night light
Nursery monitor
Old pots and pans
Personalized Christmas
   stocking
Piggy bank
Plastic key ring
Plush toys

Porcelain collectible doll
Rattlers
Riding toy
Rocking horse
Savings bond
Soft blocks
Stacking ring
Teddy Bear
Toy box
Tub toys

PRESCHOOLER

ABC blocks
Ball
Bank
Bath toys
Beginning reading books
Book and cassette collection
Children's learning aid toys
Crayons and coloring book
Doll stroller
Dress-up clothes
Flash cards
Flashlight with batteries
Footed Pajamas
Furry slippers

Jewelry
Library card
Lincoln logs
Overnight bag
Paper dolls
Personalized Bible
Play-doh
Porcelain collectible doll
Preschool magazine
   subscription
Puppets
Purse or wallet
Puzzles
Red wagon

Shape sorter
Sticker books
Stuffed animals
Tablets of paper
Tea set
Toy camera
Toy doctor kit
Toy telephone
Toy vacuum cleaner
Train set
Tricycle
Trip to museum or zoo
Video cassette of cartoons
Wind-up toys

GRADE SCHOOL AGE

Backpack
Baseball cards
Bed tent
Bike, scooter or skate board
Bird feeder and birdseed
Board and card games
Books
Cassette tape player with
   microphone
Chalk board
Charm bracelet
Chemistry set
Clothes
Comb and brush set

Craft kits
Desk
Doll house
Dolls and doll clothes
Fishing pole
Globe
Gloves and mittens
Hand-held electronic game
Jewelry box
Jump rope
Magnifying glass
Microscope
Money
Music lessons

Play appliances
Puzzle made from the child's
   photograph
Roller skates
Scented pens
Scrapbook
Sheets and pillowcases
Sleeping bag
Snowglobe
Stenciling set
Vanity set
Video cassette of favorite
   movie
Walkie Talkie

CHILDREN'S STOCKING STUFFERS

Bath bubbles
Candy
Colored pencils
Crayons
Deck of cards
Dinosaur figures
Fingernail polish

Fruit
Gloves or mittens
Gum
Hair accessories
Jacks
Jewelry
Magnets

Marbles
Mini bouncing balls
Miniature cars and trucks
Notepads
Small animal figures
Socks
Stickers

TEENAGERS

Alarm clock
Automobile emergency kit
Automobile stereo
Automobile vacuum
Books
Camera
Car care gift certificate
Cassette tapes/compact discs
Clothes
Concert tickets
Desk lamp

Diary
Dictionary, Thesaurus
Hand-held electronic game
Leather bomber jacket
Luggage
Magazine subscription
Mini-calculator
Money
Movie tickets
Pen and pencil set
Personalized car mats

Shares of stock
Silver comb and brush set
Sporting equipment
Sporting event tickets
Sports watch
Sunglasses
Telephone
Telescope
Television
Theme park season pass
Zippered sports bag

ADULTS

Address book
Art lessons
Automobile club membership
Binoculars
Bird feeder and birdseed
Blank video or cassette tapes
Book of poetry
Bottle of fine wine
Breakfast in bed
Briefcase
Camping or fishing
    equipment
Car wash
Ceramic mugs
Christmas ornament
Collection of small items
    that are habitually lost
    (pens, safety pins, needles,
    scissors, cellophane tape)
Cookbook
Copy of *Visions of
    Sugarplums*
Cordless screwdriver kit
Cotton robe

Day of maid service
Exercise equipment
FAX machine
Fire extinguisher
First aid kit
Flying lesson
Gas grill
Gift certificate
Gourmet coffees
Hammock
Hand blender set
Handbag
Handloomed throw rug
Home computer
Home medical encyclopedia
Horseback riding lessons
Hot air popcorn popper
Kaleidoscope
Kayak lessons
Limousine service for an
    evening
Load of firewood
Luggage
Magazine subscription

Miniature vacuum cleaner
Music box
Old family photos enlarged
    and framed
Packets of wildflower seeds
Peppermill
Personalized coffee cup
Scuba lesson
Smoke alarm
Self-help or motivational tapes
Snow boots
Sporting event tickets
Symphony tickets
Telephone answering machine
Tennis lessons
Theatre tickets
Tin of popcorn
Tools
Travel atlas
Video cassette of favorite
    movie
Videotape rewinder
Wallet
White water rafting trip

Our 1992 Yuletide Photographs

My favorite place in all the world is home at Christmas time,
For there is where we gather near the precious ones we love so dear,
And hold them in our hearts once more
To last throughout the coming year.

Affix Photo of
Home Here

Affix Photo of
Christmas Dinner Here

Gifts Bought Throughout the Year

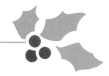

The orange has its place you know,
To fill each Christmas stocking toe.
Roseanne Russell

Gift For	Item	Where I Bought It	Where I Stored It

Our 1992 Yuletide Photographs

*T*he first toy bear was created by a German woman who saw a cartoon of President Teddy Roosevelt standing over a small bear he had shot. When offered at the Leipzig Toy Fair in 1903, the teddy bear outsold every other toy.

Affix Photo of
Tree Here

Affix Photo of
Family and Friends Here

Our 1992 Christmas Card

You cannot reach perfection though
You try however hard to;
There's always one more friend or so
You should have sent a card to.

Richard Armour

Affix
Christmas Card
Here

Our 1992 Yuletide Photographs

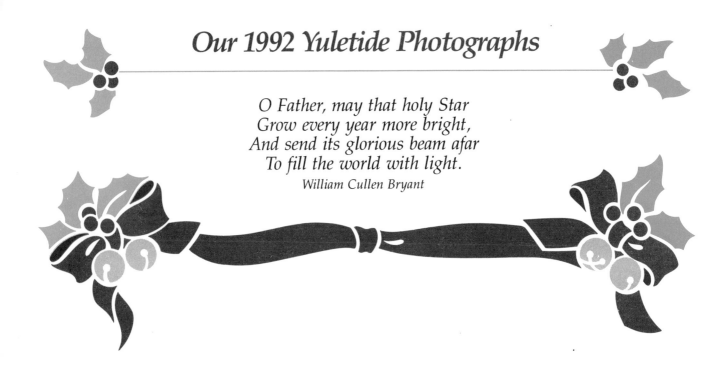

*O Father, may that holy Star
Grow every year more bright,
And send its glorious beam afar
To fill the world with light.*
William Cullen Bryant

*Affix Photo
Here*

*Affix Photo
Here*

Our Christmas Eve

*And this will be a sign for you: you will find a babe
wrapped in swaddling cloths and lying in a manger.*
Luke 2:12

This year we shared Christmas Eve with . . .

Christmas Eve Menu . . .

Santa's treat . . .

Our traditions on Christmas Eve . . .

The highlight of the evening came when . . .

Special Christmas Eve presents included . . .

Our 1992 Yuletide Photographs

*T*he Santa legend is based on the life of St. Nicholas, a bishop in the fourth century, who is said to have helped an impoverished nobleman provide his daughter with dowries by throwing sacks of gold through the windows. The gold landed in stockings that had been hung by the fire to dry.

*Affix Photo
Here*

*Affix Photo
Here*

The Night Before Christmas

*S*hare a special moment with a child by reading
aloud this delightful story by Clement C. Moore.

'Twas the night before Christmas, when all
through the house
Not a creature was stirring, not even a mouse;
The stockings were hung by the chimney
with care,
In hopes that St. Nicholas soon would be there;
The children were nestled all snug in their
beds,
While visions of sugarplums danced in
their heads;
And Mama in her 'kerchief, and I in my cap,
Had just settled our brains for a long
winter's nap;
When out on the lawn there arose such
a clatter,
I sprang from my bed to see what was
the matter.
Away to the window I flew like a flash,
Tore open the shutters and threw up the sash.
The moon, on the breast of the new-fallen
snow,
Gave the lustre of midday to objects below,
When what to my wondering eyes
should appear,
But a miniature sleigh, and eight tiny reindeer,
With a little old driver, so lively and quick,
I knew in a moment it must be St. Nick.
More rapid than eagles his coursers they came,
And he whistled and shouted, and called
them by name;
'Now, Dasher! Now, Dancer! Now, Prancer
and Vixen!
On, Comet! On, Cupid! On, Donner
and Blitzen!
To the top of the porch! To the top of the wall!
Now, dash away! Dash away! Dash away all!'
As dry leaves that before the wild
hurricane fly,
When they meet with an obstacle, mount
to the sky;
So up to the housetop the coursers they flew,
With the sleigh full of toys, and
St. Nicholas, too.
And then, in a twinkling, I heard on the roof

The prancing and pawing of each little hoof—
As I drew in my head, and was turning around,
Down the chimney St. Nicholas came
with a bound.
He was dressed all in fur, from his head to
his foot,
And his clothes were all tarnished with ashes
and soot;
A bundle of toys he had flung on his back,
And he looked like a pedlar just opening
his pack.
His eyes—how they twinkled! His dimples,
how merry!
His cheeks were like roses, his nose like
a cherry!
His droll little mouth was drawn up
like a bow,
And the beard of his chin was as white
as the snow;
The stump of a pipe he held tight in his teeth,
And the smoke it encircled his head like
a wreath;
He had a broad face and a little round belly
That shook, when he laughed, like a bowl
full of jelly.
He was chubby and plump, a right jolly old elf,
And I laughed, when I saw him, in spite
of myself;
A wink of his eye and a twist of his head,
Soon gave me to know I had nothing to dread;
He spoke not a word, but went straight
to his work,
And filled all the stockings; then turned
with a jerk.
And laying his finger aside of his nose,
And giving a nod, up the chimney he rose;
He sprang to his sleigh, to his team
gave a whistle,
And away they all flew like the down
of a thistle.
But I heard him exclaim, ere he drove
out of sight,
'Happy Christmas to all, and to all a
good night.'

Christmas Traditions

*The most essential thing for happiness
is the gift of friendship.*
Sir William Osler

The things we do year after year have a way of making family life a little more special. Every family has some traditions that are centered around the holidays. What we have for Christmas dinner or where we eat it, the stories we read on Christmas Eve, the songs we sing, are all a part of the traditions we build. We've collected the following traditions and hope you will enjoy reading them and perhaps making them a part of your families' Christmas. If developing a few traditions could help bring families a little closer together, isn't it worth the extra bit of effort?

Precious Ornaments

Collect a new ornament every year for each child. Knowing these special decorations belong to them makes the tree seem extra special. When the children grow up and have their own families, they will enjoy telling their children stories associated with each ornament.

Special Moments

As Christmas cards arrive, put them in a special container. When the family gathers for supper, let one member pick a card and read it aloud. Then say a special thought or prayer for the person who sent the card. This way you are able to enjoy each card separately for a moment before displaying it on the table or mantel.

After Dinner Gifts

After Christmas dinner is complete but the family is still gathered together, pass out one last present for each member. It can be something very small like a pocket game, colored notepad or pencils . . . Your family will come to look forward to this final time of gift-sharing as a family.

Santa's Kiss

Little ones who are especially good during the year can wake to find the print of a kiss on their cheek. When Santa kisses them his lips are ruby red (like Mom's lipstick) and it leaves a loving mark.

Storytime

Sit by the fire with a cup of coffee (try our Cappucino mix or Café Vienna recipes on page 43) and read Clement C. Moore's poem "The Night Before Christmas," page 95, aloud to the entire family.

A Year-Round Christmas

Why not fill your spouse's stocking with 12 red envelopes. Date each envelope with a different month such as "The First Day of Christmas—January 1," "The Second Day of Christmas—February 1," etc. Let your spouse open each envelope on the appropriate day. Inside will be a message detailing a special outing you'll make together such as dinner out, a ballgame, or a weekend trip. Your spouse will really look forward to these events and it's a great way to "Celebrate Christmas all year-round."

A Memory-Filled Wreath

Collect flowers from special arrangements and occasions throughout the year (example: weddings, birthdays, anniversaries). Dry them and make a keepsake wreath for yourself or a family member. This way you'll have a constant reminder of those special occasions.

Bountiful Breakfast

If your family all lives nearby, start a tradition by inviting all your family to a big Christmas breakfast. This way your married children won't have to agonize over who they will spend the day with because they can still have Christmas dinner with their in-laws.

A Clean Christmas

Help clean up the environment and have a wonderful time doing it by following some of these suggestions:

☐ Send Christmas postcards instead of cards with envelopes.

☐ Wrap your gifts in recycled paper printed with non-toxic ink.

☐ Let your kids color a brown paper grocery sack and use it to wrap your gifts.

☐ Purchase fabric ribbons and bows that can be ironed and reused.

Nature's Bounty

Take your children for a nature walk or hike outside on Christmas Eve. Talk to them about nature in the wintertime. Look for wild animal tracks in the snow, fish under frozen ice on ponds and birds in flight or sheltered in the bushes. This is a great way to use up some of that excess energy and help them have happy dreams as they await Santa's arrival.

Selfless Gifts

Last but not least, give something of yourself this season. Donate food or, better yet, some time to a food bank, homeless shelter, senior citizen center or orphanage.

Cookie Swap

Extend an invitition to your neighbors and extended family members for a cookie swap. Ask each guest to bring 6 dozen cookies along with copies of their cookie recipe. On the day of the swap provide punch and let everyone sample a few of the creations. Let everyone spend some time enjoying one anothers company, and then divide the cookies among the guests. Everyone will leave with a wonderful assortment of homemade cookies and also warm feelings towards each other.

First Foot in the Door

One old tradition that you may wish to revive is to go visiting on New Year's Day. If you are the first person to enter anothers home (first foot in the door) then you must bring a gift, usually food or drink. This is certain to be appreciated by the recipient, and the Food Gifts chapter in this book has plenty of recipes for you to choose from.

Celebrate a Birth

Make a Birthday Cake in honor of baby Jesus and serve on Christmas Eve. You may also want to read the Christmas story from the Bible or attend a special Christmas church service.

The Twelve Months of Christmas

*May there come to you at this Holiday Time
an abundance of precious things of Life;
Health, Happiness and Enduring Friendships.*
Abraham Lincoln

December

Christmas Day: Record your day's activities using your camera. Order extra prints or have your video duplicated and send to a friend or relative who could not be present.

The week following Christmas is post-holiday sale time. Take advantage of seasonal items that are marked down. Pick up extra light bulbs and decorations you'll need for next year at great savings.

Organize. Gather this year's Christmas cards and update your card list. Write and mail thank-you notes. Help your children or grandchildren write a special thank-you note to Santa.

Collect and sort your Christmas trash for disposal at your local recycling center.

Plan ahead. Start a Christmas Club Savings account for next year.

January

Back on the diet track. Begin the year with a small gathering of friends for a "back on the diet" dinner. Serve dishes that emphasize fruits and vegetables, fresh fish and grilled chicken.

Use photographs or video to record your decorating for future reference. It'll make next year's decorating much smoother. Consider making an inventory as you pack away and keep a written record of where decorations are stored.

Next year's holidays will arrive much sooner than you think. Begin long-term craft projects now.

Sort recipes. Call friends or relatives for the recipe of that delicious goody you received and add it to your recipe file.

Update your copy of Visions of Sugarplums. Place your Christmas Card, Photographs, and Christmas Eve information on the appropriate pages.

Linen and white sales are this month.

Check your poinsettia. See page 103 for 10 steps for success with poinsettias.

February

Revive your Christmas spirit. Select a craft or decorating project from this book to help pass the time during the cold wintry days.

Review last year's Christmas bills. Don't let a lack of funds dampen the spirit. Start next year's Christmas budget now.

Look for seed and plant catalogues to arrive. Your garden can provide hundreds of gift ideas. Plan to plant items that can be canned, pickled, or dried and used for gifts. Use your green thumb to create gifts with a true personal touch. Also keep in mind that seed packets can make great stocking stuffers next year.

March

Begin a long-term craft project. One good example is the Poinsettia Garland Shaw on page 58.

In some areas of the country you can begin preparing the soil for spring planting.

April

It's springtime! When the threat of frost has passed in your area, begin your gardening. Remember that flowers brighten spirits year-round. Home-grown items make great gifts.

Plan a yard sale to raise money for that extra special gift for a cherished friend or loved-one. Also shop around at yard sales and flea markets for great gift bargains.

Enjoy a warm spring afternoon. Take your children and enjoy the afternoon scouting a nearby wooded area for vines, pine cones and other materials for your handmade and heart felt decorations.

Gather a bouquet of fresh flowers for an elderly friend or shut-in.

May

It's time to harvest many varieties of fresh berries. Jams, jellies and preserves make delicious gifts with a special personal touch. Spend some time with a teenage relative or friend and share your secret recipe and techniques for the perfect finished product.

Now is the time to plan your holiday vacation. Traveling is heavy during the holiday season and contacting your travel agent now can prevent last minute mix-ups and difficulty in obtaining reservations.

June

Harvest your flowers when they are at their best. Cut and dried, they make delightful potpourri that can be used in a variety of crafts for gift-giving.

With the kids out of school take advantage of the extra help. Christmas crafts make many a rainy summer day go by faster.

Contact you local nursery for information about fertilizing your shrubbery. Extra effort now will make those clippings much more attractive.

Update the gift size chart on page 85.

July

Believe it or not, you're halfway to Christmas.

Review your progress on long-term craft projects and schedule your leisure time accordingly. The closer the holiday season becomes, the busier your schedule, so plan now to prevent last-minute rushing.

Shop festivals and craft fairs for unique and inexpensive gift ideas. (Don't forget teachers.)

August

Make your summer trips a regular part of your Christmas planning. Use them to find unique gift items and decorations. Pine cones, sea shells, berries, and driftwood are the foundations for great decorations that bring back special memories.

This is a good time to buy children's clothing for gifts. Selection is at its best. Record your purchases and where they're stored by using the chart on page 89.

Surprise an elderly friend by helping weed the garden or assisting with yard work.

Harvest delicious home-grown goodies from your garden. Or you may want to plan a visit to your local farmers market for items to prepare as gifts. Make our *Festive Fruit Jam* (see page 40) from summer's abundance.

September

Lay-away toys and other items which might be in short supply as the holiday season draws near. Catalogue items should be ordered now to allow plenty of time for delivery.

Look at unfinished craft and decorating projects. Are your goals realistic or should you move to an easier, less time-consuming project?

Start updating your Christmas card list.

Ask children/grandchildren to begin preparing their "wish lists." Provide them with your list as well.

October

Select the planting site for your live tree. Dig the hole now before the ground freezes. Store the removed dirt in the garage to prevent it from freezing and use it to backfill when planting.

Make appointments for holiday hairdos and the family Christmas portrait. Mark the dates on your holiday planning calendar on pages 82 and 83.

Be sure to ask for boxes with purchases.

A patchwork of ornaments. Every year give each of your children his or her own ornament to be opened on Christmas Eve. Through the years, your children will collect enough of these "special" ornaments to decorate their first trees away from home.

November

It's time! Update your holiday calendar.

Christmas is almost here. Your gift lists and craft projects should be near completion, and your shopping should be progressing.

Gather your wrapping supplies all in one location. Buy extra ribbon, paper and tape, if necessary.

Christmas cards should be almost ready to mail.

Test your smoke alarm.

Test your camera and have it serviced if necessary. Extra film and batteries are always a good idea.

Santa's helper. Offer your assistance to a parent of small children by assembling toys that can be picked up after children have gone to bed. This way the parents can go to bed at a decent hour on Christmas Eve rather than beginning the assembly process at midnight.

Holiday "Hellos." Make plans to visit a local nursing home in early December. Family and friends can pitch in to make Christmas cookies or take baskets of fresh fruit, jams or toilet articles. Have plenty of Christmas carols photocopied too so everyone can sing along.

December

It's not too late to make something good from the kitchen. Try our no-cook ideas such as *Sweet Garlic Pickles* (see page 42), *Fruit Salsa* (see page 42) *or Cappucino Mix* (see page 43).

Untrimming the Tree Party. Turn this most-dreaded task into a festive one by inviting friends the week after Christmas to help you undecorate. Your home will be filled with friends and your Christmas spirit will soar well into the New Year.

Thank You! Set aside one night in the week between Christmas and New Year's, and make a list of the thank-you notes that need to be written. Let the kids decorate blank postcards with stickers, messages and drawings. The note-writing task will be accomplished quickly and enjoyably.

Greenery Tips

By the late 1800s, edible ornaments of gingerbread figures, fruits, and nuts were being replaced on the Christmas tree by purchased angels, tinsel and bright shiny balls. But it wasn't until the 20th Century that we blew out the candles on the tree and began turning on the Christmas tree lights.

A TREE FOR CHRISTMAS

◻ The tree that holds pride of place for the holidays demands some forethought and special care. Most of us have our favorites—the short-needle partisans think the ornaments look best on a sparsely foliaged tree such as the Douglas fir, while others crave the green abundance of a long-needled Scotch pine. And all families have their rituals: the ceremonial drive to the street corner where the tree vendors plant their temporary forests, or the trip to the country for a cut-your-own, with a full complement of red cheeks, lost mittens and mugs of cocoa at home. Then there are those who welcome the cheery delivery person bearing the mail-order tree or who go to a shop for one of the increasingly persuasive artificial trees.

◻ Choosing a cut tree with staying power does require some guidelines. Picking the right variety helps—as beautiful as the spruces are, they are the quickest to dry out and shed; a fir is a better choice. A fresh tree shouldn't drop more than a few green needles when it's picked up and bounced on its trunk; run your hand along a branch to make sure the needles bend and don't break off. To keep the tree fresh, so that it will sprinkle the air with fragrance and not the floor with needles, cut about an inch off the trunk to allow for absorption of water. Make the cut at an angle so the base of the tree will not set flat against the bottom of the tree holder. Also make a couple of cuts in the side of the trunk to expose more water-sucking veins. Don't stint on container size—one that holds a gallon of water is good—or frequency of watering. Place the tree in the coolest part of the room.

◻ A living tree has its own special charm. Look for one labeled "root pruned," which has had its root growth stimulated by aboveground cutting for several months previous. Acclimatize it for a day or two by leaving it on a cool porch or garage, and water it thoroughly before bringing it inside. Keep it away from heat and drafts, and at the end of the holidays, return it to the porch for two days before planting it in the hole you dug before the ground froze.

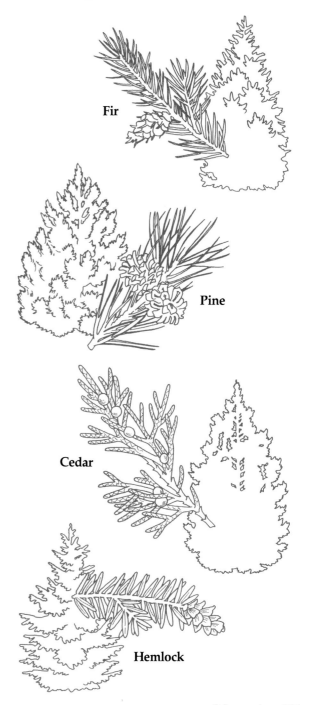

Fir

Pine

Cedar

Hemlock

□ The cut tree, too, has its uses after the Christmas season. If you have room in your backyard, your tree will make a fine bird and chipmunk shelter and feeder, especially if you stock it with bread crusts, popcorn and suet. Or sink it into a deep pond or stream to form a refuge area for fish.

□ If you're handy with pruning shears and a bow saw, cut up the branches and use them for mulch. You can burn the trunk in your fireplace. When you burn fir wood, it will hiss and pop; it's best to mix it with hardwood logs.

□ Your town or city probably has a recycling center where trees can be turned into valuable chips for mulch. Some centers let you pick up mulch for use in your own garden, or they donate it to public parks and playgrounds. You can find recycling centers listed in your local telephone directory. Your tree can keep on contributing for many seasons to come.

OLD-FASHIONED AND NEW-FANGLED TREE TRIMS AND ACCESSORIES

□ Add an old-time touch with strings of popcorn or cranberries. For a sweet new twist, string jelly beans or gummy bears. Try stringing any of the above on wire, then bend the wire into hearts, wreaths or stars.

□ Remember making chain loop garlands from strips of paper as a child? Trim your tree with this more sophisticated version. Get the family involved with gluing loops made from strips of Christmas wrapping papers or plaid ribbon.

□ Spray-paint pine cones with gold or silver paint. Add hangers, then tie red and green ribbons into bows and hot-glue them at the base of the hanger.

□ Pine cones can be used for a variety of projects. Keep in mind that not all types will be found growing in the same region. A pine cone swap with a friend living in a different state will expand your options.

Types of Pine Cones

Cedar
Cyprus
Deodar cedar
Fir
Hemlock
  Eastern
  Western
Larch
Pine
  Lodgepole
  Norway
  Pinyon
  Ponderosa
  Scotch
  White
Redwood
Sequoia
Spruce

□ For a Colonial or traditional decorating scheme, dried pomegranates are an authentic touch. To dry, simply place the fruit in a dry, dark place for several months. Or, showcase fresh ones on a table in an airy location and allow them to dry while on display. Dwarf pomegranates make lovely little ornaments hung by golden threads on the holiday tree.

□ Create hanging bouquets of dried plants by simply tying bundles with rustic twine or fancy ribbons. Hang one on a door, stair post or any other spot where you want a little Christmas cheer. Small ones can be tied to a brass drawer pull, large ones can be hung in place of wreaths above the fireplace.

□ Hang a wreath on every door *inside* the house and personalize each one. For example, attach toys to a wreath for a child's bedroom or tie sugar cookies to a wreath in the kitchen.

□ The holiday patriotic theme is very popular now. Here's a few easy suggestions on ways to achieve the look:

1. Place greenery on the top of a picture. Add a trio of flags to the center of the greenery.

2. String red, white and blue Christmas lights on the tree. Popcorn and cranberry garlands will complete the patriotic color scheme.

3. Embellish your Christmas tree with red, white and blue bows.

4. Choose candles in patriotic colors.

POINSETTIAS

The traditional Christmas plant has come a long way in the past 20 years. Not long ago the poinsettia took its place right next to the Christmas tree out on the curb after the holidays. That's not the case anymore. Here's 10 steps for success with poinsettias.

1. Select plants with green foliage all the way down to the soil line. This is a good indication that the plants have active, healthy roots.

2. Look for plants that have small green buttons (cyathia) in the center of the colored bracts. These buttons will eventually develop into little yellow flowers.

3. When transporting the plants home, make sure they are protected from temperatures below 50 degrees Fahrenheit. Chilling causes the leaves to drop.

4. Place in a room where there is sufficient natural light to read fine print. You should be able to observe a strong shadow with your hand.

5. Water plants thoroughly when you get them home. The entire soil area should be saturated so that water seeps through the drain hole. Never allow poinsettias to sit in water.

6. Check the plants daily and water only when the soil feels dry.

7. Fertilize plants within several days. They are without nutrients during the entire marketing process and will need a feeding by then. Use liquid, pills, sticks or dry fertilizer according to the directions on the label.

8. If you keep curtains drawn during the day to conserve heat, remember that poinsettias must have at least six hours of bright indirect light daily to thrive.

9. Keep plants away from drafts, radiators and hot air registers.

10. To prolong bright color of bracts, temperature should not exceed 72 degrees Fahrenheit in the day or 60 degrees Fahrenheit at night.

HOLIDAY SAFETY

Because the Christmas season has become such a hectic holiday, many of us get so tied up in the rush of buying presents or fixing our homes "just right" that safety sometimes takes a back seat to convenience. Follow these simple rules to keep your home safe.

□ If you have children in your home, keep them in mind when you decorate. All electrical lights and cords should be kept out of the reach of infants and small ones who might want to explore the tree. Although frail, beautiful decorations are tempting to have at home; keep in mind that only unbreakable decorations should be used when a child can reach and possibly break them. And make sure that Christmas bulbs, tree decorations or parts of a manger scene aren't too small since many children will be tempted to put them in their mouths.

□ When purchasing lights for your tree, be sure they are UL approved. Many inexpensive lights aren't. This listing is the consumer's assurance that their lights are safe for their intended use. If you're using a live tree, make sure the lights you use are intended for that purpose.

□ Any light and/or electric cords should be in excellent condition. If they are frayed, cracked or otherwise damaged, throw them away. When using extension cords, don't overload them. Run cords along walls, not under carpets or where people might trip or walk on them.

□ For outside decorating, use only outdoor lights; never use indoor lights outside. Outside lights are specially made to withstand the elements, unlike indoor lights.

□ Nothing feels as much like Christmas as a fire crackling in the fireplace, but don't light up until your fireplace and chimney have been professionally cleaned. Burn only fireplace-safe materials; newspapers and torn wrapping paper are not safe for kindling because they carry hot ashes out through the chimney. Dispose of fireplace ashes in metal containers; never store them in the house.

□ Finally, check your smoke detectors. With all the potential fire starters that holidays add, now is the time to replace dead batteries. Put a smoke detector outside each sleeping area and on each level of the home.

Visions of
Sugarplums

A Season for Trimming
Decorating

When it comes to Christmas tree decorations, every family has its trademark. For some, it's that special star at the peak of the tree. Others collect crystal or ceramic ornaments.

In my family, it was icicles.

They weren't real, of course, but the kind you bought at the five-and-dime store. Made of aluminum foil, the icicles were fragile, so they had to be draped over the branches one at a time. As a result, only a select few family members had ever been allowed to participate in this holiday ritual—my father, mother, and big brother Russell, who was ten. Of course, there were lots of other decorations, so there were plenty for everyone to do. That particular year, I could hardly wait to get started.

"Ho, ho, ho! Merry Christmas!" my father called out. He was balanced on a stepladder, hanging lights around the tree, while my mother held onto the back of his pants.

I was poised nearby, six years old, filled with energy, eggnog, and two slices of fruitcake.

"Now?" I asked my mother.

"Not yet, sweetheart."

Finally the lights were hung. My father plugged them in, and all at once the world started to glow.

"Now!" said Russell.

He and I plunged into the box of decorations and came out with handfuls of reflectors, which we fastened behind each of the lights. My parents hung the ornaments, spacing them evenly around the tree. Carol, my three-year-old sister, set up the Nativity scene, with the Joseph that had been glued back together and the wise man who was missing a nose. We were accompanied, as always, by Christmas carols courtesy of the Boston Pops, a group that may have been named for the surface noise on the record.

Then it was time for the icicles.

My father opened the package and gave bunches of them to Russell and my mother. Then, to my amazement, he handed some to me.

"I think you're old enough this year," he said, winking at me.

It was one of the proudest moments of my life. I was an icicle hanger!

I don't remember much of what happened after that. I know we must have opened presents and eaten turkey that year, but all I could think about was the tree. I spent the holiday in tree-trimming heaven, a magical place where smiles are bright, branches never bend, and Christmas trees sparkle with the spirit of the season.

If the icicles are hung properly.

Raffia Angel

Sublime is the only word to describe this angelic creation in eyelet, lace, and raffia. She's a wonderful accent to a newel post anchoring a bannister garland, and she would also be lovely gracing a tree top, mantel arrangement, or any other featured spot in your decor.

MATERIALS

Raffia
Hot glue gun
1 (3-inch diameter) craft foam ball
2/3 yard (45-inches wide) ecru eyelet fabric
1 1/2 yards (3-inch wide) ecru pregathered lace
21 inches heavy gauge wire
2 1/4 yards (1 1/2-inch wide) pregathered ecru lace
8 inches (1/8-inch wide) elastic
Thin quilt batting
Spanish moss
4 1/2 yards (1/8-inch wide) ecru satin ribbon
Dried and satin flowers
See Patterns

DIRECTIONS

◻ Gather a bundle of raffia and tie in middle with a raffia strip.

◻ Glue knot to top of craft foam ball and spread raffia evenly around ball to completely cover foam. Tie off around bottom of ball with a raffia strip to make head.

◻ Add more raffia if needed to make streamers 28 inches long from neck.

◻ Cut one 14-by-32-inch piece from eyelet fabric. Cut one 32-inch long piece of 3-inch wide lace. Sew lace to 1 long edge of eyelet fabric with a 1/4-inch seam.

◻ Fold lace-edged eyelet in half with right sides facing and short ends aligned and stitch short ends together with a 1/2-inch seam.

◻ Turn and run a gathering stitch along remaining raw edge. Slip dress over angel head and gather to fit neck.

◻ Cover wire with raffia strips for arms. Fold ends up for hands, and use a piece of raffia to lash strips tightly beginning 1 inch from folded ends. Glue lashing in place in center.

◻ Cut one 8 1/2-by-21-inch piece from eyelet fabric for sleeves.

◻ Cut two 8 1/2-inch long pieces of 1 1/2-inch wide lace. Sew to short ends of fabric with a 1/4-inch seam.

◻ Fold lace-edged fabric in half lengthwise with right sides facing and sew long edge with a 1/2-inch seam.

◻ Cut two 4-inch long pieces from elastic. Zig-zag stitch elastic to inside of sleeves 2 inches from lace tips of sleeves.

◻ Turn and slip sleeve piece over raffia covered wire. Glue center of piece to top center back of angel and bend arms in curve to front.

◻ Cut one 5-inch diameter circle from eyelet fabric. Mark a line from center of circle to outside edge and cut.

◻ Cut one 16-inch long piece of 1 1/2-inch wide lace. Align ends of lace with cut opening in circle. Sew lace to outside edge with a 1/4-inch seam allowance.

◻ Turning raw edges under, wrap collar around angel's neck and glue overlap in back.

◻ Transfer wing pattern to eyelet fabric and cut out 2 wing pieces. Transfer wing pattern to batting and cut out 1 wing piece. Cut one 46-inch long piece of 1 1/2-inch wide lace.

◻ Baste lace to right side of 1 eyelet fabric wing piece with raw edges aligned and ruffled edge of lace to inside.

◻ Stack other eyelet fabric wing piece on this piece with right sides facing, and place batting wing piece on top. Sew through all layers with a 1/2-inch seam, leaving an opening at bottom for turning wing.

◻ Trim excess batting from seam, clip curves, and turn. Slipstitch opening closed.

◻ Glue wings to back of angel.

◻ Make a loose garland around head with Spanish moss. Loop six 3-inch pieces of ecru satin ribbon around garland and glue ribbon ends to raffia.

◻ Make a small bow with one 7-inch long piece of ecru ribbon and glue to moss. Glue dried flowers randomly through moss.

◻ Cut one 20-inch long piece from satin ribbon and tie in a bow around angel's neck.

◻ Gather a bouquet of dried and ribbon flowers, leaving 3 inches on stems. Run a gathering stitch along gathered edge of remaining 3-inch lace. Slip over bouquet stems with gathered edge toward flowers and finished end toward stem ends. Pull gathers tightly to fit and tie off.

◻ Turn lace up to encircle flowers.

◻ Cut one 14-inch long piece of satin ribbon. Thread ends through looped angel hands and tie around lace at base of bouquet to hold in place. Tie a multi-looped bow with long streamers around base of bouquet with any remaining satin ribbon.

Bird Feeder Wreath

*E*xtend your holiday goodwill to the treetops with a wreath that contains a birdseed holder. Our version begins with a grapevine wreath that is embellished with natural materials you can cut from your own yard or purchase from your local nursery—fir, holly, magnolia, aucuba, nandina, and ivy. The feeder is a small, plastic-lined basket that's wired to the wreath. It's then surrounded by wisteria and honeysuckle vines, which are woven around it to resemble a nest. Last, we wired on a bright red bow and a couple of artificial birds. For an even easier version, fill a shallow basket with seed, embellish the handle, and choose a spot to hang it that will give you a good view of the activity inside.

Patriotic Angel Tree Topper

*I*f you're decorating with a patriotic theme and you want glorious red, white, and blue accents from the treetop down, this angel topper is just the heavenly spirit to sit on high. As every quilter will know, her pieced skirt is based on the Dresden plate pattern, and her star-studded finery can put to good use the scraps from any other Americana decorations you might make.

MATERIALS

Scrap of muslin
Polyester stuffing
1/4 yard (45-inch wide) blue star print fabric
1 (10-by-14-inch) piece ecru star print fabric
1 (10-by-14-inch) piece red star print fabric piece
Blue thread
26 inches (2-inch wide) ecru lace
Hot glue gun
Spanish moss
1¼ yards (1/8-inch wide) blue satin ribbon
See Patterns

DIRECTIONS

□ Transfer pattern for head to muslin, and cut out 2.

□ Sew together, leaving bottom open, and turn. Stuff firmly, and slipstitch opening closed.
□ Transfer pattern for skirt to blue, ecru, and red fabrics twice. Cut out 6 pieces, 2 from each print.
□ Sew skirt pieces together along long sides with right sides facing, alternating prints.
□ Stitch along scalloped edge with blue thread with sewing matchine set on appliqué. Clip fabric close to stitching line.
□ Fold top edge under ½ inch, and stitch to head.
□ Cut one 2-by-12-inch piece from blue print fabric. Fold in half lengthwise with right sides facing, and stitch together along long edge. Turn and tie knot in middle of tube for hands.
□ Turn ends of tube to inside. Tack ends to sides of dress ½ inch below head.
□ Run a gathering stitch along one long edge of lace. Gather to fit around neck, and tack to angel head just above top of dress.
□ Cover top and sides of head with glue, and attach Spanish moss.
□ Tie 30 inches of blue satin ribbon in a bow, and glue to front of lace collar.
□ Loop remaining blue ribbon around head for a halo, and glue to back of head.
□ Cut two 6-by-10-inch pieces from blue print for wings. Stitch together leaving an opening for turning with right sides facing.
□ Turn and slipstitch opening closed. Run a gathering stitch through middle of rectangle, parallel with short sides. Gather and glue gathered line to back of angel's head.

Stars and Stripes Ornaments

*T*hese Old Glory ornaments wave proudly from wreaths and trees. If you're decorating with an Americana theme, these little ornaments go together in a snap. Preprinted flag material is the secret. And when the season is over, put them where you can find them next summer—they're perfect for Fourth of July decorations, too!

MATERIALS

Purchased flag material
Polyester batting
Muslin
White quilting thread and quilting needle
1/4-inch wide blue satin ribbon
Note: Buy equal amounts of flag material, batting, and muslin, and 7 inches of ribbon per ornament

DIRECTIONS FOR STARS AND STRIPES ORNAMENT

□ Cut around flag leaving a 1/8-inch seam allowance.
□ Use flag as pattern to cut out batting and muslin.
□ Stack flag right side up, batting, and muslin.
□ Stitch, leaving an opening for turning. Turn, and blind-stitch closed.
□ Quilt along stripes and blue field.
□ Fold 7 inches of ribbon into loop, and tack to top for hanger.

Folk Art Santa Tree Trimming

This Santa can conceal himself in the woods and watch naughty and nice goings-on unobserved. Only when he blows his bugle, will you know he's there. Like all things inspired by folk art, he's simply made of bits and pieces, but he carries a big dose of imagination. Perhaps that's why folk art stays so popular. Make this little ornament, and you'll have a piece of the magic yourself.

MATERIALS

Tracing paper
Graphite or carbon paper
Scrap of 1/4-inch plywood
Jigsaw or bandsaw
Drill with 1/4-inch drill bit
Sandpaper
Tack cloth
Acrylic Paints: Spruce Green, White, Beige, Black, Dark Red
Paint brushes: medium flat, liner
Hot glue gun
1 (2-inch long) toy bugle
3 inches (1/8-inch wide) red satin ribbon
1 (9-inch) piece of thin jute rope
See Patterns

DIRECTIONS

□ Transfer pattern onto tracing paper. Place graphite paper between pattern and plywood scrap. Trace over pattern to transfer image.
□ Cut along outlines with jigsaw or bandsaw.
□ Drill a hole 3/4 inch from top.
□ Smooth plywood lightly with sandpaper. Wipe with tack cloth.

□ Apply 1 coat of green paint to both sides of ornament. Let dry.
□ Apply a second coat of paint, if desired. Let dry.
□ Paint as indicated on pattern, dabbing white paint to create wooly effect. Paint eyes, mouth, and mustache with liner brush.
□ Glue small bugle on hands. Make small bow with 1/8-inch wide ribbon and glue on bugle.
□ Thread jute through hole and tie for hanger.

Crazy-Quilt Americana Stocking

If you've made several decorations with Americana fabrics, you probably have lots of scraps. Tie your handmades together by stitching up this crazy-quilt stocking. You can make your pieces fit together any way you like, getting all the mileage possible out of them.

MATERIALS

Scraps of Americana fabrics
7 inches (1/4-inch wide) red satin ribbon
See Patterns

DIRECTIONS

□ Transfer stocking pattern to fabric of choice for backing and cut out.
□ Cut one 6-by-17-inch piece of fabric to make stocking cuff.
□ Cut fabric pieces for stocking front and sew together with a 1/4-inch seam. Transfer stocking pattern to pieced front and cut out.
□ Sew stocking front to back with right sides facing. Turn.
□ Fold cuff piece in half with right sides facing and short ends together. Stitch short ends with a 1/4-inch seam. Turn and fold tube in half with wrong sides facing. Slip over stocking with folded edge down and all raw edges aligned. Sew with a 1/4-inch seam, turn cuff up, and press.
□ Fold satin ribbon into loop, and tack ends to inside back of stocking for hanger.

Patriotic Angel Tree Topper, Stars and Stripes Ornaments, Folk Art Santa Tree Trimming, Crazy-Quilt Americana Stocking, Wooden Star Santa, Roly-Poly Americana Santa, Americana Angel, Patriotic Santa Angel, pages 108, 110, 113 and 114

Wooden Star Santa

*B*ased on Santas in folklore, this little fellow looks like he could have come from an old trunk in the attic instead of your workbench. You'll want to raid the scraps in the wood shop and make a galaxy of these star ornaments. For variety, try varnished candy canes, doll-sized toys or tiny wrapped presents in place of this Santa's pine sprig.

MATERIALS

Tracing paper
Graphite or carbon paper
Scrap of 1/4-inch plywood
Jigsaw or band saw
Drill with 1/4-inch drill bit
Sandpaper
Clean, dry cloth
Acrylic Paints: Burnt Sienna, Ivory, Tan, Gold Metallic, Black
Paint brushes: medium flat, liner
1 (1-inch long) artificial pine sprig
Hot glue gun
1 (5-inch) piece of beige cotton yarn
1 (9-inch) piece of thin jute rope
See Patterns

DIRECTIONS

☐ Transfer pattern onto tracing paper. Place graphite paper between pattern and plywood scrap. Trace over pattern to transfer image.
☐ Cut along outlines with jigsaw or band saw. Drill a hole 3/4 inch from tip on one point.
☐ Sand all surfaces and edges to even cuts. Brush off any dust with clean, dry cloth.
☐ Apply one coat of burnt sienna paint to both sides of ornament. Let dry.
☐ Apply a second coat of paint, if desired. Let dry.
☐ Paint details on face, hands and feet as indicated on pattern. Dab ivory paint to create fur effect. Shade ivory with light dabs of gold metallic paint. Paint eyes, mouth and mustache with liner brush as indicated on pattern.

Stars and Stripes Ornaments, Folk Art Santa Tree Trimming, Crazy-Quilt Americana Stocking, Wooden Star Santa, Roly-Poly Americana Santa, Americana Angel, Patriotic Santa Angel, pages 108, 110, 113 and 114

☐ Glue pine sprig between beard and waist indentation. Tie yarn around waist and over sprig.
☐ Thread jute through hole and tie for hanger.

Roly-Poly Americana Santa

*P*lop this rotund little cutie anywhere that you want to add a cheery note to your holiday decorations.

MATERIALS

1/8 yard (45-inch wide) muslin
1/4 yard (45-inch wide) red star print fabric
Scraps of navy star print fabric
Scrap of pink fabric
Polyester stuffing
Fusible web
Acrylic paints: Dark Blue, White, Red
Small round paintbrush
See Patterns

DIRECTIONS

☐ Tea-dye muslin and tear into 1/2-inch wide strips.
☐ Transfer patterns to fabric, and cut out 4 red body pieces, 2 navy mittens, and 1 pink face piece. Sew 2 red pieces together along 1 long side with right sides facing and raw edges aligned. Repeat for remaining 2 red pieces.
☐ Place 2 red halves together, and stitch remaining 2 sides, leaving an opening at bottom for turning.
☐ Turn, stuff firmly, and slipstitch closed.
☐ Transfer face and mitten patterns to fusible web and cut out.
☐ Fuse fabric mittens and face to body following manufacturer's directions, referring to photograph for placement.
☐ Paint eyes blue with white highlights and nose red.
☐ Sew a muslin strip around head at top of face with a running stitch, referring to photograph for placement. Sew another muslin strip around body 1/2-inch below hands.
☐ Cut two 1 1/2-inch long pieces of muslin. Turn ends under 1/4 inch, and sew to straight sides of gloves with a running stitch.
☐ Loop lengths of muslin 2 1/2-inches long and sew to face for beard. Begin and end at muslin strip above face.
☐ Loop an 8-inch long muslin strip into 1 1/2-inch loops and tack to top of head.

Americana Angel

*T*he twinkle in this angel's eye outshines even the galaxy of stars spangling her wings and plump little body. Americana angel is a happy addition to any decorating scheme.

MATERIALS

1/3 yard red star print fabric
Polyester stuffing
Scrap of muslin
Scrap of blue star print fabric
Thin quilt batting
Fabric paints: Red, White, Blue
Liner paintbrush
Hot glue gun
Spanish moss
18 inches (1/8-inch wide) blue satin ribbon
27 inches thin jute
White quilting thread and quilting needle
See Patterns

DIRECTIONS

□ Cut one 10-inch circle from red print fabric.
□ Turn raw edges 1-inch to wrong side and stitch with gathering stitch.
□ Gather, loosely stuff, and tie off thread.
□ Transfer head and wing patterns to fabric. Cut 2 head pieces from muslin. Cut 2 wing pieces from blue fabric and 2 wing pieces from thin batting.
□ Sew 2 head pieces together, leaving opening at bottom for turning.
□ Clip curves, turn, and stuff firmly. Slipstitch opening closed.
□ Paint eyes, cheek hearts, and mouth as indicated on pattern.
□ Cover top and back of head with hot glue, and attach Spanish moss. When dry, trim as desired.
□ Cut one 12-inch long piece of blue ribbon. Tie around head for halo.
□ Glue head to body.
□ Place jute around gathered line on body, and tie in bow in front.
□ Stack 2 wing pieces with right sides facing and batting piece on top. Stitch with a 1/4-inch seam, leaving an opening at bottom for turning.
□ Trim excess batting from seam, clip curves, and turn. Slipstitch closed.
□ Quilt around wings 1/4 from edge.
□ Loop remaining blue ribbon for hanger, and glue to center top of wings.
□ Glue hanger side of wings to back of angel.

Patriotic Santa Angel

*B*old white stars on a red field make a big impact for such a little Santa angel. His patriotism shines forth from tree or mantel.

MATERIALS

Scraps of muslin
Scraps of red star print fabric
Polyester stuffing
Black and red fine tip permanent markers
Pink blush makeup
1 (1/2-inch diameter) jingle bell
Hot glue gun
Scraps of fleece
Raffia
8 inches unbleached cotton string
See Patterns

DIRECTIONS

□ Transfer face pattern to muslin and cut out 2. Transfer body and cap patterns to red print fabric and cut out 2 body pieces and 1 cap piece.
□ Tea-dye remaining muslin and tear into 1/4-inch wide strips.
□ Sew 2 head pieces together, leaving bottom open for turning. Turn, stuff firmly and slipstitch closed.
□ Make black eyes and red nose as indicated on pattern with markers. Tint cheeks with blush.
□ Sew 2 body pieces together with right sides facing, leaving an opening at top for turning.
□ Turn, and stuff firmly.
□ Fold long sides of cap together with right sides facing and stitch with a 1/4-inch seam. Turn right side out. Position seam in center back and press. Tack jingle bell to tip.
□ Fold top edges of body 1/4 inch to inside. Slip head into opening and slipstitch head to body.
□ Slip cap over head 1/4 inch above eyes and glue in place.
□ Cut one 1/2-by-5-inch piece of fleece and glue around head, covering edge of cap above eyes.
□ Loop muslin strips into 1- to 2-inch pieces for beard, and tack to face, beginning and ending at fleece cap brim.
□ Gather a small bunch of 18-inch long raffia, and tie in bow for wings.
□ Tie string into loop for hanger and glue to back of raffia bow. Glue hanger side of bow to back of ornament below fleece.

Santa Pod and Stick Ornaments

Stars and Stripes Ornaments, Americana Angel, Santa Pod and Stick Ornaments, Patriotic Santa Tree Skirt, pages 108, 114, 115 and 116

Have a couple of okra pods that didn't wind up in the gumbo? How about a few spare cinnamon sticks? Pull out the paints and make some adorable Santa ornaments!

MATERIALS FOR SANTA POD ORNAMENT

Dried okra pod
Acrylic paints: Burnt Sienna, Beige, White, Black, Burnt Umber
Small round paintbrush
Hot glue gun
7 inches thin jute

DIRECTIONS

□ Paint entire pod with burnt sienna paint. Let dry.
□ Paint Santa's face beige approximately ⅓ way down pod.
□ Dab white paint for beard and cap fringe.
□ Dab on black eyes and a burnt sienna mouth. Let dry.
□ Antique ornament by wiping on diluted burnt umber paint.
□ Glue looped jute to back of ornament for hanger.

Cinnamon stick
Acrylic paints: Dark Red, Beige, White, Black, Gold
Paintbrushes: small round, liner
Sand or cornmeal
5 inches thin gold cord
Hot glue gun

DIRECTIONS

☐ Paint entire stick with dark red paint. Let dry.
☐ Paint Santa's face beige approximately 1/4 of the way down. Mix a dab of sand or cornmeal into some white paint, and paint cap fringe. Paint beard white. Paint black eyes, red nose and mouth with liner brush, referring to photograph for placement.
☐ Paint black belt below beard. Paint gold square for buckle on center of belt.
☐ Paint fringe on bottom of jacket below belt with sand and white paint mixture. Paint end of cinnamon stick black for feet.
☐ Loop gold cord and glue inside stick for hanger.

Patriotic Santa Tree Skirt

*I*f you collect patriotic ornaments, this tree skirt is perfect to set off your collection. It's decorated with appliquéd Santas with rag strip beards. The thick batting makes it so cuddly, you might find an eager child curled up on it waiting for the real Santa to make an appearance.

MATERIALS

1¼ yards (45-inch wide) navy star print fabric
2 yards (45-inch wide) muslin
1¼ yards polyester quilt batting
1/4 yard (45-inch wide) red star print fabric
Scraps of pink cotton fabric
6 (3/8-inch diameter) black shank buttons
3 (1/2-inch diameter) red pom-poms
4 yards (1½-inch wide) white pregathered eyelet lace
White embroidery floss
16 inches (1/4-inch wide) green satin ribbon
See Patterns

DIRECTIONS

☐ Cut 45-inch circles from navy, muslin and batting.
☐ Transfer patterns to red print fabric and pink fabric. Cut out 3 hats and 3 faces.

☐ Divide navy fabric circle into quarters and mark using long running stitch and white thread.
☐ Center appliqués on 3 of the stitched lines 8 inches from edge of circle. Slip faces 1/8-inch under bottom edges of hats and pin in place. Remove white marking thread under faces and hats.
☐ Set sewing machine for appliqué. Appliqué hats to fabric using satin stitch and red thread.
☐ Tear three 10-by-12-inch pieces from muslin.
☐ Run a gathering stitch parallel to 10-inch sides, 5 inches from edge of muslin. Gather and arrange along bottom of Santa faces, 1/4 inch from edge with 5-inch side toward hat and 7-inch side toward edge of skirt. Machine stitch in place on gathering line.
☐ Tear beards every 1/2 inch, stopping 1/4 inch from stitching line.
☐ Tear three 3/4-by-6½-inch muslin strips. Position along bottom of hats, centered lengthwise over hats and faces, and zig-zag stitch in place.
☐ Sew button eyes and pom-pom noses to faces, referring to photograph for placement.
☐ Tear nine 3/4-by-4-inch muslin strips. Fold groups of 3 strips in half, and tack along fold to top of hats.
☐ Baste lace around outside edge of skirt top with raw edges aligned and lace turned toward inside beginning at remaining quarter mark.
☐ Lay top over muslin circle and batting circle. Cut through all layers from edge to center of skirt along quarter mark. Cut a 2½-inch circle in center of skirt through all layers.
☐ Stack skirt top right side up, muslin piece, and batting piece. Stitch along all raw edges with a 1/2-inch seam, leaving an opening for turning along 1 straight side of opening.
☐ Trim excess batting from seam, clip curves, and turn. Slipstitch opening closed.
☐ Cut green ribbon into two 8-inch long pieces for skirt ties. Turn 1 end under 1/4 inch and tack to edge of opening at inside circle. Repeat on opposite side for other tie.
☐ Tack through all layers with short lengths of white embroidery floss, and knot on top to tuft skirt.

Wooden Sheep Cutouts

*P*ut a gentle gathering of sheep out to graze in your yard this holiday season. They're fashioned from wood and shearling, and dressed up for Christmas with bright bows and greenery.

MATERIALS FOR WOODEN SHEEP CUTOUTS

1 (12-by-17-inch) piece 1/8-inch plywood, for small
 sheep
1 (14-by-24-inch) piece 1/8-inch plywood, for large
 sheep
Scroll saw or bandsaw
Sandpaper
Tack cloth
Black acrylic paint
1 (1-inch) bristle paintbrush
1 (12-by-24-inch) piece black or white shearling, for
 small sheep
1 (14-by-20-inch) piece white shearling, for large sheep

Scrap of black shearling
Craft glue
White contact paper
2 (3/4-by-61/4-inch) metal stakes with nuts and bolts
Drill with bit same size as bolts
28 inches (1-inch wide) black or red satin ribbon, for
 small sheep
37 inches (11/2-inch wide) red satin ribbon, for large
 sheep
Hot glue gun
1 (3-inch long) artificial pine sprig
Berries, small cones
1 (11/4-inch diameter) red or gold bell
See Patterns

DIRECTIONS FOR SHEEP CUTOUTS

☐ Transfer body pattern to plywood and cut out. Sand lightly, and wipe with tack cloth.
☐ Paint sheep with 2 coats black paint. Let dry.
☐ Transfer coat and ear patterns to shearling, reverse, and transfer 1 each again. Cut out 2 white or black coat pieces and 2 black ear pieces.
☐ Stitch coat pieces together along top back with right sides facing. Turn.
☐ Cover sides of sheep with glue, and slip shearling coat over wood sheep.
☐ Position ears under edge of coat, referring to photograph for placement. Glue ears in place.
☐ Slipstitch coat together from chest to front leg and between front and back legs.
☐ Transfer eye pattern to white contact paper. Cut out 2 eyes, peel off backing, and press in place on sheep face, as indicated on pattern.
☐ Drill holes in legs for stakes, and attach stakes to sheep legs.
☐ Tie ribbon bow around sheep's neck. Tack to shearling at bow.
☐ Glue pine sprig, berries, and cone to bow, referring to photograph for placement.
☐ Tack bell to ribbon under chin.

Santa Wall Decoration

Recycling has really taken off lately, but crafters have always known that empty containers can be treasures. This Santa is made from a used plastic bottle. Cut in half from top to bottom, it makes a perfect form for his round pink face and bright red cap. If you aren't already recycling, this is a good place to start!

MATERIALS

1 empty (1-gallon) plastic bleach bottle, well-rinsed
1 (5-by-9-inch) pink felt piece
Craft glue
1 (14-by-20-inch) red felt piece
1 (1¼-inch diameter) white pom-pom
White yarn
White pipe cleaners
Large nail
2 (1-inch diameter) purchased eyes
1 (1¼-inch diameter) red pom-pom
Red pipe cleaner
See Patterns

DIRECTIONS

☐ Cut bottle in half from top to bottom, cutting through half of handle.
☐ Glue pink felt on side of bottle centered between side edges and 2 inches from bottom edge.
☐ Transfer pattern for hat to red felt and cut out 2. Sew sides together with a ¼-inch seam and turn. Tack white pom-pom to tip.
☐ Slip over top of bottle until bottom is ½-inch from pink felt. Glue in place.
☐ Wrap white yarn in approximately twenty 3½-inch long loops to make fringe on cap.
☐ Fold a white pipe cleaner over middle of bunch and twist tightly.
☐ Punch a hole through bottle in space between cap and face with large nail. Insert pipe cleaner ends through hole.
☐ Continue across bottle to completely cover side edges of bottle and fill space between cap and face.
☐ Twist pipe cleaner ends together across row to secure on wrong side of bottle.
☐ Trim pipe cleaners and bend flat.
☐ Continue around bottle to make beard, increasing size of loops from approximately 6 inches long to approximately 16 inches at center front of beard.
☐ Trace around 1 eye onto scrap of red felt. Cut out circle for mouth.
☐ Position eyes, nose, and mouth on face, and glue in place.
☐ Make an 8-inch long yarn loop, and attach between nose and mouth for mustache.
☐ Make a hole through felt cap and bottle about 1 inch from top on wrong side of face. Loop red pipe cleaner through it and twist ends together to make hanger.

Potpourri Pine Cone and Cinnamon Stick Garland

The scents of the season will fill your home deliciously when you hang this heady garland. Swag a fireplace with it, and the heat of your hearth will release even more of the fragrance. And if the perfume fades in future years, just lightly wipe the sticks with fine sandpaper and sprinkle a bit of essential oil onto the pine cones.

MATERIALS FOR PINE CONE GARLAND

10-inch long cinnamon sticks
1/8-inch wide satin ribbon in desired color
Hot glue gun
Potpourri
Paper bag
Pine cones
Spray adhesive
1 1/2-inch wide ribbon in desired color

DIRECTIONS

□ Lay out number of cinnamon sticks for desired length of garland.

□ Cut 2-inch long pieces of 1/8-wide ribbon, and glue ribbon ends to cinnamon sticks to link.
□ Glue 12-inch long pieces of same ribbon to ends of garland for attaching to mantel.
□ Crumble potpourri into small pieces, and place in a paper bag.
□ Coat pine cones thoroughly with spray adhesive, and shake in bag of potpourri. Let dry.
□ Glue 12-inch lengths of 1/8-inch wide ribbon to tops of pine cones.
□ Make bows from 1 1/2-inch wide ribbon, and glue to tops of pine cones.
□ Tie 1 pine cone to garland between each cinnamon stick.

Museum of American Folk Art, New York

Seasons Greetings

Wise Men Still Follow His Star

FROM ME TO THEE

Well-Feathered Birdhouses

*L*et your imagination take flight with purchased birdhouses decorated for the season. No matter what your particular craft skills are, you can show them off by cleverly embellishing houses and then nesting the results among your other seasonal decor.

MATERIALS FOR GINGERBREAD BIRDHOUSE

Purchased wooden birdhouse
Acrylic paint: White, Red, Green, Yellow, Blue
Paintbrushes: medium flat, small round, liner
3 purchased wooden gingerbread men
   (size to fit house)
Craft glue

DIRECTIONS

□ Paint roof and base of house white.
□ Paint red and white candy cane pattern along corners of house.
□ Paint wreath around hole.
□ Paint a door with garland around it, referring to photograph for placement. Let dry.
□ Paint gingerbread men as desired. Let dry.
□ Glue gingerbread men on front and sides of house as desired.

MATERIALS FOR MOSS-COVERED BIRDHOUSE

Acrylic paints: Green, Red
Purchased wooden birdhouse
Spray adhesive
Sphagnum moss
Hot glue gun
2 small artificial birds
Small purchased toys, foil-wrapped packages, stockings, candy canes, and wreath
Small purchased bird's nest
16 gauge florist's wire
Star ornament

Potpourri Pine Cone and Cinnamon Stick Garland, Moss-Covered Birdhouse, pages 118 and 121

DIRECTIONS

□ Thin acrylic paint with water and stain roof green and house red. Let dry.
□ Spray roof of house with spray adhesive and cover with sphagnum moss.
□ Glue a bird and package to roof, referring to photograph for placement.
□ Glue a bird inside opening so that head is peeking out. Glue a candy cane to bird's beak.
□ Push nest onto perch and glue to secure. Glue toys, packages, and candy canes to nest, referring to photograph for placement.
□ Glue wreath to house above opening.
□ Glue stockings to roof line.
□ Cut a 1-inch piece of wire. Glue 1 end to star ornament and other end to peak of roof.

Silent Mouse Stocking Holder

*T*his little wooden fellow evokes the spirit of the well-loved poem, *A Visit from Saint Nicholas,* even while he protects your mantel from damaging nail holes. Just survey the workshop for wood scraps, your fabric basket for a bit of wool, and your art table for a few drops of paint. Before you can name all the reindeer, you'll have a silent mouse stocking holder of your own!

MATERIALS

1 (1/2-inch-by 3-inch-by 9-inch) pine piece
1 (1-inch-by-3-inch-by-51/2-inch) pine piece
Scroll saw
Sandpaper
Wood glue
C-clamp or wood clamp
Drill with 1/4-inch bit
Tack cloth
Water base varnish
1 (4-inch, 1/4-inch diameter) screw-in metal hook
Acrylic paint: Quaker Grey, Black
Paintbrushes: medium flat, #12 shader brush
Black Tulip® Slick Paint
Scrap of dark grey wool
Fray Check™
Adhesive sealant (E-6000)
2 paper clips
12 inches (3/16-inch wide) red ribbon
See Patterns

DIRECTIONS FOR SILENT MOUSE STOCKING HOLDER

□ Cut wood according to patterns. Sand all pieces lightly. Glue smaller pieces to each side of the larger with wood glue. Clamp and let dry.
□ Drill a hole centered and 3/8 inch from back of body on the bottom of mouse for hook. Sand mouse again until smooth. Wipe with tack cloth.
□ Seal mouse with 1 coat varnish.
□ Sand the hook lightly. Paint mouse and hook with 2 to 3 coats of grey paint until smooth. Let dry.
□ Add a tiny amount of black paint to some grey and shade the mouse on all edges. Paint a 1/8-inch wide black line along front tip and sides of face for nose. Coat mouse and hook with varnish. Let dry.
□ Use Slick Paint to squeeze an eye on each side. Let dry.
□ Cut ears from wool. Use Fray Check™ around edges. Fold over base of each ear and glue with acrylic sealant as shown (Figure 13). Secure with a paper clip until dry. Remove clips and using a small amount of acrylic sealant, attach ears to mouse as indicated on pattern.
□ Screw hook into hole on base of mouse for tail.
□ Tie ribbon into a bow. Glue bow to base of tail with acrylic sealant.

Figure 13

● Drops of glue

Jumbo Christmas Stocking

*I*f you need lots of room for the goodies Santa's bringing, this is the stocking for you. Its bold burgundy and white design sparkles thanks to gold rickrack and shiny holiday braid accents. You'll enjoy the color it adds to your mantel; it's owner will appreciate all the bounty it holds on Christmas morning.

MATERIALS

1 yard (45-inches wide) white fabric
1/4 yard (45-inches wide) burgundy fabric
1 1/4 yards (1/2-inch) gold rickrack
23 inches Christmas braid
See Patterns

DIRECTIONS

□ Cut 4 stockings from white fabric using pattern. (2 pieces for stocking and 2 pieces for lining.)
□ Cut 1 cuff from burgundy fabric and 1 cuff from white fabric using pattern.
□ Cut 2 toe pieces from burgundy fabric using pattern.
□ Turn straight sides of toe pieces under 1/4 inch and press.
□ Position toe pieces on toes of 2 stockings with gold rickrack between toe piece and stocking, referring to photograph. Stitch 1/8 inch from edge along straight side, catching rickrack in seam.
□ Stitch along sides with a 1/2-inch seam allowance with right sides of stocking pieces facing, leaving top open. Turn.
□ Stitch remaining 2 stockings together with 1/2-inch seam allowance for lining, leaving top open. Do not turn.
□ Stitch white and burgundy cuff pieces together along scalloped edge with a 1/2-inch seam allowance. Turn and press.
□ Pin rickrack on white side of cuff along scallop so half of it extends past edge, referring to photograph. Stitch in place.
□ Fold short ends of cuff together with burgundy sides facing. Stitch short edge with a 1/2-inch seam. Do not turn.
□ Insert stocking lining inside stocking. Insert cuff in stocking so that raw edges of cuff and raw edges of stocking top are aligned. Pin in place. Stitch through all layers with a 1/2-inch seam allowance.
□ Turn cuff to outside of stocking and press.
□ Cut a 3-inch piece from braid, loop, and tack to inside back of stocking for hanger.
□ Tie knots in ends of remaining 20-inch piece of braid. Tie braid in bow and tack to cuff, referring to photograph for placement.

Gingerbread Birdhouse, Silent Mouse Stocking Holder, Jumbo Christmas Stocking, pages 121 and 122

Cheery Christmas Tree Tablecloth

Setting a festive table begins with a cheery tablecloth like this one. Plump little trees cut from a bright holiday print becomes appliqués that herald the season. And white eyelet edging adds a feminine touch. Hate to pack it away with the ornaments? You can keep enjoying your handiwork after the season has passed. Just flip the cloth over to its solid green back—St. Patrick's Day will be here before you know it!

MATERIALS

1¼ yards (45-inch wide) red fabric
½ yard (36-inch wide) holiday print fabric
Green thread
1¼ yards (45-inch wide) green fabric
4 yards (1-inch wide) pregathered white eyelet lace
See Patterns

DIRECTIONS

□ Cut one 45-inch circle from red fabric. Transfer tree pattern to holiday fabric and cut out 4 trees.
□ Position appliqués 3 inches from edge on right side of red circle as shown (Figure 14).
□ Set sewing machine for appliqué. Appliqué trees with green thread using satin stitch.
□ Cut one 45-inch circle from green fabric.
□ Pin green circle to red circle with right sides facing, inserting eyelet lace between layers around outside edge. Make sure all raw edges are aligned.
□ Sew with a ¼-inch seam allowance, leaving a 6-inch opening for turning. Clip seam and turn. Blind-stitch opening closed.

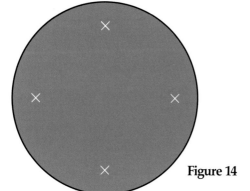

Figure 14

Santa-in-the-Moon Plate

This time of year the man in the moon sometimes bears a distinct resemblance to You Know Who. Here, Santa appears to be having one last nap before the big night begins. A purchased wooden serving plate reflects the light of our Santa moon thanks to a wink-of-the-eye application of acrylic paints protected by varnish. Top the server with a clear glass plate to hold holiday treats, or prop it on a plate stand to add a celestial note to your holiday decor.

MATERIALS

Tracing paper
Graphite or carbon paper
1 (14-inch diameter) wooden serving plate
Acrylic paints: Red, Royal Blue, White, Beige, Gold
Paintbrushes: medium flat, liner
Black paint pen
Clear spray varnish
See Patterns

DIRECTIONS

□ Transfer pattern onto tracing paper. Place graphite or carbon paper between pattern and plate. Trace over pattern to transfer image onto plate.
□ Paint as indicated. Let dry.
□ Add additional coats of paint until colors are desired brightness, letting paint dry thoroughly between coats.
□ Trace over details on Santa's hat, face, and beard with black paint. Let dry.
□ Finish with a light coat of clear spray varnish.

Lollipop Door Delights

Visions of sugarplums leave the world of fantasy to dance before your eyes each time you answer the call of the doorbell. It's not a dream. It's a dream-come-true door decoration. And these giant lollipops are guaranteed to sweeten each entry and exit without souring your budget or decorating timetable.

MATERIALS FOR LOLLIPOP DOOR DELIGHTS

White spray paint
2 (7/8-by-36-inch) dowels
2 (7/8-by-117/8-inch) styrofoam circles
Hot glue gun
Red cellophane wrapping paper
31/2 yards (7/8-inch wide) plaid satin ribbon
Green cellophane wrapping paper
3 yards (11/2-inch wide) white satin ribbon
3 yards (5/16-inch wide) green satin ribbon
Masking tape
Florist's wire

DIRECTIONS

□ Spray dowels with white paint. Let dry.
□ Cut a hole into the side of each styrofoam circle, wide enough and deep enough to fit end of the dowel snuggly into the hole.
□ Cover end of dowel with hot glue, and insert dowel into hole in styrofoam. Let dry.
□ Cover styrofoam with red cellophane, leaving 6 inches at bottom around dowel.
□ Gather cellophane around dowel like a lollipop wrapper. Tie with a small piece of plaid ribbon.
□ Repeat procedure with green cellophane to make second lollipop.
□ Form large multi-looped bow with white ribbon in back, green ribbon in middle and plaid ribbon in center of bow.
□ Cross dowels in an "X" shape.
□ Secure with masking tape at the intersection.
□ Wire multi-looped bow to dowels, covering masking tape.

Bandana Barnyard Animals

Howdy, pardner! Grab a critter and help decorate the tree. These barnyard ornaments are so cute, you'll want a corral-full. Shucks, you might even want to enter 'em in the county fair.

MATERIALS

Scraps of bandana fabric
Black perle cotton
Polyester stuffing
Pinking shears
Black buttons
See Patterns

DIRECTIONS

□ Fold fabric in half. Transfer animal pattern to fabric. Do not cut out.
□ Take small running stitches using 1 strand of black perle cotton around body along outline, leaving a small opening for stuffing. Do not clip thread.
□ Firmly stuff animal. Continue running stitches to close opening.
□ Cut with pinking shears around each animal, 1/4 inch outside stitching line.
□ Sew on button eyes.
□ Sew two 4-inch lengths of perle cotton through rear and knot in middle for tails.
□ Sew a 6-inch length of perle cotton through top and knot for hanger.

Doggone Cute Ornaments

Man's best friend inspired these happy little ornaments. Santa Fido is really a dog biscuit wearing felt accessories. Enlist the kids as workshop elves for extra fun. But when it comes time to hang the finished ornaments, you might want to make sure they're up high and out of temptation's way for your pup!

MATERIALS

Scraps of red and green felt
Craft glue
1 (21/2-inch long) dog biscuit
2 (1/2-inch diameter) white pom-poms
Purchased eyes
6-inches (1/4-inch wide) white satin ribbon
See Patterns

DIRECTIONS

□ Transfer hat, tongue, and bow tie patterns to red felt. Cut out.
□ Transfer ear patterns to green felt. Cut out.
□ Fold band of hat up 1/4 inch and glue to secure. Glue hat to end of biscuit.
□ Fold tip over to hatband and attach with glue. Glue 1 pom-pom to tip.
□ Position eyes, tongue, remaining pom-pom for nose, and bow tie on biscuit, and glue in place.
□ Glue white ribbon ends to each side of biscuit behind hatband.
□ Glue ears over ribbon.

Checker Bear Playmate

*M*any a joke has been told and many a problem solved over a good old-fashioned game of checkers. Little checker bear will look so cute propped up in a den or playroom that you won't be able to resist sitting down for a game, with all the closeness that goes along, on a regular basis.

MATERIALS

2 feet (1-by-12) pine shelving piece
Bandsaw or scroll saw
Sandpaper
Tack cloth
Walnut stain
Water base varnish
Tracing paper
Graphite or carbon paper
Acrylic paints: Red, White, Black
Paintbrushes: medium flat, small round
24 (1-inch diameter) wooden toy wheels
30 inches thin jute rope
See Patterns

DIRECTIONS

❑ Transfer pattern to wood, and cut out.
❑ Sand lightly, and wipe with tack cloth.
❑ Stain with walnut stain. Let dry.
❑ Apply a coat of water base varnish. Let dry.
❑ Transfer patterns for checkerboard, facial features, and bow tie onto tracing paper. Place graphite paper between pattern and bear. Trace over pattern to transfer image onto bear.
❑ Paint as indicated. Let dry.
❑ Paint 12 wheels black. Apply a coat of varnish to both unpainted and black wheel checkers.
❑ Thread checkers on jute rope, and knot ends of rope.

Fido Photo Ornaments

*P*rove your fidelity to Fido by hanging his picture on the tree. You shouldn't have any trouble enlisting your children's help on this project—not only will they enjoy working with pictures of their pets, it's quick and easy enough for even the shortest attention spans.

MATERIALS

Photograph of your dog
Mat board in desired color
Spray mount adhesive
Stickers
Dog biscuits
Scraps of ribbon
Craft glue

DIRECTIONS FOR SQUARE ORNAMENT

❑ Trim picture to desired size. Add 2 inches to horizontal and vertical measurements, and cut a piece of mat board this size.
❑ Spray mount adhesive to back of photograph, and center photo on front of mat board.
❑ Place stickers in corners.
❑ Glue biscuits between stickers on sides and top.
❑ Make a small bow with ribbon and glue to center bottom between stickers.
❑ Loop thin ribbon and glue to top back for hanger.

DIRECTIONS FOR RECTANGULAR ORNAMENT

❑ Mount photograph to mat board with spray adhesive.
❑ Trim to desired size.
❑ Make a large bow for top.
❑ Wrap thin ribbon around a dog biscuit and loop for hanger. Glue to center front of bow.

Jacob Bear's Christmas Ladder

*I*nvite a fluffy white bear into your home to frolic for the holidays. This ladder, decorated with greenery and little packages, is a heavenly backdrop for a happy teddy.

MATERIALS

4 small gold-wrapped packages
Hot glue gun
3 (5-by-7-inch) artificial greenery sprigs predecorated with pine cones, baby's-breath, and red berries
3 (7-by-9-inch) artificial greenery sprigs
1 (8-inch tall) white stuffed bear
1 (3-by-36-inch) red and green ladder
18 inches (5/16-inch wide) green satin ribbon
2 gold bells

DIRECTIONS FOR JACOB BEAR'S CHRISTMAS LADDER

☐ Glue 1 gold wrapped package to each predecorated greenery sprig.
☐ Glue each decorated sprig to the front of each large plain greenery sprig.
☐ Glue bear to center front of ladder.
☐ Glue 1 gold wrapped package to bear's right paw.
☐ Glue 2 greenery sprigs to ladder above bear.
☐ Glue 1 greenery sprig to ladder below bear.
☐ Cut satin ribbon into 2 pieces, 1 to measure 6 inches and 1 to measure 12 inches.
☐ Thread 1 gold bell onto each ribbon piece. Overlap ends around bottom rung of ladder and tie in knot.
☐ Glue ribbon to ladder rung to hold in place.

Naughty and Nice Wreath

There he is, checking it twice. Delight friends and family with your version of Santa's list on this novel holiday wreath. Best of all, you don't have to spend hours putting it together. You can use purchased decorations, old ornaments that might benefit from a new venue, and artificial greenery to make a wall or door decoration that's a keeper. To prevent the bow from getting crushed, stuff the loops with wadded paper before carefully packing it away. You'll earn a standing reservation at the top of Santa's nice list!

MATERAILS

Hot glue gun
Craft wire
Artificial greenery
Excelsior
Artificial clusters of berries
Pine cones
1 (22-inch diameter) grapevine wreath
1 large red bow
1 (35-inch long) adding machine tape piece
1 (12-inch) Santa doll
Miscellaneous ornaments

DIRECTIONS

☐ Glue and wire various lengths of greenery, bundles of excelsior, berries, and pine cones around wreath, referring to photograph.
☐ Wire bow to lower right-hand side of wreath.
☐ Write list of names on adding machine tape, and position it with Santa on the wreath, adjusting until it balances well with the bow. Wire Santa in place, and glue list in his hands.
☐ Fill in remaining spots with glued or wired ornaments and decorations, referring to photograph for placement.

Santa's Goodies Plate

Remember how you worried when you were little about putting out Santa's goodies? There had to be a nice big plateful and they had to be somewhere he couldn't miss seeing. This year, set your little elves' minds at rest with a festive goodies plate. A plain wooden serving plate, available at craft stores or kitchen shops, is easily transformed into the plate of honor. And the train cars nod to old-fashioned spongeware.

MATERIALS

1 (14-inch diameter) wooden serving plate
Acrylic paints: White, Red, Blue, Yellow, Green
Medium flat paintbrush
4 (1 1/8-inch-by-1 1/2-inch) synthetic or craft sponges
Black paint pen
Clear spray varnish
See Patterns

DIRECTIONS

☐ Paint top of plate white; let dry. Apply a second coat, if needed.
☐ Sponge blocks for train cars around edge of plate referring to photograph and using 1 sponge for each color. Let dry.
☐ Transfer train car details to sponged cars and lettering to center of charger using patterns. Paint details and letters with paint pen. Let dry.
☐ Finish with a light coat of clear spray varnish.

Love Knot Angel

Here's an angel that carries a lovely tradition. The rope forming her wings is looped in a Swedish love knot. Tradition has it that the love knot brings good luck and happiness to the home in which it hangs. Make a love knot angel for your home, and usher in 1993 with this sweet good luck charm watching over your shoulder.

MATERIALS

¹/4 yard (45-inch wide) muslin
Polyester stuffing
Fabric paint: Red, White, Light Blue
Liner paintbrush
³/4 yard (2-inch wide) pregathered ecru lace
Hot glue gun
Spanish moss
18 inches (¹/8-inch wide) ecru satin ribbon
18 inches (¹/8-inch wide) light blue satin ribbon
Pink satin ribbon rose
42 inches (³/8-inch thick) sisal rope
See Patterns

DIRECTIONS

◻ Transfer angel pattern to muslin and cut out 2 angel pieces.
◻ Stitch together with a ¹/4-inch seam, leaving bottom open for turning.
◻ Clip curves and turn. Stuff firmly, working stuffing well into hands. Slipstitch opening closed.
◻ Paint face according to pattern.
◻ Transfer pattern for dress to muslin and cut out 2 dress pieces. Stitch side seams from sleeve openings to skirt edge. Turn skirt edge under ¹/2 inch and press. Cut 18 inches of ecru lace. Position lace inside skirt with raw edge aligned with raw edge of skirt hem. Machine topstitch lace in place.
◻ Run gathering stitches along neck and sleeve openings on dress. Slip dress over angel. Gather openings to fit, tuck raw edges to inside, and tack to angel.
◻ Cover top and back of head with glue, and attach Spanish moss.
◻ Tie satin ribbon pieces into a bow and tack ribbon rose to knot. Glue to front of angel's dress.

◻ Tie remaining ecru lace into bow, and glue to back of angel's head.
◻ Loop rope into love knot as indicated (Figure 15). Glue to back of angel.

Figure 15

Sweetheart Frames

Small enough to tuck into a pocket, these little picture frames take on a special charm when their subject is a lovely snippet of lace. If you have an heirloom remnant, show it off on a field of deep cranberry velvet or crimson moire. But if your treasured pieces of lace are intact, you can get the same effect with purchased tatting and lace. Then let your imagination guide your display—prop a grouping on a dresser, loop ribbon around their supports and hang them from the tree, or attach them to a beautiful chain or ribbon and wear them around your neck. Once you've assembled a few of your own, you'll come up with dozens of ways to enjoy them.

Visions of
Sugarplums

A Season for Celebrating
Entertaining

Whenever I entertain during the holidays, my thoughts drift back to my grandmother.

Grandma had a favorite saying: "I never worry about being too rich or too thin." She was neither. Her home was modest. Her size was ample. Her favorite outfit was a comfortable housedress and an apron that was faded but clean. Her wrinkled face was not beautiful until you noticed her eyes. They carried the smile of a warm, welcoming soul.

When the holidays rolled around, Grandma would put on her Christmas apron, swap the red-and-white checked tablecloth for white linen, and open her door to the world. And the world came. Her house would fill up with people, with spirited conversation, with the good smells that accompany the foods of southern Italy. Stepping into her kitchen was like dancing through the pages of an Italian cookbook. Eggplant parmigiana. Fried cauliflower. Homemade Italian sausage. There was also a turkey, of course, but what was turkey without appetizers?

Holiday visitors always felt at home in Grandma's house. They would gather around the table and talk about the exorbitant price of produce; the good man (or woman) whom their daughter (or son) was dating; the untimely death of a friend from church. No topic was too trivial or too personal for the dinner table.

Whatever the conversation, Grandma's contribution was always the same: "What else can I get for you?"

No matter who you were—a next-door neighbor, the mailman, a business associate, an impressionable grandchild—the treatment was the same. You left energized, full of wonderful food and holiday spirit.

Despite Grandma's mild manner, chaos often threatened to take over. Perhaps because of all the Italian friends and relatives, the decibel level could reach ear-splitting proportions. Phones would ring. Dogs would bark. Friends would drop in unannounced with Christmas wishes. But Grandma remained rock solid and in control—the calm at the center of the storm.

Today, I'm far removed in time and place from those events at my grandmother's house. Grandma passed away more than a decade ago. When I entertain, I lean toward fine china and crystal, and recipes that come from a cookbook instead of from memory. But as this Christmas season approaches, I can't help but reflect on what I learned from this special woman.

The true secret of holiday entertaining is not in the food or the accessories. It's in the heart.

All-American Christmas Dinner

The traditional red and green colors of Christmas turn red, white and blue when you salute the holidays with our All-American Christmas Dinner. We've collected choice recipes from across the United States for a fresh angle on holiday classics, from a new way to serve everyone's favorite feathered friend to a new pumpkin pie. These instant classics are accompanied by a whole painter's palette of colorful seasonal vegetables, salads and desserts for an especially thankful celebration.

Menu

Shoreline Cocktail
Sunshine State Salad
Herb-Roasted Turkey with
San Francisco Stuffing
Sweet Potatoes Southern-Style
Down Home Corn Pudding
Broccoli in Horseradish Sauce
Country Squash Casserole
Fresh Cranberry Relish
Cheese and Herb Biscuits
Mincemeat-Glazed Apples
Christmas Carrot Cake or
Sour Cream Pumpkin Pie
Christmas Cider

SHORELINE COCKTAIL

1 egg white, beaten	1/4 cup whipping cream
2 tablespoons chopped parsley	2 tablespoons Irish or Scotch whiskey
1/2 cup shredded lettuce	Tabasco sauce to taste
1 pound cooked shrimp	Lemon slices
1/2 cup mayonnaise	Cucumber slices
2 tablespoons catsup	

☐ Dip rims of 8 champagne glasses into egg white; dip into parsley, coating well. Layer lettuce and shrimp in glasses.
☐ Combine mayonnaise, catsup, cream, whiskey and Tabasco sauce in bowl; mix well.
☐ Spoon over shrimp. Garnish with slices of lemon and cucumber.
☐ Yield: 8 servings.

SUNSHINE STATE SALAD

1 1/2 cups cranberries	Prepared mustard to taste
1/3 cup water	4 oranges
1/4 cup honey	2 avocados, sliced
1 1/2 teaspoons vegetable oil	Lettuce leaves

☐ Combine cranberries, water and honey in small saucepan.
☐ Cook over medium heat until half the cranberries pop, stirring frequently.
☐ Cool to room temperature. Stir in oil and prepared mustard.
☐ Chill in refrigerator.
☐ Peel and section oranges, reserving any juice.
☐ Brush avocado slices with reserved orange juice.
☐ Arrange orange and avocado slices on lettuce-lined plates. Drizzle with cranberry dressing. Serve with remaining dressing.
☐ Yield: 8 servings.

HERB-ROASTED TURKEY

1 (12-pound) turkey	1 medium onion, cut into quarters
6 fresh thyme sprigs	
4 fresh rosemary sprigs	2 stalks celery, cut into quarters
4 fresh sage sprigs	
1/2 teaspoon poultry seasoning	Parsley sprigs
	Orange sections
1/4 teaspoon salt	Green and red grapes
1/4 teaspoon pepper	

☐ Preheat oven to 325 degrees.
☐ Rinse turkey inside and out, discarding neck, giblets and excess fat; pat turkey dry.
☐ Loosen skin carefully from breast and drumsticks. Arrange 1 thyme sprig beneath skin on each drumstick. Arrange 2 sprigs each of thyme, rosemary and sage beneath skin on breast.
☐ Mix poultry seasoning, salt and pepper together. Sprinkle into neck and body cavities. Place onion, celery and remaining thyme, rosemary and sage into cavities.
☐ Secure body cavity with skewers and truss turkey; tuck wings under back. Place breast side up on rack sprayed with nonstick cooking spray in shallow roasting pan. Spray turkey with cooking spray.
☐ Insert meat thermometer in meaty part of thigh, making sure it does not touch bone. Cover loosely with foil.
☐ Roast for 2 hours. Remove cover. Roast for 1 1/2 hours longer or to 185 degrees on meat thermometer.
☐ Let stand, loosely covered, for 20 minutes. Place on serving plate. Garnish with parsley, oranges and grapes.
☐ Yield: 12 servings.

Herb-Roasted Turkey with San Francisco Stuffing,
pages 137 and 138

SAN FRANCISCO STUFFING

6 cups sourdough bread cubes	1¹/3 cups chopped green onions
1¹/2 cups chopped dried apricots	1 cup chicken broth
1 cup chopped celery	¹/4 cup olive oil
1 cup coarsely chopped pine nuts	1 tablespoon fresh basil
	1 clove of garlic, minced

□ Preheat oven to 375 degrees.
□ Combine first 5 ingredients in large bowl; mix gently. Combine chicken broth, olive oil, basil and garlic in small bowl; mix well.
□ Sprinkle chicken broth mixture over bread cube mixture; toss lightly to mix well. Spoon into baking dish.
□ Bake for 40 minutes. May microwave for 5 minutes if preferred.
□ Yield: 8 servings.

SWEET POTATOES SOUTHERN-STYLE

3 eggs	²/3 cup half and half
2 tablespoons (or more) light brown sugar	6 tablespoons melted butter or margarine
2 teaspoons grated orange rind	²/3 cup coarsely chopped pecans
¹/4 teaspoon nutmeg	Miniature marshmallows
1 teaspoon salt	Pecan halves
6 sweet potatoes, cooked, peeled, mashed	Maraschino cherry halves, drained

□ Preheat oven to 325 degrees.
□ Combine eggs with brown sugar, orange rind, nutmeg and salt in bowl; beat until light and fluffy.
□ Add sweet potatoes, half and half, butter and chopped pecans; mix well. Spoon into 1¹/2-quart baking dish.
□ Bake for 50 minutes. Top with marshmallows, pecan halves and cherries.
□ Yield: 8 servings.

DOWN HOME CORN PUDDING

1 (12-ounce) can whole kernel corn, drained	1¹/2 teaspoons seasoned salt
2 (17-ounce) cans cream-style corn	¹/2 teaspoon dry mustard
5 eggs, slightly beaten	1 teaspoon onion flakes
¹/2 cup sugar	¹/2 cup milk
¹/4 cup cornstarch	¹/2 cup melted butter or margarine

□ Preheat oven to 400 degrees.
□ Combine corn and eggs in bowl; mix well. Mix sugar, cornstarch, seasoned salt, dry mustard and onion flakes in bowl. Add to corn; mix well.

□ Stir in milk and butter. Spoon into greased 3-quart baking dish.
□ Bake for 1 hour, stirring once.
□ Yield: 8 servings.

BROCCOLI IN HORSERADISH SAUCE

3 egg yolks	2 tablespoons prepared horseradish
3 tablespoons vinegar	Flowerets of 1 large bunch broccoli
³/4 cup cold water	
2 tablespoons sugar	Grated radishes or red bell pepper strips
1 tablespoon cornstarch	
³/4 teaspoon salt	

□ Process first 6 ingredients in blender until smooth. Pour into double boiler.
□ Cook until thickened, stirring constantly; remove from heat. Stir in horseradish. Chill in refrigerator.
□ Cook broccoli in boiling water in saucepan just until tender-crisp but still bright green. Rinse and drain. Chill in refrigerator.
□ Arrange broccoli on serving platter. Spoon horseradish sauce over broccoli. Garnish with grated radishes or red bell pepper strips.
□ Yield: 8 servings.

COUNTRY SQUASH CASSEROLE

1 pound yellow squash, sliced	3 tablespoons melted butter or margarine
8 ounces zucchini, sliced	1 (10-ounce) can cream of chicken soup
1 cup water	
¹/2 cup chopped onion	1 (8-ounce) can water chestnuts, drained, chopped
¹/4 cup chopped green bell pepper	
3 tablespoons chopped green onions	¹/2 cup plain low-fat yogurt
1 tablespoon butter or margarine	¹/4 cup chopped pimento
	1 large carrot, grated
1 cup herb-seasoned stuffing mix	¹/2 teaspoon salt
	¹/4 teaspoon pepper

□ Preheat oven to 350 degrees.
□ Bring squash, zucchini and water to a boil in saucepan; cover and reduce heat. Simmer for 8 minutes or until tender; drain.
□ Sauté onion, green pepper and green onions in 1 tablespoon butter in skillet until tender; set aside.
□ Mix stuffing mix and 3 tablespoons butter in large bowl. Reserve ¹/3 cup mixture for topping.
□ Add squash mixture, sautéed mixture, soup, water chestnuts, yogurt, pimento, carrot, salt and pepper to remaining stuffing mixture; mix well.
□ Spoon into lightly greased 8-by-12-inch baking dish. Sprinkle with reserved stuffing.
□ Bake for 30 minutes or until heated through.
□ Yield: 8 servings.

CHEESE AND HERB BISCUITS

2 cups all-purpose flour
1 tablespoon baking powder
1/2 teaspoon cream of tartar
1/2 teaspoon each oregano, basil, savory and marjoram

2 teaspoons sugar
1/4 teaspoon salt
1/2 cup shortening
1/2 cup shredded Cheddar, Swiss or Monterey Jack cheese
2/3 cup milk

□ Preheat oven to 450 degrees.
□ Sift flour, baking powder, cream of tartar, oregano, basil, savory, marjoram, sugar and salt into large bowl.
□ Cut in shortening until mixture resembles coarse crumbs. Mix in cheese.
□ Make well in center.
□ Pour milk into well. Mix with fork just until mixture forms ball.
□ Knead 10 to 12 times on lightly floured surface.
□ Pat 1/2 inch thick. Cut with 2 1/2-inch cutter. Place on ungreased baking sheet.
□ Bake for 10 to 12 minutes or until golden brown.
□ Yield: 8 servings.

CRANBERRY RELISH

1 orange, cut into quarters, seeded
1 cup chopped unpeeled apple
1 (8-ounce) can juice-pack crushed pineapple
1/3 cup sugar
2 cups fresh cranberries

□ Process unpeeled orange in food processor until coarsely ground. Combine with apple, drained pineapple and sugar in medium bowl; mix well.
□ Process cranberries in food processor until coarsely ground. Add to orange mixture; mix well.
□ Chill, covered, for 8 hours.
□ Yield: 3 cups.

Invite a family of Teddys—dressed for the season—to decorate your holiday table for kids of all ages.

MINCEMEAT-GLAZED APPLES

1 (3-ounce) package
cherry gelatin
1 (3-ounce) package
orange gelatin
1 1/2 cups boiling water

1 cup cold water
8 baking apples
1 1/2 cups prepared
mincemeat

□ Dissolve gelatins in boiling water in bowl. Stir in cold water.
□ Core apples and peel top 1/3.
□ Arrange apples peeled end up in large skillet.
□ Fill apple cores with mincemeat. Pour gelatin mixture over apples.
□ Bring to a boil over medium heat; reduce heat.
□ Simmer, covered, for 15 minutes or until apples are tender.
□ Preheat broiler.
□ Broil for 15 minutes or until apples are glazed and light brown, basting frequently.
□ Serve warm or cool with ice cream. Spoon cooking syrup over top.
□ Yield: 8 servings.

CHRISTMAS CARROT CAKE

2 cups all-purpose flour
2 cups sugar
2 teaspoons baking soda
1 tablespoon cinnamon
Allspice and salt to taste
4 eggs

1 cup vegetable oil
4 cups finely shredded
carrots
1/2 cup apricot preserves
Cream Cheese Frosting

□ Preheat oven to 350 degrees. Grease and flour three 8-inch cake pans.
□ Sift flour, sugar, baking soda, cinnamon, allspice and salt into bowl.
□ Beat eggs in mixer bowl until light and foamy.
□ Add oil very gradually, beating constantly at medium speed. Add dry ingredients; mix until smooth.
□ Stir in carrots. Spoon into prepared pans.
□ Bake for 20 to 35 minutes or until cake layers test done.
□ Cool in pans for 10 minutes. Remove to wire rack to cool completely.
□ Spread preserves between layers of cake. Spread Cream Cheese Frosting over top and side.
□ Yield: 16 servings.

CREAM CHEESE FROSTING

8 ounces cream cheese,
softened
1/3 cup unsalted butter or
margarine, softened

1/2 teaspoon vanilla
extract
3 cups (about) sifted
confectioners' sugar

□ Beat cream cheese, butter and vanilla in mixer bowl until light and fluffy.
□ Add enough confectioners' sugar to make of spreading consistency, mixing until smooth.
□ Yield: 3 1/2 cups.

SOUR CREAM PUMPKIN PIE

1 unbaked 9-inch pie shell
1/4 cup chopped pecans
1 (16-ounce) can
solid-pack pumpkin
1 cup sour cream
3 eggs

2/3 cup sugar
1/2 teaspoon cinnamon
1/4 teaspoon ground cloves
1/4 teaspoon nutmeg
1/4 teaspoon ginger
12 pecan halves

□ Preheat oven to 375 degrees.
□ Bake pie shell for 8 minutes. Sprinkle with 1/4 cup chopped pecans.
□ Combine pumpkin, sour cream, eggs, sugar, cinnamon, cloves, nutmeg and ginger in medium bowl; mix well.
□ Pour into prepared pie shell.
□ Bake for 40 minutes. Top with pecan halves.
□ Bake for 5 to 10 minutes longer or until set. Cool to room temperature.
□ Yield: 8 servings.

CHRISTMAS CIDER

9 cups water
1 (12-ounce) can frozen
apple juice concentrate,
thawed
1 (12-ounce) can frozen
cranberry juice
concentrate, thawed

1 (6-ounce) can frozen
lemonade concentrate,
thawed
7 whole cloves
1 teaspoon nutmeg
5 (3-inch) sticks cinnamon
1/2 cup rum (optional)

□ Combine water, apple juice concentrate, cranberry juice concentrate, lemonade concentrate, cloves, nutmeg and cinnamon in heavy saucepan.
□ Simmer for 15 minutes. Remove cloves and cinnamon sticks.
□ Stir in rum. Ladle into punch cups.
□ Yield: 3 quarts.

Shrimp Oriental, Tangy Salmon Kabobs, page 147

Light-Hearted Open House

*I*n these health-conscious times we're often confronted with a new holiday dilemma: how to serve great food that doesn't sabotage our guests' (and our own!) diets. The answer, fortunately, is no longer boring raw veggies with cottage cheese dip. At our Light-Hearted Open House, guests can indulge in great finger foods without a moment's guilt. Look for fabulous healthy recipes and special "lighten up" hints on ways to cut down on fats, sodium or cholesterol without sacrificing flavor. Once you get in the habit of making easy substitutions, you may find all your cooking becomes "light-hearted."

SALMON MOUSSE

1 envelope unflavored
  gelatin
3 tablespoons milk
1/2 cup boiling water
1/4 cup lightly packed
  fresh dill sprigs or 1
  tablespoon dried dill
1/4 cup (1-inch) scallion
  pieces
1 (14-ounce) can pink
  salmon, drained, flaked

1 cup low-fat plain yogurt
1/2 cup reduced-calorie
  mayonnaise
2 teaspoons paprika
1/2 teaspoon salt
1/4 teaspoon pepper
Sliced radishes
Fresh dill sprigs
Assorted crackers

☐ Soften gelatin in milk in blender container for 5 minutes. Process until smooth.
☐ Add boiling water. Process for 20 seconds or until gelatin is dissolved. Add 1/4 cup dill and scallions; process for 20 seconds.
☐ Add salmon, yogurt, mayonnaise, paprika, salt and pepper; process for 1 minute. Spoon into lightly buttered 4-by-7-inch loaf pan or 1-quart mold.
☐ Chill for 3 hours or until firm. Unmold onto serving plate. Garnish with radishes and additional dill sprigs. Serve with assorted crackers.
☐ Yield: 3 1/2 cups.

FRESH SALSA DIABLO

6 tomatoes, peeled,
  chopped
1/4 cup chopped red onion
1/4 cup chopped yellow
  onion
1/2 cup beef consommé
3 tablespoons vodka
1 tablespoon lime juice

1 (2-ounce) can chopped
  green chilies
1 teaspoon cumin
1 teaspoon chopped fresh
  cilantro
1 teaspoon salt
Tortilla chips

☐ Combine tomatoes, onions, consommé, vodka, lime juice, green chilies, cumin, cilantro and salt in bowl; mix well. Let stand for 1 hour.
☐ Spoon into serving dish. Serve with tortilla chips.
☐ Yield: 3 cups.

ROAST BEEF CANAPÉS AND KIWIFRUIT

4 ounces sliced rare roast
  beef
1/4 cup finely chopped
  walnuts, toasted
1 tablespoon fresh lemon
  juice
1 tablespoon wine
  vinegar
1 tablespoon chopped
  fresh dill

1 tablespoon olive oil
1 small clove of garlic,
  crushed
Salt to taste
1/4 teaspoon freshly
  ground pepper
12 (1/4-inch) thick slices
  French bread
2 kiwifruit, peeled, sliced
Pimento

☐ Cut roast beef into 12 uniform slices; arrange in glass dish. Sprinkle with walnuts.
☐ Combine lemon juice, vinegar, dill, olive oil, garlic, salt and pepper in bowl; mix well. Pour over beef and walnuts, lifting beef to coat well.
☐ Marinate, covered, for 30 minutes; drain.
☐ Place 1 piece of beef on each bread round; top with walnuts and slice of kiwifruit. Garnish with pimento.
☐ Yield: 12 appetizers.

BROCCOLI PUFFS

2 (10-ounce) packages
  frozen chopped broccoli,
  thawed, drained
2 tablespoons minced
  onion
3/4 cup shredded
  mozzarella cheese
3/4 cup grated Parmesan
  cheese

2 egg whites, beaten
1 teaspoon garlic powder
1 teaspoon thyme
1/2 cup melted butter
2 1/2 cups fresh bread
  crumbs
1/2 cup seasoned Italian
  bread crumbs

☐ Preheat oven to 350 degrees.
☐ Combine first 7 ingredients in bowl; mix well.
☐ Add butter and 2 1/2 cups bread crumbs; mix well.
☐ Mixture will be very moist.
☐ Shape into 1-inch balls. Coat with 1/2 cup seasoned bread crumbs. Place 1 inch apart on baking sheet.
☐ Bake for 25 minutes.
☐ Yield: 72 appetizers.
☐ *Lighten Up:* Substitute margarine for butter and use skim milk and light cheeses.

RICOTTA AND BLUE CHEESE IN ENDIVE SPEARS

1/2 cup chopped walnuts
1/2 cup part-skim ricotta
  cheese
2 tablespoons crumbled
  blue cheese

Salt and red pepper to
  taste
2 heads endive, separated
  into spears

☐ Toast walnuts in single layer in skillet over low heat for 5 minutes or until brown, stirring occasionally.
☐ Combine ricotta cheese, blue cheese, salt and red pepper in food processor container fitted with metal blade. Process for 15 seconds or until smooth.
☐ Spoon 1 teaspoon cheese mixture onto stem end of each endive spear; garnish with walnuts.
☐ Yield: 32 appetizers.

Salmon Mousse, Ricotta and Blue Cheese in Endive Spears, page 142

CHICKEN AND PASTRAMI PINWHEELS

4 large chicken breast filets	2 tablespoons mayonnaise
4 teaspoons coarse-grained mustard	2 tablespoons coarse-grained mustard
4 slices pastrami	12 slices dark party rye or pumpernickel bread
Paprika to taste	

☐ Preheat oven to 350 degrees.
☐ Rinse chicken and pat dry. Pound 1/4 inch thick between sheets of plastic wrap with meat mallet.
☐ Spread each filet with 1 teaspoon mustard; top each with 1 slice pastrami. Roll from narrow side to enclose filling.
☐ Arrange chicken rolls seam side down in 6-by-10-inch baking dish. Brush with water; sprinkle with paprika.
☐ Bake for 30 minutes or until chicken is tender.
☐ Chill, covered, in refrigerator. Cut rolls into 3/8-inch slices.
☐ Combine mayonnaise and 2 tablespoons mustard in bowl. Spread on bread rounds. Top with chicken slices.
☐ Yield: 24 servings.
☐ *Lighten Up:* Substitute turkey pastrami for pastrami and use nonfat mayonnaise.

BAKED BRIE BITES

2 sourdough French rolls	1/2 cup packed light brown sugar
1/2 cup margarine, softened	15 ounces Brie, cut into thin wedges
1/4 cup chopped almonds	

☐ Preheat oven to 375 degrees.
☐ Cut French rolls into 1/2-inch slices, discarding end rounds. Spread 1 side of slices with margarine.
☐ Combine almonds and brown sugar in bowl; mix well. Spread half the almond mixture on slices.
☐ Top with wedge of Brie and remaining almond mixture. Arrange on baking sheet.
☐ Bake for 6 to 7 minutes or until heated through.
☐ Yield: 24 appetizers.

HAM AND CHEESE APPETIZERS

2 cups baking mix	2 tablespoons chopped parsley
1/4 cup sour cream	3/4 cup chopped smoked ham
2/3 cup milk	
1 egg	1 cup shredded Cheddar cheese
1/2 teaspoon salt	
1/2 cup chopped onion	1/2 cup grated Parmesan cheese
2 cloves of garlic, minced	

☐ Preheat oven to 350 degrees.
☐ Combine baking mix, sour cream, milk, egg and salt in bowl; mix well.
☐ Add onion, garlic, parsley, ham and cheeses; mix well. Spread in greased 9-by-13-inch baking pan.
☐ Bake for 25 to 30 minutes or until golden brown.
☐ Cut into rectangles.
☐ Yield: 36 servings.
☐ *Lighten Up:* Substitute turkey ham for ham, sour cream substitute for sour cream, skim milk for milk, 1/4 cup egg substitute for egg and skim milk cheese for Cheddar.

GENOA APPETIZER SQUARES

1 (8-count) can crescent rolls	1 clove of garlic, finely chopped
1 (4-ounce) can pimento	3 tablespoons finely chopped Bermuda onion
12 ounces Genoa salami, coarsely chopped	
1 pound extra-sharp Cheddar cheese, shredded	2 tablespoons finely chopped black olives
	5 eggs, at room temperature, beaten
1 medium green bell pepper, finely chopped	2 tablespoons poppy seed
3 tablespoons finely chopped parsley	5 tablespoons grated Parmesan cheese

☐ Preheat oven to 350 degrees.
☐ Line 9-by-13-inch baking pan with roll dough, pressing perforations to seal.
☐ Push up dough 1/4 inch around edges of pan to form rim.
☐ Process pimento and salami in food processor until finely chopped.
☐ Combine with Cheddar cheese, green pepper, parsley, garlic, onion, olives, eggs, poppy seed and 3 tablespoons Parmesan cheese in large bowl; mix well.
☐ Spoon over dough; sprinkle with remaining 2 tablespoons Parmesan cheese.
☐ Bake for 30 to 40 minutes or until top is golden brown and knife inserted in center comes out clean.
☐ Cool on wire rack for 15 minutes. Cut into 1-inch squares.
☐ Yield: 117 appetizers.
☐ *Lighten Up:* Use light Cheddar cheese and substitute 1 1/4 cups egg substitute for eggs and turkey salami for salami.

SHERRIED ONIONS AND OLIVES

1/2 cup sherry
1/4 cup red wine vinegar
2 tablespoons vegetable
  oil
1 clove of garlic, minced
1/2 teaspoon oregano
1/2 teaspoon basil

1 cup thawed frozen
  small whole onions
1 (6-ounce) can pitted
  black olives
1 (2 1/2-ounce) jar
  pimento-stuffed green
  olives

☐ Combine sherry, vinegar, oil, garlic, oregano and basil in bowl; mix well. Add onions and olives; mix gently.
☐ Chill, covered, for 1 to 3 days, stirring mixture occasionally.
☐ Drain onions and olives. Place in serving bowl.
☐ Yield: 8 servings.

OYSTER-STUFFED MUSHROOMS

8 ounces oysters, chopped
3 tablespoons bread
  crumbs
1/4 cup margarine
2 cloves of garlic, crushed
2 teaspoons mixed basil,
  rosemary and parsley

Salt and pepper to taste
24 mushroom caps
White wine
1/3 cup shredded Swiss,
  Gruyère or Parmesan
  cheese

☐ Preheat oven to 350 degrees.
☐ Coat oysters with bread crumbs. Melt margarine in skillet. Add garlic, herbs, salt, pepper and oysters.
☐ Sauté until oysters are light brown. Spoon mixture into mushroom caps.
☐ Arrange mushrooms in greased baking dish. Drizzle with pan drippings and a small amount of wine. Sprinkle with cheese.
☐ Bake, covered, for 15 minutes. Broil for 1 minute.
☐ Yield: 24 appetizers.

POTATOES WITH DILLED SOUR CREAM

1 pound whole small new
  potatoes
1/4 cup plain nonfat
  yogurt
6 tablespoons light sour
  cream
1/4 cup finely chopped
  green onions

1/4 cup grated Parmesan
  cheese
2 teaspoons chopped
  fresh dill or 1/4 teaspoon
  dried dill
Pepper to taste
Lemon slices
Fresh dill

☐ Scrub potatoes well; pierce with fork.
☐ Arrange on glass plate.
☐ Microwave on High just until potatoes are tender.
☐ Cut potatoes into halves and scoop out centers; reserve pulp for another use.
☐ Combine yogurt, sour cream, green onions, cheese, 1 teaspoon dill and pepper in bowl; mix well. Spoon into potato shells.
☐ Arrange on serving plate.
☐ Garnish with lemon slices and fresh dill.
☐ Yield: 10 servings.

Fill a basket with an assortment of colorful peppers, vegetables, pine cones and candles for a festive centerpiece.

Turkey Antipasto

TURKEY ANTIPASTO

1 green bell pepper, cut
  into halves
1 (6-ounce) jar marinated
  artichoke hearts
4 ounces jalapeño
  Monterey Jack cheese,
  cut into 1/2-inch cubes
1/2 yellow bell pepper
1 (7-ounce) can capanato
  (eggplant relish)
8 ounces oven-roasted
  turkey breast slices
1 (5-ounce) can jumbo
  pitted black olives,
  drained
8 ounces turkey pastrami
  slices

1 (3-ounce) package
  sesame breadsticks
2 tablespoons prepared
  mustard
1 pound smoked turkey
1 (6-ounce) jar cocktail
  onions, drained
8 ounces turkey ham slices
1 (16-ounce) jar sweet
  gherkin pickles
8 ounces turkey salami
  slices
6 ounces provolone
  cheese, sliced
1 (7-ounce) jar tiny corn
  ears, drained

□ Fill green pepper halves with marinated
artichokes and cheese cubes.
□ Fill yellow bell pepper half with capanato.
Arrange pepper halves in center of serving tray.
□ Cut oven-roasted turkey slices into 1/2-by-3-inch
strips; fold strips in half. Stuff turkey into holes of
black olives.
□ Cut turkey pastrami slices into 1/2-inch wide
strips. Spread breadsticks with mustard. Wrap
turkey strips around breadsticks.
□ Cut smoked turkey into 1/2-inch cubes. Thread
alternately with onions onto frilled toothpicks.
□ Cut turkey ham slices into halves; roll each half
into cone. Place 1 pickle into center of each cone;
secure with round wooden picks.
□ Stack turkey salami and provolone cheese,
alternating 3 slices turkey salami with 2 slices
provolone cheese. Cut stacks into 8 wedges; secure
with wooden picks.
□ Arrange hors d'oeuvres on serving tray.
□ Fill spaces on serving tray with tiny corn.
□ Yield: 20 servings.

REUBEN ROLLS

4 ounces deli sliced corned beef	1 tablespoon Dijon mustard
1/2 cup rinsed drained sauerkraut	7 sheets frozen phyllo dough, thawed
4 ounces low sodium Swiss cheese, shredded	3 tablespoons vegetable oil

□ Preheat oven to 375 degrees.
□ Combine first 4 ingredients in bowl; mix well.
□ Place 1 sheet phyllo dough on waxed paper, leaving remaining dough covered with damp towel to prevent drying out. Brush sheet of dough with oil.
□ Spoon 3 tablespoons corned beef mixture in thin strip 1/2 inch from narrow edge of dough. Roll up dough from narrow edge to enclose filling, folding in edges.
□ Place seam side down on baking sheet sprayed with nonstick cooking spray. Score crosswise into 4 equal portions; brush with oil. Repeat with remaining dough and corned beef mixture.
□ Bake for 13 to 15 minutes or until brown. Cut into scored portions. Serve warm.
□ Yield: 28 appetizers.

SHRIMP ORIENTAL

1/2 cup dark soy sauce	2 pounds (21 to 25 count) shrimp, peeled, deveined
1/2 cup rice wine	
1 tablespoon hoisin sauce	
1/2 teaspoon hot bean paste	48 snow peas

□ Blend soy sauce, wine, hoisen sauce and bean paste in bowl. Add shrimp; mix gently.
□ Marinate in refrigerator for 3 to 6 hours; drain. Preheat broiler. Place shrimp on rack in broiler pan. Broil 4 inches from heat source for 4 minutes, turning halfway through cooking time. Chill in refrigerator.
□ Thread 1 shrimp and 1 snow pea on each toothpick. Arrange appetizers on serving plate.
□ Chill until serving time.
□ Yield: 48 appetizers.
□ *Lighten Up:* Use reduced-sodium soy sauce.

TANGY SALMON KABOBS

12 ounces salmon filets, skinned	1/2 teaspoon vegetable oil
1/2 cup grapefruit juice	1 tablespoon minced fresh ginger
2 teaspoons lime juice	Salt and pepper to taste
1 teaspoon red wine vinegar	30 bamboo skewers or wooden picks
Several drops of hot pepper sauce	2 or 3 small zucchini Cucumber-Yogurt Sauce

□ Rinse salmon under cold water and pat dry. Slice into 1/4-inch pieces.
□ Combine grapefruit juice, lime juice, vinegar, pepper sauce, oil, ginger, salt and pepper in bowl; mix well. Add salmon; mix gently.
□ Marinate in refrigerator for 30 minutes to overnight. Drain salmon.
□ Preheat broiler.
□ Soak skewers or wooden picks in warm water; drain. Slice zucchini into 60 slices.
□ Thread 1 piece salmon between 2 slices zucchini on each skewer. Place on rack in broiler pan.
□ Broil for 45 seconds or just until salmon is cooked through.
□ Serve with Cucumber-Yogurt Sauce.
□ Yield: 30 appetizers.

CUCUMBER-YOGURT SAUCE

1 cup plain yogurt	1 clove of garlic, minced
1/4 cup finely chopped cucumbers	2 teaspoons olive oil
	1/4 teaspoon salt
1/4 cup finely chopped onion	1/4 teaspoon pepper

□ Combine yogurt, cucumbers, onion, garlic, olive oil, salt and pepper in bowl; mix well.
□ Spoon into serving dish. Chill until serving time.
□ Yield: 1 1/2 cups.

SPINACH AND CHEESE TRIANGLES

8 ounces soft cream cheese with chives and onion	1/3 cup chopped roasted red peppers, drained
1 (10-ounce) package frozen chopped spinach, thawed, drained	9 sheets frozen phyllo dough, thawed
	6 tablespoons melted margarine
Black pepper to taste	

□ Preheat oven to 375 degrees.
□ Combine cream cheese, spinach, black pepper and red peppers in bowl; mix well.
□ Place 1 sheet phyllo dough on work surface, leaving remaining dough covered with damp cloth to prevent drying out. Brush sheet with margarine. Cut lengthwise into 4 equal strips.
□ Spoon about 1 tablespoon filling 1 inch from end of each strip. Fold end over filling at 45-degree angle. Continue to fold into triangles as for flag. Repeat with remaining phyllo and filling. Place triangles on baking sheet. Brush with margarine.
□ Bake for 12 to 15 minutes or until golden brown.
□ Yield: 36 appetizers.
□ *Lighten Up:* Use light cream cheese and substitute butter-flavored cooking spray for margarine.

CHEESY BLACK OLIVE PUFFS

2 cups coarsely chopped black olives	Tabasco sauce to taste
1½ cups shredded Monterey Jack cheese	1 teaspoon pepper
	2 sheets frozen puff pastry, thawed
½ cup chopped scallions	1 egg yolk, beaten
½ cup mayonnaise	1 tablespoon water

□ Preheat oven to 400 degrees.
□ Combine first 6 ingredients in bowl; mix well.
□ Cut pastry lengthwise into 3 equal strips. Spoon filling evenly along strips, leaving ½-inch edges. Roll up strips from long side to enclose filling.
□ Brush ends with mixture of egg yolk and water; seal ends. Place seam side down on ungreased baking dish. Brush with egg yolk mixture.
□ Bake for 15 minutes or until golden brown. Cool for 10 minutes. Slice diagonally into 1-inch pieces.
□ Yield: 10 to 12 servings.
□ *Lighten Up:* Use light mayonnaise and cheese and substitute phyllo dough for puff pastry.

LIGHT PARTY MIX

5 cups pretzels	2 (½-ounce) envelopes butter substitute mix
4 cups bite-sized wheat or bran cereal squares	¼ cup reduced-sodium Worcestershire sauce
4 cups bite-sized shredded wheat cereal	2 tablespoons canola oil
3 cups oyster crackers	Several drops of hot pepper sauce
2 cups bite-sized round butter crackers	½ teaspoon garlic powder
¼ cup water	½ teaspoon seasoned salt

□ Preheat oven to 300 degrees.
□ Combine first 5 ingredients in roasting pan sprayed with nonstick cooking spray.
□ Combine water, butter substitute mix, Worcestershire sauce, oil, pepper sauce, garlic powder and seasoned salt in saucepan.
□ Cook until heated through, stirring to mix well. Drizzle evenly over cereal mixture; toss to mix well.
□ Bake for 45 minutes, stirring every 15 minutes.
□ Spread on foil to cool.
□ Yield: 32 servings.

SPRING GARDEN DIP

¼ cup minced green bell pepper	¼ cup mayonnaise
¼ cup minced green onions	2 teaspoons sugar
	1 clove of garlic, minced
¼ cup minced cucumber	½ teaspoon salt
¼ cup minced radishes	¼ teaspoon white pepper
¼ cup minced celery	Bite-sized fresh vegetables or crackers
1 cup sour cream	

□ Drain green pepper, green onions, cucumber, radishes and celery on paper towels.
□ Combine sour cream, mayonnaise, sugar, garlic, salt and white pepper in bowl; mix well. Stir in drained vegetables.
□ Spoon into serving bowl. Serve with bite-sized vegetables or crackers.
□ Yield: 16 servings.
□ *Lighten Up:* Substitute sour half and half for sour cream and use light mayonnaise.

TACO PIZZA

16 ounces cream cheese, softened	½ head lettuce, shredded
2 envelopes taco seasoning mix	2 or 3 green onions, chopped
1 cup plain yogurt, drained	2 cups shredded Cheddar cheese
2 tomatoes, chopped	Toasted Italian bread rounds

□ Combine cream cheese, taco seasoning mix and yogurt in bowl; mix well. Spread in pizza pan.
□ Top with tomatoes, lettuce, green onions and Cheddar cheese. Serve with bread rounds.
□ Yield: 20 servings.
□ *Lighten Up:* Substitute Neufchâtel cheese for cream cheese and use nonfat yogurt and light Cheddar cheese.

SMOKED TURKEY SPREAD

1 pound deli smoked turkey	Pepper to taste
⅓ cup coarsely chopped celery	½ (10-ounce) package frozen chopped spinach, thawed, drained
8 ounces soft cream cheese with chives and onion	1 tablespoon lemon juice
	¼ cup toasted sliced almonds
¼ cup milk	Assorted flatbreads
Spicy mustard to taste	

□ Line 4-cup mold or 4-by-8-inch loaf pan with plastic wrap.
□ Chop turkey and celery in food processor.
□ Combine with half the cream cheese, milk, mustard and pepper in bowl; mix well.
□ Combine spinach, lemon juice and remaining cream cheese in bowl; mix well.
□ Layer half the turkey mixture, all the spinach mixture and remaining turkey mixture in prepared mold.
□ Chill, covered, for several hours to overnight.
□ Unmold onto serving plate. Garnish with almonds. Serve with assorted flatbreads.
□ Yield: 16 servings.
□ *Lighten Up:* Substitute Neufchâtel cheese for cream cheese, use skim milk and omit almonds.

Simply spectacular—a tray filled with brown bags of special treats for a party nibbling center or to welcome guests all season long.

HONEY-MUSTARD BRIE

1 (15-ounce) round Brie
  cheese
1/4 cup honey-mustard
1/2 cup sliced almonds,
  toasted
2 red unpeeled apples,
  cut into wedges

2 green unpeeled apples,
  cut into wedges
1 (6-ounce) can pineapple
  juice

□ Remove rind from top of cheese, leaving 1/2-inch border. Place on large serving tray.
□ Spread mustard over top of cheese; sprinkle with almonds. Let stand at room temperature for 1 hour or longer.
□ Toss apple wedges with pineapple juice in bowl; drain. Arrange on tray around cheese. Serve immediately.
□ Yield: 10 to 14 servings.

ROASTED CORN AND AVOCADO DIP

1 cup frozen whole
  kernel corn, thawed
2 teaspoons vegetable oil
2 large avocados
1 medium tomato, finely
  chopped
2 tablespoons minced
  onion
2 cloves of garlic, minced

1 (2-ounce) can jalapeño
  peppers, chopped
3 tablespoons lime juice
1/4 teaspoon cumin
1/2 teaspoon salt
Tomato wedges
Yellow and blue
  cornmeal chips

□ Preheat oven to 400 degrees.
□ Combine corn and oil in shallow baking dish; mix well.
□ Bake for 8 minutes or until light brown, stirring twice. Set aside to cool.
□ Chop 1 avocado. Mash remaining avocado in bowl. Add chopped avocado, corn, chopped tomato, onion, garlic, jalapeño peppers, lime juice, cumin and salt; mix gently.
□ Chill, covered, for up to 24 hours.
□ Spoon into serving bowl. Garnish with tomato wedges. Serve with chips for dipping.
□ Yield: 3 cups.

Golden Glow Punch, Florida Fizz, Fruity Grapefruit Spritzers, Spicy Citrus Toddy, Hot Mulled Cranberry Orange Cup, pages 151 and 152

RACLETTE CHEESE SPREAD

1½ cups shredded
　process Swiss cheese
1 cup shredded Gouda
　cheese
1 tablespoon chopped
　fresh basil or oregano
2 teaspoons Dijon
　mustard

1 teaspoon dry white
　wine Worcestershire
　sauce
Hot pepper sauce to taste
Bite-sized cauliflower
　and broccoli
Tiny new potatoes
Pita bread wedges

□ Combine cheeses in small mixer bowl or food processor container. Let stand until softened.
□ Add next 4 ingredients. Beat or process until mixed; mixture will be crumbly.
□ Shape into round 4½ inches across and 1 inch high. Wrap in plastic wrap.
□ Chill for several hours to overnight.
□ Preheat oven to 325 degrees.

□ Blanch cauliflower and broccoli in saucepan. Boil potatoes in water in saucepan until tender.
□ Drain vegetables and cut potatoes into halves. Keep warm.
□ Place cheese in 9-inch pie plate. Cut into 6 wedges; separate wedges slightly.
□ Bake for 10 to 12 minutes or just until cheese begins to melt. Serve with warm vegetables and pita bread wedges.
□ May microwave cheese wedges on Medium for 2 to 3 minutes, rotating dish once.
□ Yield: 6 servings.

MUSHROOM PÂTÉ

8 ounces fresh
　mushrooms, chopped
2 tablespoons unsalted
　butter or margarine
1½ teaspoons chopped
　garlic
¼ cup chopped scallions
⅓ cup chicken broth
4 ounces cream cheese,
　softened

2 tablespoons unsalted
　butter or margarine,
　softened
2 tablespoons chopped
　chives
Salt and freshly ground
　pepper to taste
Chopped chives
Toast points

□ Sauté mushrooms in 2 tablespoons butter in skillet over medium heat for 2 to 3 minutes. Add garlic and scallions.
□ Sauté for 1 minute. Stir in chicken broth.
□ Cook over high heat until all liquid has evaporated. Cool to room temperature.
□ Combine cream cheese and 2 tablespoons butter in bowl; mix until smooth. Add mushroom mixture, 2 tablespoons chives, salt and pepper; mix well. Spoon into 1-cup serving bowl.
□ Chill, covered, until serving time. Garnish with additional chopped chives. Serve with toast points.
□ Yield: 1 cup.
□ *Lighten Up:* Substitute margarine for butter and use Neufchâtel cheese for cream cheese.

ROASTED PEPPER DIP

1 (5-ounce) jar roasted red
　peppers, drained, finely
　chopped
1 (4-ounce) can chopped
　green chilies, drained
1 cup sour cream

1 cup mayonnaise
1 tablespoon lemon juice
½ teaspoon garlic powder
Bite-sized fresh
　vegetables

□ Combine first 6 ingredients in bowl; mix well.
□ Spoon into serving bowl. Chill until serving time.
□ Serve with vegetables for dipping.
□ Yield: 3 cups.
□ *Lighten Up:* Use sour half and half and cholesterol-free reduced-calorie mayonnaise.

HONEY-CRANBERRY DIP

1 (16-ounce) can jellied
  cranberry sauce
3 tablespoons prepared
  horseradish
2 tablespoons honey
1 tablespoon
  Worcestershire sauce
1 tablespoon lemon juice

1 clove of garlic, minced
1/2 teaspoon ground red
  pepper
Orange sections
Pineapple chunks
Smoked turkey link
  sausage, cooked

□ Combine cranberry sauce, horseradish, honey, Worcestershire sauce, lemon juice, garlic and red pepper in saucepan; mix well.
□ Bring to a boil; reduce heat. Simmer, covered, for 5 minutes.
□ Serve warm with oranges, pineapple and sausage for dipping.
□ Yield: 24 servings.

CHOCOLATE CHIP-CREAM CHEESE LOAVES

24 ounces cream cheese,
  softened
11/2 cups semisweet
  miniature chocolate
  chips
1 tablespoon cinnamon

1 cup sifted confectioners'
  sugar
11/4 cups chopped pecans
2 (11/2-ounce) bars
  chocolate candy
Gingersnaps

□ Line two 3-by-7-inch loaf pans with plastic wrap.
□ Combine first 4 ingredients in bowl; mix well. Press evenly into prepared pans.
□ Chill, covered, for 5 hours or until serving time.
□ Invert onto serving plates; remove plastic wrap.
□ Press pecans around sides of loaves. Shave chocolate bars into curls with vegetable peeler.
□ Sprinkle curls over tops of loaves.
□ Serve with gingersnaps.
□ Yield: 30 servings.
□ *Lighten Up:* Substitute Neufchâtel cheese for cream cheese and carob chips and bars for chocolate chips and bars.

POLYNESIAN DIP

8 ounces cream cheese,
  softened
1/4 cup sour cream
1 (8-ounce) can crushed
  pineapple, drained
2 tablespoons sugar

1/2 cup chopped
  mandarin oranges
1/2 cup chopped
  macadamia nuts
Gingersnaps

□ Combine cream cheese, sour cream, pineapple, sugar, oranges and half the macadamia nuts in bowl; mix well. Spoon into serving dish.
□ Chill until serving time. Sprinkle with remaining macadamia nuts. Serve with gingersnaps.
□ Yield: 21/2 cups.

□ *Lighten Up:* Substitute Neufchâtel cheese for cream cheese, sour half and half for sour cream and almonds for macadamia nuts.

ORANGE-PECAN DIP

8 ounces cream cheese,
  softened
1/4 cup thawed frozen
  orange juice concentrate
1/2 teaspoon lemon juice

2 tablespoons whipping
  cream
2 tablespoons sugar
1/2 cup chopped pecans
Sliced apples and pears

□ Combine first 5 ingredients in bowl; mix well. Stir in pecans. Spoon into serving dish.
□ Chill until serving time. Serve with sliced apples and pears tossed with additional lemon juice.
□ Yield: 2 cups.
□ *Lighten Up:* Substitute Neufchâtel cheese for cream cheese and evaporated skim milk for whipping cream.

GOLDEN GLOW PUNCH

3 cups grapefruit juice
1 cup tangerine juice
1/2 cup light corn syrup
2 cups chilled seltzer
  water

1 grapefruit, peeled,
  sliced
1 cup sliced strawberries

□ Blend grapefruit juice, tangerine juice and corn syrup in pitcher. Chill, covered, until serving time.
□ Pour over ice cubes in small punch bowl. Add seltzer water; mix gently. Garnish with grapefruit and strawberry slices.
□ Yield: 8 cups.

FLORIDA FIZZ

2 cups orange juice
1 cup grapefruit juice
1 cup tangerine juice

2 cups chilled ginger ale
Fresh fruit chunks

□ Blend orange juice, grapefruit juice and tangerine juice in pitcher. Chill, covered, until serving time.
□ Stir in ginger ale. Pour over ice cubes in glasses.
□ Garnish with fruit on skewers.
□ Yield: 6 cups.

FRUITY GRAPEFRUIT SPRITZERS

1 (10-ounce) package
  frozen mixed fruit in
  syrup, thawed

2 cups grapefruit juice
1 cup chilled club soda

□ Combine undrained mixed fruit and grapefruit juice in pitcher. Chill, covered, until serving time.
□ Stir in club soda. Pour over ice cubes in glasses.
□ Yield: 4 cups.

SPICY CITRUS TODDY

4 whole cloves	2/3 cup tangerine juice
2 cups water	1/3 cup grapefruit juice
1/3 cup honey	Orange slices
1 cup orange juice	Whole cloves

□ Bring 4 cloves and water to a boil in saucepan. Simmer, covered, for 10 minutes.
□ Stir in honey, orange juice, tangerine juice and grapefruit juice.
□ Heat just until heated through; do not boil. Ladle into cups. Garnish with orange slices studded with additional cloves.
□ Yield: 4 cups.

HOT MULLED CRANBERRY ORANGE CUP

2 cups cranberry juice cocktail	8 whole cloves
1/3 cup sugar	1 (2-inch) cinnamon stick
Peel of 1 orange, cut into strips	3 cups orange juice
	Cinnamon sticks

□ Combine cranberry juice, sugar, orange peel, cloves and 1 cinnamon stick in 2-quart saucepan.
□ Bring to a boil; reduce heat. Simmer for 10 minutes; strain. Combine with orange juice in saucepan.
□ Heat just until heated through. Ladle into cups.
□ Garnish with additional cinnamon sticks.
□ Yield: 5 cups.

SPICY LEMONADE WARMER

6 whole cloves	1 1/4 to 1 1/2 cups sugar
2 (2-inch) cinnamon sticks	1 cup lemon juice
1 (32-ounce) bottle of cranberry juice cocktail	2 tablespoons honey
4 cups water	1 lemon, sliced

□ Tie cloves and cinnamon sticks in cheesecloth bag. Combine spice bag with cranberry juice cocktail, water, sugar, lemon juice, honey and lemon slices in slow cooker.
□ Cook on Low for 4 hours or on High for 2 hours.
□ Discard spices and lemon slices. Ladle into cups.
□ Yield: 10 cups.

WHITE SANGRIA SLUSH

1 (12-ounce) can frozen lemonade concentrate, thawed	1 (750-milliliter) bottle of Chablis or nonalcoholic white wine, chilled
1 (6-ounce) can frozen orange juice concentrate, thawed	1 (10-ounce) bottle of club soda, chilled
1 1/2 cups water	Lemon, lime and orange slices

□ Combine lemonade concentrate, orange juice concentrate and water in pitcher; mix well. Pour into 9-by-13-inch pan.
□ Freeze until firm.
□ Spoon frozen mixture into punch bowl. Add wine and club soda; mix gently. Garnish with fruit slices.
□ Yield: 2 quarts.

BANANA CRUSH

1 banana, cut up	1 teaspoon fresh lemon or lime juice
2 tablespoons frozen pineapple juice concentrate	1 cup crushed ice

□ Combine banana, pineapple juice concentrate and lemon juice in blender container; process until well mixed.
□ Add crushed ice gradually, processing until thickened and smooth.
□ Pour into glasses; serve immediately.
□ Yield: 2 servings.

FAUX KIR

3 ounces (about) white grape juice, chilled	Raspberry ginger ale or cherry 7-up, chilled
1 tablespoon grenadine syrup	

□ Fill large wine glass half full with grape juice. Stir in 1 tablespoon grenadine syrup.
□ Fill glass with ginger ale. Serve immediately.
□ Yield: 1 serving.

CREME EGGNOG

1 (7-ounce) jar marshmallow creme	1/4 cup rum or rum flavoring to taste
1 cup skim milk	8 ounces whipped topping
2 cups egg substitute	Nutmeg to taste
1 teaspoon vanilla extract	

□ Spoon marshmallow creme into mixer bowl. Add milk gradually, beating constantly until smooth.
□ Beat in egg substitute. Stir in vanilla and rum.
□ Fold in whipped topping.
□ Chill until serving time. Spoon into punch cups. Garnish with nutmeg.
□ Yield: 10 servings.

Clam Roll-Ups, Chili-Chicken Appetizer Cheesecake, Marinated Pork Loin, pages 154 and 156

Luminaria Supper

*I*f you think Christmas is strictly evergreens, snow and sleighbells, take a cue from south of the border and expand your holiday horizons with a neighborhood Mexican fiesta. Decorate front walks and porches with store-bought luminaries, those enchanting paper-bag candle lanterns, or make your own with plain brown bags, decorated with a paper punch and weighted with sand. Throw a serape across your dining room table, nestle a few candles into rustic artichoke holders, and invite the neighbors in for a Southwestern version of a sledding party.

Menu

Clam Roll-Ups
Mexican Shrimp Cocktail
Chili-Chicken Appetizer Cheesecake
Spicy Hot Wings
Guacamole   Barbecue Sauce
Southwestern Chili Dip with
Vegetable Dippers
Endive with Red Pepper Cheese
Marinated Pork Loin
Blue and Gold Cornmeal Muffins
Chocolate Tortilla Torte
Miraculous Pralines
Coffee Punch

CLAM ROLL-UPS

2 (6¹/2-ounce) cans minced clams, drained	8 slices white sandwich bread, crusts trimmed
¹/2 cup mayonnaise	Melted margarine
1 tablespoon grated onion	Chopped parsley or toasted sesame seed
¹/4 to ¹/2 teaspoon curry powder	

□ Combine first 4 ingredients in bowl; mix well.
□ Flatten bread slices with rolling pin. Spread 2 tablespoons clam mixture on each bread slice. Roll up to enclose filling. Brush with margarine.
□ Chill or freeze, wrapped in plastic wrap.
□ Preheat oven to 350 degrees.
□ Coat rolls with parsley; cut each roll into 4 pieces. Place on rack in shallow baking pan.
□ Bake for 8 to 10 minutes or until golden brown. Serve immediately.
□ Yield: 32 appetizers.

MEXICAN SHRIMP COCKTAIL

3 large tomatoes, chopped	1 green chili pepper, seeded, chopped
2 avocados, chopped	
1 bunch green onions, chopped	1¹/2 tablespoons chopped garlic
1¹/2 cups chopped celery	Salt to taste
1 (46-ounce) can tomato juice	2 pounds cooked medium shrimp
³/4 cup chopped cilantro	Celery leaves

□ Combine tomatoes, avocados, green onions, celery, tomato juice, cilantro, green chili pepper, garlic and salt in bowl; mix well. Add shrimp.
□ Marinate in refrigerator for 2 to 8 hours. Drain. Arrange shrimp on serving plate. Garnish with celery leaves.
□ Yield: 16 servings.

CHILI-CHICKEN APPETIZER CHEESECAKE

2 teaspoons chicken-flavored instant bouillon	2 eggs
	1 cup finely chopped cooked chicken
¹/2 cup hot water	1 (4-ounce) can chopped green chilies, well drained
24 ounces cream cheese, softened	
1¹/2 teaspoons chili powder	Salsa
	Shredded cheese
¹/2 to 1 teaspoon hot pepper sauce	Sliced green onions
	Tortilla chips

□ Preheat oven to 325 degrees.
□ Dissolve bouillon in water in cup.
□ Beat cream cheese with chili powder and pepper sauce in bowl. Beat in eggs. Add bouillon; mix well.
□ Stir in chicken and green chilies. Spoon into 9-inch springform pan.
□ Bake for 30 minutes or until set. Cool in pan for 15 minutes. Place on serving plate. Run knife around side of pan; remove side.
□ Top with salsa, cheese and green onions. Serve warm or chilled with tortilla chips.
□ Yield: 16 servings.

SPICY HOT WINGS

24 chicken wings	¹/4 teaspoon ground cloves
1 cup beer	3 tablespoons honey
¹/3 cup vegetable oil	Fresh Salsa Diablo (page 142)
1 tablespoon Worcestershire sauce	Guacamole (page 155)
¹/2 teaspoon cinnamon	Barbecue Sauce (page 155)

□ Rinse chicken and pat dry. Cut each wing into 3 joints, discarding wing tips.
□ Mix beer, oil, Worcestershire sauce and spices in shallow dish. Add chicken, coating well.
□ Marinate, covered, for several hours to overnight. Drain, reserving marinade. Stir honey into reserved marinade.
□ Preheat broiler.
□ Place chicken wings on rack in broiler pan.
□ Broil 3 to 4 inches from heat source for 8 minutes; turn chicken. Broil for 8 to 10 minutes longer, brushing with marinade during last 5 minutes.
□ Serve with Fresh Salsa Diablo, Guacamole or Barbecue Sauce.
□ Yield: 4 dozen.

GUACAMOLE

1 large avocado, peeled, mashed
3 small green onions, chopped
2 tablespoons lemon juice
1/2 (10-ounce) can tomatoes with green chilies, drained
Salt to taste
Tortilla chips

□ Combine first 5 ingredients in bowl; mix well.
□ Chill, tightly covered, until serving time. Serve with tortilla chips or Spicy Hot Wings.
□ Yield: 1 1/2 cups.

BARBECUE SAUCE

1 (6-ounce) jar prepared mustard
1/2 cup sugar
1/4 cup packed light brown sugar
1/2 cup margarine
1/2 cup apple cider vinegar
1/3 cup catsup
Salt and pepper to taste

□ Combine all ingredients in saucepan.
□ Simmer for 30 minutes. Serve sauce with Spicy Hot Wings.
□ Yield: 3 cups.

SOUTHWESTERN CHILI DIP

2 cups shredded Cheddar cheese
1 cup mayonnaise
1 (4-ounce) can chopped green chilies, drained
1/4 teaspoon garlic powder
Hot pepper sauce to taste
1 (4-ounce) can chopped black olives, drained
1 medium tomato, chopped
1/4 cup sliced green onions
Bite-sized vegetables
Corn chips

□ Preheat oven to 350 degrees.
□ Combine first 5 ingredients and half the olives in large bowl; mix well.
□ Spread in 9-inch quiche dish or pie plate.

□ Bake for 20 minutes or until heated through.
□ Sprinkle with tomato, remaining olives and green onions. Serve with assorted fresh vegetable dippers or corn chips.
□ May microwave on High for 4 to 6 minutes or until heated through.
□ Yield: 16 servings.

ENDIVE WITH RED PEPPER CHEESE

1 (8-ounce) jar roasted red peppers
2 ounces Neufchâtel cheese
1 clove of garlic, crushed
1/4 teaspoon oregano
3 heads endive

□ Rinse red peppers with cold water and drain well.
□ Purée next 3 ingredients in blender. Add red peppers; purée.
□ Spoon into small bowl. Chill, covered, overnight.
□ Separate endive into 36 leaves. Fill with cheese mixture. Chill until serving time.
□ Yield: 3 dozen appetizers.

Use artichokes gilded or not, for unusual candle holders at each place—or group for maximum effect.

MARINATED PORK LOIN

1/2 cup bottled lemon juice	1/3 cup sliced green onions
1/4 cup packed light brown sugar	2 (1 1/2-pound) pork tenderloins
1/4 cup orange juice	1 cup peach or apricot preserves
1/4 cup soy sauce	Thinly sliced jicama
1/3 cup vegetable oil	Fresh pea pods
1 tablespoon finely chopped fresh ginger	Red pepper strips

☐ Process lemon juice, brown sugar, orange juice and soy sauce in blender until smooth.
☐ Add oil gradually, blending constantly. Reserve 1/4 cup marinade.
☐ Add ginger and green onions to remaining marinade. Pour over tenderloins in shallow dish.
☐ Marinate, covered, for 4 hours to overnight.
☐ Combine reserved 1/4 cup marinade with preserves in saucepan.
☐ Cook over low heat until preserves melt, stirring to mix well.
☐ Chill, covered, until serving time.
☐ Preheat oven to 450 degrees.
☐ Drain tenderloins, reserving marinade. Arrange tenderloins on rack in foil-lined baking pan. Insert meat thermometer.
☐ Bake for 10 minutes. Reduce oven temperature to 350 degrees. Bake for 25 to 30 minutes or to 155 degrees on meat thermometer, basting frequently with reserved marinade.
☐ Chill in refrigerator. Slice tenderloins thin.
☐ Arrange on serving plate. Serve with chilled preserve sauce. Garnish with jicama, pea pods and red pepper strips.
☐ Yield: 16 servings.

BLUE AND GOLD CORNMEAL MUFFINS

2 tablespoons natural wheat and barley cereal	1 egg, beaten
2 tablespoons finely chopped walnuts	1/2 cup milk
1/2 cup all-purpose flour	2 tablespoons chopped chives
2 teaspoons sugar	3 tablespoons melted butter or margarine
1 1/2 teaspoons baking powder	1/4 cup blue cornmeal
1/4 teaspoon salt	1/4 cup yellow cornmeal

☐ Preheat oven to 425 degrees.
☐ Mix cereal and walnuts in bowl. Mix flour, sugar, baking powder and salt in bowl. Beat egg, milk, chives and butter in bowl until smooth. Add to dry ingredients; mix just until moistened.
☐ Divide batter into 2 portions. Stir blue cornmeal into 1 portion. Stir yellow cornmeal into remaining portion.
☐ Spoon batters side by side into greased 1 3/4-inch muffin cups, filling 2/3 full. Sprinkle with cereal and walnut mixture.
☐ Bake for 8 to 10 minutes or until muffins test done.
☐ Yield: 18 muffins.

CHOCOLATE TORTILLA TORTE

1 cup semisweet chocolate chips	6 (8-inch) flour tortillas
1 cup sour cream	1 tablespoon seedless red raspberry preserves

☐ Melt chocolate chips in double boiler; remove from heat. Stir in sour cream. Cool to room temperature.
☐ Spread chocolate mixture over 5 tortillas. Spread preserves over 1 tortilla. Stack tortillas, placing tortilla with preserves in center of stack.
☐ Chill, covered, for 4 to 24 hours. Cut into wedges.
☐ Yield: 12 servings.

MIRACULOUS PRALINES

1 cup whipping cream	1 teaspoon vanilla extract
1 (1-pound) package light brown sugar	2 tablespoons melted butter or margarine
2 cups broken pecans	

☐ Combine whipping cream and brown sugar in glass bowl; mix well.
☐ Microwave on High for 8 to 12 minutes or until mixture boils. Stir in pecans, vanilla and butter.
☐ Drop by spoonfuls onto foil-lined tray. Let stand until firm.
☐ Yield: 3 dozen.

COFFEE PUNCH

2 ounces instant coffee powder	2 quarts vanilla ice cream, softened
1 cup sugar	4 quarts milk
2 cups boiling water	16 ounces whipped topping
2 quarts chocolate ice cream, softened	

☐ Dissolve coffee powder and sugar in water in pitcher; mix well. Chill until serving time.
☐ Combine with ice cream and milk in punch bowl; mix gently.
☐ Top with whipped topping. Ladle into punch cups.
☐ Yield: 50 servings.

Banana Pistachio French Toast, Rich Caramel Sauce, page 158

Make-Ahead Christmas Brunch

*F*inding the right date and time to host a holiday party can be a problem, given friends' busy schedules and your own holiday plans. Our brunch is just the solution. It offers guests a welcome breather from the round of evening parties, and our well-planned menu allows you to relax and do most of the preparation far in advance. There are goodies for everyone from seven-year-olds to sophisticates. For a pull-out-the-stops brunch, offer your guests the whole array of sumptuous breakfast dishes we've assembled here, or choose several you especially like for smaller, more intimate get-togethers.

Menu

Banana Pistachio French Toast
Rich Caramel Sauce
Holiday Müeslix
Yuletide Breakfast Pie or
Monterey Strata
Christmas Scones
Pumpkin and Apple Streusel Muffins
Orange Cream Fruit Salad or
Fruit Sampler with Yogurt Sauce
Festive Blueberry Pizza or
Strawberry Waffle Sundaes
Blintz Soufflé
Hot Apricot Tea
Cranberry Sparkler

BANANA PISTACHIO FRENCH TOAST

1 cup sugar	1 cup mashed banana
1/2 cup shortening	1 cup coarsely chopped
2 eggs	pistachios
1 tablespoon milk	9 eggs, beaten
2 cups all-purpose flour	3 tablespoons milk
1 teaspoon baking soda	Butter or margarine
1/4 teaspoon salt	Rich Caramel Sauce

□ Preheat oven to 350 degrees.
□ Combine sugar, shortening, 2 eggs and 1 tablespoon milk in bowl; beat until smooth. Add mixture of flour, baking soda and salt. Fold in banana and 3/4 cup pistachios. Spoon into greased 5-by-9-inch loaf pan. Sprinkle with remaining 1/4 cup pistachios.
□ Bake for 1 hour or until wooden pick inserted in center comes out clean; cover with foil if necessary to prevent overbrowning. Remove to wire rack to cool.
□ Cut bread into 3/4-inch slices. Dip into mixture of 9 eggs and 3 tablespoons milk, saturating well.
□ Cook in melted butter in skillet until brown on both sides. Serve with Rich Caramel Sauce.
□ May freeze coated bread slices, brush with melted butter and bake at 500 degrees for 20 minutes, turning once and brushing with butter again.
□ Yield: 9 servings.

RICH CARAMEL SAUCE

1/2 cup melted butter or	1 cup packed light brown
margarine	sugar
1/2 cup whipping cream	

□ Combine butter, whipping cream and brown sugar in saucepan.
□ Bring to a boil over medium heat, stirring to mix well; reduce heat. Cook for 5 minutes; do not stir. Set aside.
□ Yield: 1 1/4 cups.

HOLIDAY MÜESLIX

2 cups plain yogurt	1/2 cup sliced grapes
4 ounces cream cheese,	1 banana, sliced
softened	1 apple, chopped
3/4 cup quick-cooking oats	1/2 cup coconut
3/4 cup sliced hazelnuts	2 teaspoons lemon juice
1/3 cup raisins	3/4 cup whipping cream
1/2 cup sliced strawberries	Sugar to taste

□ Combine yogurt and cream cheese in bowl; mix well. Add next 9 ingredients; mix well.
□ Whip cream with sugar in mixer bowl until soft peaks form. Fold into fruit mixture.
□ Yield: 8 servings.

YULETIDE BREAKFAST PIE

1 (8-count) can crescent	1/2 teaspoon salt
rolls	1/8 teaspoon pepper
1 pound chopped cooked	1/2 cup chopped onion
ham or sausage	1/4 cup chopped green
1 cup loose-pack frozen	bell pepper
hashed brown potatoes	1 (2-ounce) can chopped
1/2 cup shredded sharp	mushrooms, drained
Cheddar cheese	2 tablespoons chopped
1/2 cup shredded Swiss	pimento
cheese	2 tablespoons grated
6 eggs, beaten	Parmesan cheese
1/3 cup milk	

□ Preheat oven to 375 degrees.
□ Separate roll dough into 8 triangles. Arrange in ungreased 12-inch pizza pan to form crust; press edges to seal.
□ Sprinkle ham, potatoes, Cheddar cheese and Swiss cheese over crust.
□ Combine eggs, milk, salt and pepper in bowl; mix well. Stir in onion, green pepper, mushrooms and pimento. Pour over layers. Sprinkle with Parmesan cheese.
□ Bake for 25 to 30 minutes or until bubbly.
□ Yield: 8 servings.

MONTEREY STRATA

4 cups cheese-flavored tortilla chips	1 (4-ounce) can chopped green chilies
2 cups shredded Monterey Jack cheese	1 cup chopped onion
6 eggs, beaten	3 tablespoons catsup
2 1/2 cups milk	1/4 teaspoon Tabasco sauce
	1/2 teaspoon salt

□ Layer tortilla chips and cheese in greased 9-by-13-baking dish.
□ Combine remaining ingredients in bowl; mix well. Pour over layers. Chill overnight.
□ Preheat oven to 325 degrees.
□ Bake casserole for 50 minutes or until set.
□ Yield: 8 servings.

CHRISTMAS SCONES

4 cups all-purpose flour	2/3 cup butter or margarine
3 tablespoons sugar	1 1/3 cups buttermilk
1 tablespoon baking powder	8 teaspoons cherry jam or preserves
1/2 teaspoon baking soda	1 tablespoon sugar
1/2 teaspoon salt	Red sugar sprinkles

□ Preheat oven to 425 degrees.
□ Combine flour, sugar, baking powder, baking soda and salt in bowl. Cut in butter until crumbly. Add buttermilk; mix lightly with fork until mixture forms soft dough.
□ Knead dough gently 5 or 6 times on lightly floured surface. Roll 1/4 inch thick; cut into sixteen 3-inch circles.
□ Place 8 circles on greased baking sheet. Spoon 1 teaspoon cherry jam into center of each. Moisten edges with water; top with remaining circles, pressing edges to seal. Sprinkle with mixture of 1 tablespoon sugar and red sugar sprinkles.
□ Bake for 15 to 18 minutes or until golden brown. Serve warm.
□ Yield: 1 dozen.

PUMPKIN AND APPLE STREUSEL MUFFINS

2 1/2 cups all-purpose flour	2 cups chopped peeled apples
2 cups sugar	1 cup chopped pecans
1 tablespoon pumpkin pie spice	2 tablespoons all-purpose flour
1 teaspoon baking soda	1/4 cup sugar
1/2 teaspoon salt	1/2 teaspoon cinnamon
2 eggs, beaten	4 teaspoons butter or margarine
1 cup canned pumpkin	
1/2 cup vegetable oil	

□ Preheat oven to 350 degrees.
□ Mix 2 1/2 cups flour, 2 cups sugar, pumpkin pie spice, baking soda and salt in large bowl.

□ Beat eggs with pumpkin and oil in bowl. Add to dry ingredients; mix just until moistened. Stir in apples and pecans.
□ Fill greased muffin cups 3/4 full.
□ Combine 2 tablespoons flour, 1/4 cup sugar and cinnamon in small bowl. Cut in butter until crumbly. Sprinkle over muffin batter.
□ Bake for 35 to 40 minutes or until golden brown.
□ Freeze muffins if desired. Reheat in microwave before serving.
□ Yield: 1 1/2 dozen.

ORANGE CREAM FRUIT SALAD

1 (20-ounce) can pineapple chunks, drained	1 (4-ounce) package vanilla instant pudding mix
1 (16-ounce) can sliced peaches, drained	1 1/2 cups milk
1 (11-ounce) can mandarin oranges, drained	1/3 cup thawed frozen orange juice concentrate
2 apples, peeled, chopped	3/4 cup sour cream
3 bananas, sliced	Lettuce cups
	Mandarin oranges

□ Combine pineapple, peaches, 1 can oranges, apples and bananas in large bowl.
□ Combine pudding mix, milk and orange juice concentrate in mixer bowl. Beat at high speed for 1 to 2 minutes. Beat in sour cream. Add to fruit; mix well.
□ Chill, covered, in refrigerator. Serve in lettuce cups. Garnish with additional orange segments.
□ Yield: 8 to 12 servings.

FRUIT SAMPLER WITH YOGURT SAUCE

3 cups plain or vanilla yogurt	2 apples, peeled, cored
1/4 cup honey	2 pears, peeled, cored
1 teaspoon grated orange rind	2 kiwifruit, peeled, sliced
4 large navel oranges	4 ounces seedless red grapes, in small clusters
	Lemon leaves

□ Combine yogurt, honey and orange rind in bowl; mix well. Chill, covered, until serving time.
□ Cut oranges into halves horizontally. Remove orange sections carefully; reserve juice and orange shells.
□ Cut apples and pears into wedges. Sprinkle with reserved orange juice.
□ Spoon yogurt sauce into reserved orange shells; place on 8 individual serving plates.
□ Arrange orange sections, apple wedges, pear wedges, kiwifruit and grapes around orange shells. Garnish with lemon leaves.
□ Yield: 8 servings.

FESTIVE BLUEBERRY PIZZA

8 ounces cream cheese, softened	3/4 cup all-purpose flour
1/2 cup sugar	1/2 cup sugar
1 egg, beaten	6 tablespoons margarine
1 teaspoon vanilla extract	1/4 teaspoon butter extract
1 loaf frozen bread dough, thawed	1 cup confectioners' sugar
2 cups blueberries	2 tablespoons milk
	1/2 teaspoon vanilla extract

□ Beat cream cheese with 1/2 cup sugar in small mixer bowl until light and fluffy. Beat in egg and 1 teaspoon vanilla.
□ Press thawed bread dough into 14-inch pizza pan. Spread with cream cheese mixture. Sprinkle with blueberries.
□ Mix flour and 1/2 cup sugar in small bowl. Cut in margarine and butter extract until crumbly. Spoon over blueberries.
□ Let rise for 30 minutes.
□ Preheat oven to 375 degrees.
□ Bake pizza for 30 minutes or until golden brown.
□ Blend confectioners' sugar with milk and 1/2 teaspoon vanilla in bowl. Drizzle over warm pizza.
□ Yield: 8 to 10 servings.

BLINTZ SOUFFLÉ

1 1/2 cups sour cream	16 ounces small curd cottage cheese
1/2 cup orange juice	8 ounces cream cheese, softened
6 eggs	
1/4 cup butter or margarine, softened	2 egg yolks, slightly beaten
1 cup all-purpose flour	1 teaspoon vanilla extract
1/3 cup sugar	Apricot preserves
2 teaspoons baking powder	Sour cream
1 tablespoon sugar	

□ Combine 1 1/2 cups sour cream, orange juice, eggs, butter, flour, 1/3 cup sugar and baking powder in blender container. Process until smooth. Pour half the batter into greased 9-by-13-inch baking dish.
□ Combine 1 tablespoon sugar, cottage cheese, cream cheese, egg yolks and vanilla in mixer bowl; beat until smooth. Drop by teaspoonfuls onto batter in baking dish. Spread evenly; mixture will mix slightly. Top with remaining sour cream batter.
□ Chill, covered, for 2 hours to overnight.
□ Preheat oven to 350 degrees.
□ Bake soufflé for 50 to 60 minutes or until puffed and light brown. Top with apricot preserves and additional sour cream.
□ Yield: 8 to 12 servings.

STRAWBERRY WAFFLE SUNDAES

2 (10-ounce) packages quick-thaw frozen strawberries or raspberries, thawed	1/4 cup Framboise or other fruit-flavored liqueur
	8 frozen waffles
	Vanilla ice cream
2 tablespoons cornstarch	1 pint fresh strawberries, sliced
2 tablespoons sugar	

□ Combine thawed strawberries with syrup, cornstarch and sugar in 2-quart saucepan; mix well.
□ Cook mixture until thickened, stirring constantly.
□ Strain into small bowl, discarding pulp and seed. Stir in liqueur.
□ Chill, covered, for 2 hours or longer.
□ Bake waffles using package directions.
□ Place waffles on individual plates. Top with ice cream, sliced strawberries and chilled sauce.
□ Yield: 8 servings.

HOT APRICOT TEA

1 cup sugar	1 cup strong tea
3 cups water	1/2 cup lemon juice
2 cinnamon sticks	2 (12-ounce) cans apricot nectar
6 whole cloves	

□ Bring sugar, water, cinnamon sticks and cloves to a boil in saucepan. Stir in tea, lemon juice and apricot nectar.
□ Cook until heated through; strain. Serve hot.
□ Yield: 8 servings.

CRANBERRY SPARKLER

1 (6-ounce) can frozen grape juice concentrate, thawed	1 (6-ounce) can frozen orange juice concentrate, thawed
1 (6-ounce) can frozen lemonade concentrate, thawed	1 (32-ounce) bottle of cranberry juice cocktail
1 (6-ounce) can frozen pink lemonade concentrate, thawed	1 (3-liter) bottle of lemon-lime soda

□ Combine first 5 ingredients in large freezer container; mix well. Freeze until slushy.
□ Spoon frozen mixture into punch bowl. Add lemon-lime soda; mix gently.
□ Yield: 16 servings.

Golden Cauliflower Soup, Winter Salad with Lemon Vinaigrette, Coconut-Glazed Ham, Merry Cherry Pie, Southern Sunshine, pages 162 and 163

Easy Holiday Potluck

*C*oordinating a potluck supper can be tricky business: keeping hot dishes hot, cold salads cold and getting everything to the table—and edible—at the same time. Our menu takes all the guesswork out of bring-a-dish dinners, with recipes that include a bit of "holding" time. Coconut-Glazed Ham can finish baking just before serving. Spinach Pâté and Holiday Potatoes are refrigerated until just before baking at the same temperature. Soup and salad chill until the last moment, and desserts come from the freezer ready to serve—whenever you are.

Menu

Golden Cauliflower Soup
Winter Salad with
Lemon Vinaigrette
Coconut-Glazed Ham
Spinach Pâté
Holiday Potatoes
Starfruit Muffins
Merry Cherry Pie
Chocolate Malt Ice Cream Torte
Southern Sunshine

GOLDEN CAULIFLOWER SOUP

2 (10-ounce) packages frozen cauliflower or 4 cups fresh cauliflowerets	1 cup water
	2 cups milk
	1 tablespoon chicken-flavored instant bouillon
1 cup water	
1/2 cup chopped onion	2 cups shredded mild Cheddar cheese
1/3 cup margarine	
1/3 to 1/2 cup all-purpose flour	Nutmeg to taste
	Chopped green onions

□ Cook cauliflower in 1 cup water in medium saucepan until tender. Reserve 1 cup cauliflower.
□ Process remaining cauliflower and liquid in food processor until smooth; set aside.
□ Sauté onion in margarine in large heavy saucepan. Stir in flour. Add 1 cup water, milk and bouillon.
□ Cook until slightly thickened, stirring constantly. Stir in cheese, puréed cauliflower, reserved 1 cup cauliflower and nutmeg; mix well.
□ Cook until heated through and cheese melts.
□ Spoon into chafing dish or chill until buffet time and reheat; do not boil. Garnish servings with green onions.
□ Yield: 12 servings.

WINTER SALAD WITH LEMON VINAIGRETTE

1/2 cup vegetable oil	1 head Bibb lettuce, torn
1/3 cup bottled lemon juice	8 ounces spinach, torn
1/4 cup sliced green onions	8 ounces mushrooms, sliced
1 tablespoon Dijon mustard	
1 teaspoon sugar	1 cucumber, sliced
1/2 teaspoon salt	1 small red onion, sliced into rings

□ Combine oil, lemon juice, green onions, mustard, sugar and salt in 1-pint jar with tight-fitting lid; shake to mix well. Chill until serving time.
□ Combine lettuce, spinach, mushrooms, cucumber and onion in salad bowl. Chill, covered, until serving time.
□ Drizzle desired amount of dressing over salad; toss gently to mix well.
□ May also use dressing as marinade for asparagus, broccoli, poultry or seafood.
□ Yield: 12 servings.

COCONUT-GLAZED HAM

1 (10- to 12-pound) ham	2 tablespoons prepared mustard
Whole cloves	
3/4 cup Coco Lopez® cream of coconut	1 1/2 teaspoons cornstarch

□ Prepare and bake ham using directions on wrapper, removing ham from oven 30 minutes before end of baking time. Score top of ham and stud with cloves.
□ Bring cream of coconut, mustard and cornstarch to a boil in small saucepan. Cook for 2 to 3 minutes or until thickened, stirring constantly.
□ Brush glaze over ham.
□ Bake for 30 minutes longer.
□ May microwave glaze in glass dish on Medium-High for 4 to 6 minutes or until thickened, stirring every 2 minutes and let stand for 5 minutes.
□ Yield: 24 servings.

SPINACH PÂTÉ

2 (10-ounce) packages chopped spinach	1/2 to 1 cup bread crumbs
	1/3 cup vegetable oil
4 eggs, slightly beaten	1/3 cup grated Romano cheese
12 ounces Cheddar cheese, shredded	
	1/3 cup grated Parmesan cheese
12 ounces Velveeta cheese, shredded	
	1/3 cup cracker crumbs
16 ounces cottage cheese, drained	

□ Cook spinach using package directions; drain.
□ Combine eggs, Cheddar cheese, Velveeta cheese and cottage cheese in large bowl; mix well. Add spinach gradually, mixing well. Add enough bread crumbs to make of desired consistency.
□ Spoon into greased 9-by-13-inch baking dish.
□ Drizzle with oil. Top with mixture of Romano cheese, Parmesan cheese and cracker crumbs.
□ Chill until baking time.
□ Preheat oven to 350 degrees.
□ Bake for 1 hour or until set.
□ Yield: 12 servings.

HOLIDAY POTATOES

1/2 cup chopped green bell pepper	1 teaspoon paprika
1/4 cup chopped green onions	2 teaspoons salt
1/4 cup chopped pimento	1/4 teaspoon pepper
1/2 cup margarine	3 to 4 cups milk
6 tablespoons all-purpose flour	1 cup shredded Cheddar cheese
1 tablespoon parsley flakes	6 cups chopped cooked potatoes
	1 cup shredded Cheddar cheese

☐ Sauté green pepper, green onions and pimento in margarine in skillet for 1 minute.
☐ Stir in flour, parsley flakes, paprika, salt and pepper. Stir in milk gradually.
☐ Cook over medium heat until thickened, stirring constantly. Stir in 1 cup cheese.
☐ Place potatoes in 9-by-13-inch baking dish. Pour cheese sauce over potatoes; stir gently to coat well. Top with remaining 1 cup cheese.
☐ Chill casserole until baking time.
☐ Preheat oven to 350 degrees.
☐ Bake casserole for 30 to 40 minutes or until potatoes are tender.
☐ Yield: 12 servings.

STARFRUIT MUFFINS

1/2 cup butter or margarine, softened	1 teaspoon baking soda
1/3 cup sugar	1/2 teaspoon cinnamon
1 tablespoon molasses	1/4 teaspoon salt
1 egg	1 cup buttermilk
1 cup all-purpose flour	1/4 cup chopped starfruit
1/2 cup whole wheat flour	1/4 cup sweetened coconut
1/2 cup quick-cooking oats	1 tablespoon grated lemon rind
1/2 teaspoon baking powder	12 slices starfruit
	Confectioners' sugar

☐ Preheat oven to 375 degrees.
☐ Cream butter and sugar in mixer bowl until light and fluffy. Beat in molasses and egg.
☐ Mix all-purpose flour, whole wheat flour, oats, baking powder, baking soda, cinnamon and salt together. Add to creamed mixture alternately with buttermilk, beginning and ending with dry ingredients and mixing well with spoon. Fold in chopped starfruit, coconut and lemon rind.
☐ Spoon into 12 greased 2 1/2-inch muffin cups filling 2/3 full. Top each with starfruit slice.
☐ Bake for 20 to 25 minutes or until golden brown. Cool in pan for 5 minutes. Remove to wire rack to cool completely. Sprinkle with confectioners' sugar if desired.
☐ Yield: 15 muffins.

MERRY CHERRY PIE

8 ounces cream cheese, softened	1 teaspoon vanilla extract
1 (14-ounce) can Eagle® Brand sweetened condensed milk	1 (9-inch) graham cracker or baked pie shell
1/3 cup bottled lemon juice	1 (21-ounce) can cherry pie filling, chilled

☐ Beat cream cheese in mixer bowl until light. Add condensed milk, beating constantly until smooth.
☐ Stir in lemon juice and vanilla. Spoon mixture into pie shell.
☐ Chill for 3 hours or until set. Top with pie filling. Chill until serving time.
☐ Yield: 8 servings.

CHOCOLATE MALT ICE CREAM TORTE

1 cup finely crushed graham cracker crumbs	1/2 gallon vanilla or fudge marble ice cream, softened
3 tablespoons sugar	1/2 cup malted milk powder
1 teaspoon cinnamon	4 ounces chocolate-covered malted milk balls, coarsely chopped
3 tablespoons melted butter or margarine	
2 tablespoons finely grated semisweet chocolate	

☐ Combine cracker crumbs, sugar and cinnamon in bowl; mix well. Stir in butter and chocolate. Press over bottom and halfway up side of greased springform pan.
☐ Blend ice cream and malted milk powder in bowl. Spread in prepared pan.
☐ Sprinkle with chopped malted milk balls, pressing in lightly.
☐ Freeze, covered, for 4 hours or until firm. Loosen from side of pan with knife dipped in hot water.
☐ Place on serving plate; remove side of pan. Cut into wedges.
☐ Yield: 12 servings.

SOUTHERN SUNSHINE

2 cups orange juice	1 (32-ounce) bottle of lemon-lime soda, chilled
1/2 cup bottled lemon juice	
1/4 cup sugar	
3/4 cup Southern Comfort (optional)	

☐ Combine orange juice, lemon juice and sugar in pitcher; mix until sugar dissolves.
☐ Chill until serving time.
☐ Add liqueur and lemon-lime soda at serving time; mix gently. Serve over ice.
☐ Yield: 7 cups.

After Caroling Warm-Up

What could be more warming after an evening of caroling or attending *The Nutcracker* than a steaming cup of rich coffee or tea, fragrant with the spirits of faraway places? We've taken an elegant afternoon tea and expanded it, with an assortment of special drinks your guests can make for themselves. Set the table with your most festive linens and silver, and then arrange pots and pitchers of coffees, liqueurs and other ingredients, along with one-cup instructions written on small cards. Add delicate sweets served from silver baskets for a magical and memorable party.

Menu

Lemon Shortbread
Apricot Pecan Tassies
Chocolate-Peppermint Pretzels
Brownie Bonbons
Hot Freshly Brewed Tea with
Lemon, Cream and Sugar
Café Brûlot
Irish Coffee
Buttered Rum Coffee
South of the Border Coffee
Schnappy Coffee

LEMON SHORTBREAD

1/2 cup hazelnuts or pecans	1/2 cup confectioners' sugar
1/2 cup butter or margarine, softened	1/4 cup cornstarch
2 teaspoons grated lemon rind	1/8 teaspoon nutmeg
1 egg yolk	1/4 teaspoon salt
1 cup all-purpose flour	4 ounces yogurt-flavored white chocolate coating

□ Preheat oven to 375 degrees.
□ Toast hazelnuts in baking pan for 7 to 8 minutes; rub with kitchen towel to remove skins.
□ Reduce oven temperature to 325 degrees.
□ Line 9-by-9-inch baking pan with foil; spray foil with nonstick cooking spray.
□ Chop hazelnuts medium-fine in food processor.
□ Add butter, lemon rind, egg yolk, flour, confectioners' sugar, cornstarch, nutmeg and salt. Process until crumbly. Press evenly into prepared baking pan.
□ Bake for 25 to 30 minutes or until light brown. Cool in pan on wire rack for 10 minutes. Lift out of pan using foil. Cut into diamonds. Let stand until cooled completely.
□ Melt white chocolate coating in double boiler. Pipe onto shortbread.
□ Store in airtight container in cool spot for up to 2 weeks.
□ Yield: 1 dozen.

APRICOT PECAN TASSIES

1 cup all-purpose flour	1 tablespoon butter or margarine, softened
1/2 cup butter or margarine, cut into pieces	1/2 teaspoon vanilla extract
6 tablespoons light cream cheese	1/4 teaspoon salt
3/4 cup packed light brown sugar	2/3 cup dried apricots, finely chopped
1 egg, slightly beaten	1/3 cup chopped pecans

□ Process flour, 1/2 cup butter and cream cheese in food processor until mixture forms ball.
□ Chill, wrapped in plastic wrap, for 15 minutes.
□ Preheat oven to 325 degrees.
□ Combine brown sugar, egg, 1 tablespoon butter, vanilla and salt in mixer bowl; beat until smooth. Stir in apricots and pecans.
□ Shape dough into twenty-four 1-inch balls. Press over bottoms and sides of greased miniature muffin cups. Fill with apricot filling.
□ Bake for 25 minutes or until filling is set. Cool in pan.
□ Yield: 2 dozen.

CHOCOLATE-PEPPERMINT PRETZELS

1/2 cup butter or margarine, softened	1 teaspoon salt
1/2 cup shortening	2 tablespoons butter or margarine
1 cup confectioners' sugar	2 ounces unsweetened chocolate
1 egg	2 cups confectioners' sugar
11/2 teaspoons vanilla extract	3 to 4 tablespoons water
21/2 cups all-purpose or unbleached flour	1/4 cup crushed peppermint candy
1/2 cup baking cocoa	

□ Preheat oven to 375 degrees.
□ Combine 1/2 cup butter, shortening, 1 cup confectioners' sugar, egg and vanilla in mixer bowl; beat at medium speed until smooth. Add flour, cocoa and salt; mix well.
□ Knead by level tablespoonfuls until of desired consistency. Shape into 9-inch rolls. Twist into pretzels on ungreased baking sheet.
□ Bake for 9 minutes or until set. Let stand for 1 to 2 minutes. Remove to wire rack to cool.
□ Melt 2 tablespoons butter and chocolate in medium saucepan, stirring until smooth. Beat in 2 cups confectioners' sugar and enough water to make of glaze consistency.
□ Dip tops of cooled pretzels into chocolate glaze. Sprinkle with peppermint candy. Let stand on waxed paper until coating is firm.
□ Yield: 4 dozen.

Apricot Pecan Tassies, page 165

BROWNIE BONBONS

2 (10-ounce) jars
  maraschino cherries
  with stems
Cherry liqueur
4 ounces unsweetened
  chocolate
3/4 cup butter or
  margarine

2 cups sugar
4 eggs
1 teaspoon vanilla extract
1 cup all-purpose flour
Chocolate Fudge Filling
1/2 cup sifted
  confectioners' sugar

□ Drain liquid from cherries, leaving cherries in jars. Fill jars with cherry liqueur; seal. Let stand for 24 hours or longer.
□ Preheat oven to 350 degrees.
□ Combine chocolate and butter in large glass bowl.
□ Microwave on High for 2 minutes or until melted; stir to mix well. Stir in sugar, eggs and vanilla. Add flour; mix well. Spoon into greased or paper-lined 1 3/4-inch muffin cups filling 2/3 full.
□ Bake for 20 minutes or until wooden pick inserted in center comes out covered with fudgy crumbs. Cool in pan for several minutes. Remove to waxed paper.
□ Make 1/2-inch indentation in each brownie bonbon with end of wooden spoon. Cool completely.
□ Drain cherries, reserving liqueur; dry cherries on paper towels.
□ Pipe Chocolate Fudge Filling into indentations of brownies. Press 1 cherry gently into filling.
□ Combine confectioners' sugar with enough reserved liqueur to make of glaze consistency. Drizzle over bonbons.
□ Yield: 4 dozen.

CHOCOLATE FUDGE FILLING

3 ounces cream cheese,
  softened
1 teaspoon vanilla extract
1/4 cup light corn syrup

3 ounces unsweetened
  chocolate, melted, cooled
1 cup sifted confectioners'
  sugar

□ Beat cream cheese and vanilla at medium speed in small mixer bowl until smooth. Beat in corn syrup.
□ Add chocolate; beat until smooth. Add confectioners' sugar gradually, beating constantly to blend well.
□ Yield: 1 1/2 cups.

CAFÉ BRÛLOT MIX

Zest of 1 orange, cut into
  thin strips
Zest of 1 lemon, cut into
  thin strips
4 cinnamon sticks

1 tablespoon whole cloves
24 sugar cubes
3/4 cup Cognac
Hot coffee

□ Combine orange and lemon zests, cinnamon sticks and cloves in chafing dish. Add sugar cubes.
□ Pour Cognac over sugar cubes; ignite. Let flames die down. Remove cloves and cinnamon sticks.
□ Stir desired amount into demitasse cups of hot coffee.
□ Yield: Enough mix for 12 demitasse servings.

IRISH COFFEE

1/3 cup Irish whiskey
2/3 cup hot coffee

Whipped cream

□ Stir whiskey into hot coffee in Irish coffee cup.
□ Top with whipped cream; do not stir. Sip coffee through cream.
□ Yield: 1 serving.

BUTTERED RUM COFFEE MIX

1 cup butter or margarine,
  softened
1 cup packed light brown
  sugar
1 pint vanilla ice cream,
  softened

1/2 teaspoon vanilla extract
1/2 teaspoon nutmeg
1/2 teaspoon cinnamon
Hot coffee
Rum

□ Combine butter, brown sugar, ice cream, vanilla, nutmeg and cinnamon in bowl; mix until smooth.
□ Spoon into freezer container. Freeze until firm.
□ Place 1 tablespoon mix in 1 serving of hot coffee. Stir in 1 tablespoon rum.
□ Yield: Enough mix for 64 servings.

SOUTH OF THE BORDER COFFEE

1/2 cup hot coffee
1/2 cup hot chocolate

1 cinnamon stick

□ Combine coffee and hot chocolate in mug.
□ Stir and serve with cinnamon stick.
□ Yield: 1 serving.

SCHNAPPY COFFEE

1 cup hot coffee
1/2 ounce cinnamon
  schnapps

1/2 ounce coffee liqueur
1 tablespoon whipped
  cream

□ Combine coffee, schnapps and coffee liqueur in mug; stir to mix well.
□ Top with whipped cream.
□ Yield: 1 serving.

Chocolate Strawberry Tart, Royal Chocolate Cake, Strawberry Sugarplums, pages 168 and 169

Sugarplum Dessert Party

As any child can tell you, Christmas is just
not Christmas without sugary cookies,
dark chocolatey cakes, nutty pies and creamy
puddings. While we may be good all the rest of
the year, there aren't many of us who can, or even
really want to, resist our sweet tooth completely
during the holidays. In the following pages,
you'll find a special assortment of desserts which,
besides being delicious and decorative, have
another advantage. They are easy to do ahead—
a real plus during the holiday rush. Serve several
desserts to an intimate gathering of neighbors or
dazzle a large group with a tableful—your own
"vision of sugarplums."

CHOCOLATE STRAWBERRY TART

3/4 cup butter or margarine, softened	1 cup Hershey's premium milk chocolate chunks
1/2 cup confectioners' sugar	1 cup Hershey's premium semisweet chocolate chips
1 1/2 cups all-purpose flour	1/3 cup sugar
2/3 cup milk	1 tablespoon cornstarch
2 egg yolks, beaten	1/2 cup water
1/4 cup sugar	2 teaspoons lemon juice
1/4 teaspoon salt	1 pint fresh strawberries

□ Preheat oven to 350 degrees.
□ Cream butter and confectioners' sugar in mixer bowl until light and fluffy. Add flour; mix well. Press over bottom and side of 11-inch tart pan with removable bottom.
□ Bake for 20 to 25 minutes or until light brown. Cool completely.
□ Microwave milk in glass bowl on High for 1 to 1 1/2 minutes or until hot but not boiling. Whisk a small amount into egg yolks; whisk eggs yolks into hot mixture. Whisk in 1/4 cup sugar and salt.
□ Microwave on High for 30 to 60 seconds or until hot and thickened; stir until smooth. Stir in chocolate until smooth. Spoon into prepared crust.
□ Place plastic wrap directly on surface of filling. Chill for several hours to overnight.
□ Mix 1/3 cup sugar and cornstarch in small saucepan. Stir in water and lemon juice.
□ Cook over medium heat until thickened and clear, stirring constantly. Cool completely.
□ Cut strawberries vertically into 1/4-inch slices; pat dry. Arrange over tart. Drizzle or brush glaze over strawberries. Chill until serving time. Remove side of tart pan; place tart on serving plate.
□ Yield: 10 to 12 servings.

ROYAL CHOCOLATE CAKE

3 eggs	1 teaspoon baking powder
1 cup sugar	1/2 teaspoon salt
1/3 cup water	Confectioners' sugar
1 teaspoon vanilla extract	Strawberry Filling
3/4 cup all-purpose flour	2/3 cup Hershey's semisweet chocolate chips
1/4 cup Hershey's premium European style cocoa	1/4 cup whipping cream

□ Preheat oven to 375 degrees.
□ Grease 10-by-15-inch cake pan. Line pan with waxed paper; grease waxed paper.
□ Beat eggs at high speed in small mixer bowl for 5 minutes or until thick and lemon-colored. Add sugar gradually, beating constantly. Beat in water and vanilla at low speed.

□ Mix flour, cocoa, baking powder and salt together. Add to batter gradually, beating just until smooth. Spoon into prepared pan.
□ Bake for 10 to 13 minutes or until cake tests done.
□ Invert immediately onto towel sprinkled with confectioners' sugar; remove waxed paper carefully. Invert onto wire rack covered with waxed paper to cool completely.
□ Cut cake into four 3 1/2-by-10-inch layers. Spread Strawberry Filling on 3 layers. Chill, covered, until firm. Stack layers, topping with unfilled layer.
□ Microwave chocolate chips and whipping cream in small glass bowl on High for 30 to 60 seconds or until chips are melted; mix until smooth. Cool for 5 to 10 minutes or until thickened.
□ Spread glaze over top of cake. Chill in refrigerator.
□ Yield: 8 servings.

STRAWBERRY FILLING

1 cup sliced fresh strawberries	1 cup whipping cream, chilled, whipped
1/4 cup strawberry syrup	
1 envelope unflavored gelatin	

□ Process strawberries with strawberry syrup in food processor until smooth. Sprinkle with gelatin. Let stand for 5 minutes or until softened. Process for several seconds. Spoon into glass dish.
□ Microwave on High for 30 to 60 seconds or until hot but not boiling; stir to dissolve gelatin completely. Cool. Fold in whipped cream.
□ Yield: 3 cups.

CRÈME BRÛLÉE AMANDINE

2 cups whipping cream	1/2 cup finely chopped toasted blanched almonds
7 egg yolks	
1 teaspoon vanilla extract	3/4 cup packed light brown sugar
1/3 cup packed light brown sugar	
Salt to taste	

□ Scald whipping cream in double boiler.
□ Beat eggs yolks in mixer bowl until thick and lemon-colored. Stir in next 3 ingredients.
□ Stir a small amount of hot cream into egg yolk mixture; stir egg yolk mixture into hot cream.
□ Cook over hot water to the consistency of mayonnaise, stirring constantly. Stir in almonds. Spoon into greased round 8-inch baking dish.
□ Chill in refrigerator.
□ Preheat broiler. Sift remaining 3/4 cup brown sugar over top of custard.
□ Broil for several seconds or until brown sugar melts into even glaze. Chill for 2 hours.
□ Yield: 4 to 6 servings.

STAR OF THE EAST LOAVES

1/2 cup butter or
  margarine, softened
1 cup sugar
2 eggs
1 teaspoon vanilla extract
2 cups all-purpose flour
1 teaspoon baking soda
1/4 teaspoon salt
3 medium bananas,
  mashed
1/2 cup chopped figs

1/2 cup chopped
  maraschino cherries,
  drained
1 (11-ounce) can
  mandarin oranges,
  drained
1 cup Hershey's
  semisweet chocolate
  chips
Cocoa Glaze

☐ Preheat oven to 350 degrees.
☐ Cream butter and sugar in large mixer bowl until light and fluffy. Beat in eggs and vanilla.
☐ Mix flour, baking soda and salt together. Add to creamed mixture alternately with bananas, mixing well after each addition.
☐ Stir in figs, cherries, oranges and chocolate chips. Spoon into 2 greased 4-by-8-inch loaf pans.
☐ Bake for 40 to 50 minutes or until golden brown. Cool in pans. Remove to serving plates.
☐ Drizzle Cocoa Glaze over loaves.
☐ Store tightly covered.
☐ Yield:
2 loaves.

COCOA GLAZE

2 tablespoons butter
3 tablespoons Hershey's
  premium European
  style cocoa
3 tablespoons water

2 tablespoons light corn
  syrup
2 teaspoons vanilla extract
11/2 cups confectioners'
  sugar

☐ Melt butter in small saucepan over low heat. Stir in cocoa, water and corn syrup.
☐ Cook until smooth and slightly thickened, stirring constantly; remove from heat.
☐ Stir in vanilla. Add confectioners' sugar gradually, beating until of desired consistency.
☐ Yield: 2 cups.

STRAWBERRY SUGARPLUMS

12/3 cups Hershey's
  vanilla milk chips
1 tablespoon shortening
2 pints fresh strawberries,
  chilled

1 cup Hershey's
  semisweet chocolate
  chips
1 tablespoon shortening

☐ Combine vanilla milk chips and 1 tablespoon shortening in medium glass bowl or measuring cup.
☐ Microwave on High for 1 minute or until chips are melted; stir to mix well.
☐ Pat strawberries dry. Dip bottom 2/3 of each strawberry into vanilla mixture, shaking gently to remove excess coating.
☐ Place on waxed paper-lined tray. Chill for 10 minutes or until coating is firm.
☐ Combine chocolate chips and 1 tablespoon shortening in medium glass bowl.
☐ Microwave on High for 1 minute or until chips are melted; stir to mix well.
☐ Dip bottom 1/3 of each strawberry into chocolate mixture. Chill until firm. Store in refrigerator.
☐ Yield: 2 to 3 dozen.

For a holiday double-dip, "favor" your guests with these delightful holiday decorations to enjoy a second time at home.

*Star of the East Loaves, Black Forest Cherry Torte,
Celebration Cake, pages 169, 170 and 171*

BLACK FOREST CHERRY TORTE

2/3 cup unsalted butter
  or margarine
6 eggs, at room
  temperature
1 cup sugar
1 teaspoon vanilla extract
1/2 cup all-purpose flour
1/2 cup Hershey's
  premium European
  style cocoa

1/4 cup light corn syrup
1/4 cup kirsch
3 cups whipping cream
1/2 cup confectioners'
  sugar
1 teaspoon almond extract
2 (10-ounce) jars
  maraschino cherries,
  rinsed, drained
Shaved chocolate

□ Preheat oven to 350 degrees.
□ Melt butter in saucepan over very low heat;
discard milky solids. Beat eggs, sugar and vanilla
at high speed in mixer bowl for 10 minutes.

□ Mix flour and cocoa in small bowl. Fold gradually
into egg mixture. Fold in butter. Spoon into 3
greased and floured 8-inch cake pans.
□ Bake for 10 to 15 minutes or until layers test
done. Cool in pans for 5 minutes. Remove to wire
rack to cool completely.
□ Place cooled cake layers on waxed paper. Pierce
holes at 1-inch intervals with fork. Drizzle with
mixture of corn syrup and kirsch.
□ Beat chilled whipping cream with confectioners'
sugar and almond extract in mixer bowl until soft
peaks form. Pat cherries dry with paper towel.
□ Spread 1/2 inch whipped cream on 2 cake layers.
□ Arrange cherries over whipped cream, leaving
1 inch edge. Stack cake layers, placing plain layer
on top.
□ Spread remaining whipped cream mixture over
top and side of cake. Press shaved chocolate
lightly into side of cake. Chill, covered, until
serving time.
□ Yield: 10 to 12 servings.

CELEBRATION CAKE

1 (16-ounce) pound cake
3 tablespoons orange
   liqueur or orange juice
15 ounces ricotta cheese,
   drained
3 tablespoons candied
   mixed fruit
1/2 cup Hershey's
   miniature semisweet
   chocolate chips
2 teaspoons instant coffee

3 tablespoons warm
   water
2 1/2 cups confectioners'
   sugar
1/3 cup Hershey's
   premium European
   style cocoa
1/2 cup butter or
   margarine, softened
Whipped cream

□ Slice cake horizontally into 3 equal layers.
Sprinkle layers with liqueur.
□ Press ricotta cheese through sieve into medium
bowl. Fold in candied fruit and chocolate chips.
□ Spread filling between layers of cake; press down
gently on top layer.
□ Chill, wrapped with foil, for 2 to 3 hours.
□ Dissolve instant coffee in warm water in small
cup. Mix confectioners' sugar and cocoa together.
□ Cream butter in small mixer bowl until light.
□ Add cocoa mixture alternately with coffee,
beating until smooth after each addition.
□ Spread over top and sides of cake. Pipe whipped
cream around top edge of cake. Chill, covered,
until serving time.
□ Yield: 10 to 12 servings.

CRANBERRY UPSIDE-DOWN CAKE

1 1/3 cups sugar
4 cups fresh cranberries
5 egg yolks
1 1/2 cups sugar
3/4 cup water
1/2 cup vegetable oil
2 teaspoons grated lemon
   rind
2 teaspoons vanilla extract
2 cups all-purpose flour

1 tablespoon baking
   powder
1 teaspoon salt
7 egg whites
1/2 teaspoon cream of
   tartar
2 cups whipping cream
2 tablespoons
   confectioners' sugar
2 teaspoons cream sherry

□ Preheat oven to 350 degrees.
□ Sprinkle 1/3 cup sugar in each of 2 greased
8-by-8-inch cake pans. Arrange cranberries in
prepared pans. Sprinkle each with 1/3 cup sugar.
□ Bake, covered with foil, for 30 minutes. Cool .
□ Combine next 6 ingredients in mixer bowl;
mix well.
□ Add mixture of flour, baking powder and salt;
mix well.
□ Beat egg whites with cream of tartar in mixer
bowl until soft peaks form. Fold gently into batter.
Spoon over cranberries.
□ Bake for 35 minutes or until layers test done. Cool
in pans for 5 minutes. Invert onto wire rack.

□ Beat whipping cream, confectioners'
sugar and sherry in mixer bowl until soft peaks
form. Spread between layers; pipe around sides.
□ Yield: 16 servings.

CREAMY PEANUT BUTTER CHIP CHEESECAKE

1/3 cup melted butter or
   margarine
1 1/4 cups graham cracker
   crumbs
1/3 cup Hershey's baking
   cocoa
1/3 cup sugar
24 ounces cream cheese,
   softened
1 1/2 cups sugar

4 eggs
2 teaspoons vanilla extract
1 10-ounce package
   Reese's peanut butter
   chips
1/2 cup Hershey's
   semisweet chocolate
   chips
1 tablespoon shortening

□ Preheat oven to 350 degrees.
□ Combine first 4 ingredients in bowl; mix well.
Press over bottom of 9-inch springform pan.
□ Beat cream cheese with 1 1/2 cups sugar until
smooth. Beat in eggs and vanilla. Stir in peanut
butter chips. Pour into prepared pan.
□ Bake for 50 to 55 minutes or until slightly puffed
and center is set except for 4-inch circle in center.
Cool for 30 minutes. Loosen from edge of pan.
Cool completely.
□ Microwave chocolate chips and shortening in
small glass bowl on High for 30 seconds or until
melted; blend well. Drizzle over cheesecake.
□ Chill for several hours to overnight. Remove
side of pan.
□ Yield: 10 to 12 servings.

PUNCH BOWL TRIFLE

1 (6-ounce) package
   vanilla pudding and
   pie filling mix
1 teaspoon almond extract
1 (8-ounce) can crushedm
   pineapple
1 (8-ounce) can pineapple
   chunks
2 bananas, sliced
1 angel food cake, torn

1 (10-ounce) package
   frozen strawberries,
   thawed, drained
1 package strawberry
   glaze
1 (16-ounce) can
   juice-pack sliced
   peaches, drained
12 ounces whipped
   topping

□ Prepare and cook pudding using package
directions. Add almond extract; mix well.
□ Drain pineapple, reserving juice. Combine
banana slices with reserved juice in bowl.
□ Layer half the cake, pineapple, strawberries,
half the glaze and half the pudding in glass punch
bowl. Add remaining cake, peaches, drained
bananas, remaining glaze and remaining pudding.
Top with whipped topping.
□ Yield: 15 to 20 servings.

Craft and Project Index

Recipe Index

Photograph Index